Multiple Sarcasm

MULTIPLE SARCASM

Alice Kahn

Ten Speed Press

1☉
TEN SPEED PRESS
PO Box 7123
Berkeley, California 94707

ISBN: 0-89815-148-1

Book Design by Nancy Austin
Cover Design by Brenton Beck
Illustrations by Pat Adler

Library of Congress Cataloging-in-Publication Data

Kahn, Alice, 1943–
        Multiple sarcasm.

        1. United States—Social life and customs—
1971–   —Anecdotes, facetiae, satire, etc.   I. Title.
E169.02.K25 1985   973.927′0207   85-17281
ISBN 0-89815-148-1 (pbk.)

Printed in the United States of America

10 9 8 7 6 5 4 3 2 1

To Silk and Fonzo

Acknowledgements

I would like to thank Dr. Edward P. Kahn for constant criticism and loving friendship. My thanks to Hannah Rose Kahn and Emma R. Kahn for inspiration and keeping their parents in line. I will always be indebted to John Raeside and the entire staff of *The East Bay Express* for the opportunity to make a fool of myself in public. Most of these pieces originally appeared in that paper. Some were written for *West Magazine* (*San Jose Mercury News*) and I thank Jeffrey Klein (and Bob Thompson, now gone to *Inc.*) for letting my shrill female voice loose in the Valley of the Silicons. Most of all I want to thank all the people who wrote me personal letters. The kindness of strangers is all a fool really wants.

Contents

Sense of Place

Upward Mobility, Heterosexuality, and More Bizarre Trends

Parenting and Kidding

Foreword

Alice Kahn's writings offer guidance for life's really important moments. She is the Empirin with Codeine for the menstrual cramps of life. It's a pleasure for me to introduce—or should I say foreword?—her to you.

I first met Alice Kahn several years ago. I had already been motivated to explore and question the world I lived in (in this case the wacky world of Berkeley, California) by reading her articles in *The Express*. When I met her she was totally different than I expected. She was not a typical "groovy" Berkeley person—you know, a hefty earthmother. Instead, she looked more like me.

Alice has inspired me and other people to look at things in a new glaring light and to see the humor in these things and ourselves. Sometimes it's enough to stop us from making stupid moves or to encourage us to take a stand on significant issues no one is exploring, like bugs in our cereal. Once, during an important interview with a Manhattan mover and shaker, I bit into my sandwich, the aptly named "Steak Surprise." When I saw an enormous insect peering at me from under the bun, I thought: what would Alice Kahn do at a moment like this?

When I first read her description of Yuppies two years ago, I thought that would make her a household word. Instead, others claimed the phenomenon but her original description's still the greatest.

Kahn's comedic writing includes satire with an edge. But rather than make the reader turn away with self-consciousness or anger at identifying with the joke, she makes it possible for us to see and accept our own ridiculousness. From New Sensitive Males to leftwing sacred cows, Alice has the 4-1-1 on 'em all. I mean it from my heart: the bitch is funny.

—WHOOPI GOLDBERG

An Imitation
of Lifestyles

High School Nympho

I think of her often. Every high school had one and we had ours. She went down for our sins. She put out so that others could live. She was Mandy Slitkin—high school nympho.

Mandy was a martyr in the golden age of foreplay. To understand her significance, let us put Mandy down for a moment (lots of people did), and talk about what it was like in the bad old days before birth control. Foreplay, or necking and petting, was as far as most girls dared to go before The Pill made its spectacular appearance in 1963. Prior to that time, a mental cold shower haunted the backseats of America. It was called: fear of pregnancy.

Certainly there were always contraceptives. We have all read about how the pharoahs used camel bladders or somesuch as a penile raincoat. I'm sure you have seen those articles describing remote coastal tribes where the women fashioned IUDs from whalebones. It's enough to make you glad you never came of age in Samoa.

I hadn't even heard of a diaphragm until I got to college, and I'm sure that if I saw one back then, I would have wondered what the little rubber *yarmulka* was used for. But once I heard what you had to do to get one, it was perfectly clear to me I'd never do *that* I could imagine doing it to the entire football team before I'd let a gynecologist do that to me.

Are you someone who remembers a certain kind of boy who would flash a wallet full of rubbers at you on the first date? Was there a girl alive before 1963 who did not experience that little rush that came when you noticed a small foil packet when he went to pay the check? It took a certain kind of cool guy who could keep a straight face to walk into Pop's Drug Store and say in a deep, far-beyond-puberty voice, "Trojans, please." To ask for condoms in public then was equivalent to ripping off your clothes and yelling "fuck me" in a crowded theater.

At my first summer job, I learned a great deal about condom sense. I worked at a so-called "gift shop" in the lobby of a large motel on the lakefront in Chicago. My job was tending a small counter that stocked a few items—gum, lifesavers, aspirin, cosmetics, souvenirs, and a one night's supply of condoms for the entire US Army. Oddly enough, however, I only sold one packet all summer. But I got really good at spotting a condom-wanter. He would walk up to the counter, pick up a pack of Chiclets, and take one look at me—fifteen years old, ponytail, saddle shoes, freckles—and ask, "You don't have a pharmacist on duty here, do you?" (The 80's version of this story, of course, would have the condom-wanter solicit the ponytail girl, who would then take him in the back room and roll him.)

The point is that before The Pill, no one really talked of birth control, because no one really believed you could *control* it. And being an unmarried pregnant teenager in most communities meant a choice between having an illegal abortion or being an outcast. It was against this background that we girls would sit there in the backseat arguing between our passions and our survival instincts. But we'd spend *a lot* of time arguing. Hours. Boys would neck almost indefinitely. They were really patient in those thrilling days of yesteryear.

There was pretty much a stepwise progression that couples followed back then. First, there was the goodnight kiss, which was also known as first base. This was followed by extensive necking, possibly, but not inevitably, leading to petting up to the psychological Maginot line. Petting above the waist, referred to as second base, was generally shunned by a certain group of girls who happened to wear "falsies." Somewhere along with conversations about love, marriage, and do-you-believe-in-God? came the lost art of petting below the waist. This was followed (often rather quickly at this point) by sexual intercourse—a social homerun for boys and a social strike three for girls (or, possibly, if she had a really good time—a base on balls.)

In addition to Mandy Slitkin, I can never forget Natalie Schwab, the Girl Who Got Pregnant. One day she was a cheerleader, president of the French Club, and the lucky girlfriend of Barry "Biff" Hoffman. Then, as in a Kafka story, she was transformed overnight into a slut. She had gotten pregnant. She was called a "skank," Barry left her. None of her friends would talk to her. People would wipe off her desk seat before sitting on it.

I was a freshman and she was a senior. She had been one of the girls I looked up to and tried to emulate. I was just astounded. She still looked so beautiful to me with her blond ponytail in a perfect corkscrew down to her waist and her peach cashmere sweaterset. The teachers had a meeting and told her to leave school. Hester Prynne's life was a sitcom next to what people did to Natalie.

Thus, inevitably it was Natalie who first came to mind when I'd be sitting there out in front of the pizza parlor with my boyfriend. One time, when we were locked in embrace, I opened my eyes and, through the wrap-around windshield of his Olds 88, I saw a sign in the supermarket window. It was three feet high, and it said, "Breasts 19¢." The boyfriend, who was heading for second base, saw it around the same time too. I don't know why I mention this. I guess it's because it was the one time that laughter saved me from the tense debate over whether I wanted to risk pulling a Natalie.

Frequently, boys would take time out from kissing and panting to present learned arguments as to why you'd either, 1) not get pregnant from them or, 2) would want to take that chance for them. Now that there's scientific proof that "pulling out" doesn't work (sperm precedes ejaculate), I can feel vindicated for not buying that one. "I'll marry you" and "I love you" actually sounded like fine reasons to chance it to me, especially as compared to: "Prove your love or I'll break up with you," or "We may only have seven hours to live." But the argument that would most touch my tender young heart was the suggestion that necking without a climax could lead the boy to have an excruciatingly painful condition known as "blue balls."

That's where Mandy Slitkin, high school nympho, played her

part in this American tragedy. She was the one girl set aside to go all the way. She was an angel of mercy whose only mission in life was to save boys from pain. She was the Jonas Salk of blue balls. Why she was a nympho or exactly what a nympho was were hazy areas. I only know that one day someone described her to me this way: "Oh, Mandy—she's a nympho. She has to have sex."

After that I was just fascinated with her. I'd watch her like a hawk. She looked great all the time—tall, thin, black curly hair in a pageboy that fell over one eye; terrific clothes—pleated skirts and matching Shetland sweaters. It wasn't even like she was a tramp. A tramp was someone who let boys have their way with her. But Mandy appeared to be having a good time. *She had to have sex!*

I'm not sure what divine auspices prevented her from getting pregnant. I suppose she only *looked* happy. But the rest of us needed her. As we sat there into the fourth hour of necking, while the Penguins sang "Earth Angel" over and over again, I would get a little pang of guilt when I thought about how I might be leading him to this awful pain. Then I'd think about Natalie, the girl who got pregnant, and tell myself: what the hell, he can always go see Mandy.

8

Lifestyles of
the Middle-Class
and Obscure

The public's right-to-know sank to a new low with the success of the television show *Lifestyles of the Rich and Famous*. I don't know how you spend your Sunday afternoons, but I have been spending mine watching "celebrity interviewer" Robin Leach tell me about "conspicuous consumption, playboys and polo, dowagers and diamonds, pagan proportions" and "the agony and the ecstasy of megabuck realities."

In prose pickled in hyperbole (and alluringly alive with alliteration), Leach travels the world to bring back intimate portraits of the rich, famous and frequently fatuous. The show is a cliche collector's wet dream: We're taken to Hollywood parties "where the stars really come out at night," to a famous plastic surgery clinic "just a samba beat away from Rio" and to a charity ball where a wealthy philanthropist asks his wife, "What disease are we celebrating tonight, dear?"

Each week we thrill to the Days and Deeds of the Decadently Disgusting—and anticipation is half the fun. In one of the most heavily promoted segments of the show, we're told that Terry Moore will play, for the first time anywhere, "the secret tape recordings of (her) midnight love conversations" with her husband, Howard Hughes. How much, we wonder, will we learn about the

9

legendary reclusive billionaire in this "extraordinary revelation and confession"?

Finally, Moore plays the love tapes:

Howard Hughes: Did you decide which ring you wanted?

Terry Moore: I like the little ring. It's just darling.

Howard Hughes: It is cute. I knew you'd like the little one.

Not quite up there with the "modified limited hang-out" of the Watergate tapes, but never fear. Things get spicier when Moore reveals more about Hughes' notorious bra fetish. We already know about the famous cantilever job he engineered for sprucy, goosey Jane Russell. But now Moore confesses—*for the first time anywhere*—that when she and Hughes went horseback riding, the great man insisted she wear two bras "because he was afraid I would break down."

Underwear of the Rich and Famous is a recurrent theme on *Lifestyles*. Another show takes us to the London salon that sells "the most sought-after underwear in the world"—the very stuff that Bianca Jagger, Britt Ekland and Princess Di park it in. In yet another segment we learn that when Tom Jones performs in Las Vegas, "women throw their room keys at him in lace panties." Jones, alas, has to console himself with these perks because, as we later discover, he is far from being the highest salaried performer on The Strip. That honor goes to none other than "Mr. Las Vegas" himself, Wayne Newton—who, we are told, earns a whopping $9,250,000 a month for two shows nightly. Kind of makes you want to go around erasing the moustache on his posters.

Another innovative feature of the show is the use of captions after each segment to tell you what kind of lifestyle you have just seen. One week we see Famous Amos himself as he "spreads the gospel of chocolate chips" in what is described as the Rags-to-Riches Lifestyle. In another segment, we see how actress Valerie Harper handles stress with the help of her "live-in lover," exercise expert Tony Caccioti. This one gets captioned the Unique Fitness Lifestyle. And TV actor Mark Harmon (son of Tom) shocks Robin Leach by revealing that he handles stress by—guess what?—*working!* He has a part-time job as a carpenter, which gives him a Surprising Lifestyle.

Of course, *Lifestyles* is not all who's got the biggest hot tub in Tinsel Town, or whose 3-year-old daughter has her own mink coat (kids are occasionally seen but never heard on the show) or what strange magic happens at nightfall in Rio. Periodically, we do get a glimpse of the nobler aspirations of the R & F. Thus, we learn that "supervixen" Joan Collins' recent spread in *Playboy* was more than skin deep. "I did it not just for myself but to help other women deal with aging fear," Joan explains. Where else would you learn about stars who strip for feminism?

What motivates people to bare their souls and closets on television? Isn't being spared the intrusion of such Leaches one of the real benefits of riches? Well, it often turns out that the R & F are plugging something that they hope will make them even richer and more famous—perhaps an autobiography (Star Birth), or a new line of designer paper products (Handiwipes to the Stars) or a chain of fitness salons (Star Sweat). But most of the time what we get are stars whose careers are on the skids and who are hoping to attract renewed interest. One such segment featured a washed-out-looking Omar Sharif, who explained how he lost all his money gambling. This was called Changing Lifestyles.

Another obvious question presents itself. Why, given my lack of reverence for the show, do I bother to watch? I have a whole range of reasons that fall somewhere between jealousy and snobbery. I suppose I find myself thinking that if I were rich and famous, I'd have more tasteful furniture. I'd certainly have a live-in lover you could talk to—perhaps Norman Mailer or Steve Wozniak—someone amusing. I'd probably keep the third house on a quiet 50 acres of the Sonoma Coast rather than one of the old nouveau scenes like Palm Springs. But I think the thing that keeps me glued to my set is the ongoing fantasy that some day, some time when I least expect it, Robin Leach will be knocking at my door saying, "May I and the rest of Televisionland come in and just take a look around?"

"Tonight," says Leach, "on Lifestyles we are visiting the fabulous San Francisco Bay Area (where everyone comes out each night) to see the home of one of the most mediocre writers in America, Alice Kahn. It is here in this house that could certainly use a paint job, situated on a quiet street where real estate values have not kept pace with the market, that Kahn sits knocking out articles on her primitive Olympia typewriter. When she's not hoping to sell out to a high-paying girlie magazine, Kahn is hard at

11

work on a new book about the wine industry, *The Name of the Rosé.*

"Tell us, Alice," he asks, poking his microphone into my office as I quickly brush the cherry pits into my top drawer, "how do you start your day?"

"Well, Pigeon . . ." I begin.

"Er, Robin," he interrupts.

"Yes, well, Robin, I know it's kind of wild and crazy but the first thing I like to get into is some clothes."

"Fantastic!" he bellows in his Cockney-but-kissing-his-way-up accent. "Let's see the underwear collection."

"Collection? You mean here—now?" I ask with a shyness bred of obscurity.

"Don't worry," he reassures me, "I don't want you to model anything. Just let us look in your drawers. Come on, now, just a look-see."

In minutes, the camera crew is squeezed into my bedroom. I'm now regretting the fact that I never got the coffee stains out of the comforter. The husband, of course, has last night's Dos Equis prominently lined up next to his side of the bed. Then, to my horror, I notice the gargantuan dust bunnies in the corner. What will this be labeled—Total Slob Lifestyle?

The director is now cueing in the zoom for a close-up of my underwear drawer. "Tell us about it," Leach insists.

"Well, what you see is what you get, Robin. You're looking at 14 pairs of size 38 briefs, white, 100 percent cotton exclusive of decorations."

"Camera Three, close up on the label," shouts the director as Robin asks me, "14 pairs, huh? Is there some significance there?"

"As a matter of fact there is, Robin. The reason I have so many of them is so I only have to do my laundry every two weeks. I mean I might do it more often but this way I don't have to."

"Take another shot of the drawer," says the director as Leach adds the voice-over: "White cotton briefs—the least-sought-after underwear in the world."

Then Leach asks me to demonstrate my fitness routines. I explain that I like to jog a few miles in the neighborhood every day, but I demand that the camera following me on the road avoid the back-of-the-leg shots. I don't want everyone in Televisionland counting the rings on my thighs and guessing my age.

12

"But mostly what I do to keep in shape," I explain as I walk through my daughters' bedrooms, "is bend over and pick up the stuff my kids leave on the floor after they clean their rooms. I just pick up stuff until I feel the burn."

"Fitness Fetishes of the Imperfect and Unaerobic," Leach says, "not exactly the direct route to the lap of luxury. And tell us, Ms. Nobody and Never Amount to Nothing, what is it that you do to cool down after you work out? May we have a glimpse of the Secret Spa of the Mundane Many?"

"Yes, Robin, this here's what we call the bathtub," I say, noting that the rings on my tub put it squarely in the middle of the Paleolithic Age. "You see, in the days before Jacuzzi and Pia Zadora, this was all we knew. I'm part of that back-to-the-tub movement you've probably read about, the Simple Lifestylers. It's really an amazing piece of machinery. You turn this little knob and what you've got is a kind of tight-fit swimming pool. By the time the summer's over, we'll probably be calling this Olympic size. Also, I figure if the Kennedys ever come to dinner, this will do."

Leach, now lurking in my hallway and holding his cigarette dangerously close to my smoke alarm, asks, "Where are your collectibles? Barbie Benton showed me her unusual collection of eggs and James Brolin let me see his amazing backyard wildlife collection. What have you got along that line?"

He almost has me there—but then I remember the last time guests oohed and aahed over something in my house. "Certainly, Robin, if you'll follow me into the kitchen and get a close-up shot inside the fridge, I'd like to show you my antique food collection."

I open the refrigerator door rapidly, knocking all my daughters' cute little magnets to the floor. "See that large green rock?" I ask a wide-eyed Leach. "Well, that started out as a hunk of Cheddar. And that glistening blue plate over there—why, that was once an ordinary tortilla. And, if you'd care to open up the vegetable bin, I'll show you things I've done with celery that you simply wouldn't believe."

"That's enough!" shouts the director. "OK, Camera One, ready to pan out from the house. Robin, ready with the voice-over. Go . . ."

"And so, as the neighbor's stereo plays too loudly just a heavy-metal beat away, we leave the world of putrid pantries and parsimonious panties, of leaky garbage bags and unwiped bathtubs, of faulty smoke alarms and feisty children, of wiped-out writers and willy-nilly work-outs, the entire pathetic panorama of minibuck miseries. Join us next week as we jet from Sunnyvale to Schenectady in search of more *Lifestyles of the Middle-Class and Obscure*."

The Surprise Package

It was a week of surprises. I used to like surprises. I used to think that life consisted of going through the motions waiting for the next exciting surprise. Now, the unpredictable has taken on the quality of an act of aggression—not necessarily deliberate aggression but, worse yet, *random* aggression, like the 2:00 a.m. phone caller who asks, "Is this KSOL?"

I will describe for you the Big One, the Monday morning, let's-start-the-week-out-shell-shocked incident. I'm talking 8:00 a.m. on Monday morning—the point of maximum walking unconsciousness. . . .

But let me digress for a moment. I am now, and have been for some time, addicted to a product called Skinner's Raisin Bran. This may sound weird to you, but I have encountered other SRB addicts in the course of my travels through life. We aren't all necessarily cereal lovers, and we wouldn't be caught dead eating Kellogg's Raisin Bran. Would a Quaalude aficionado be caught dead taking Tylenol?

The affaire d'Skinner's may have started out as an attempt to eat a healthy breakfast, but it is now a full-blown dependency. I'd eat it with Twinkies if I had to. I'm nothing until I have my morning bowl. Don't talk to me until the first chewy bite is safely in my mouth. I have been known to run out to the supermarket for a new box as soon as I reach the lower fourth. The lower fourth is a rough time. The raisins are few and the bran is plentiful. Often, I've been

15

tempted to ditch the box when there are two raisin-scarce, branny bowls left. But that would be wrong.

Opening a new box, however, is the highlight of an SRB addict's life. As I tear into the cardboard with the wanton abandon of one who never cares if she can insert tab here to close, I hear a distant orchestra playing, "Another opening, another show . . ." My mouth begins to water as I anticipate the cream of my raisin bran box—that first bowl of fertile topsoil loaded with plump, juicy raisins and crisp, crunchy wheat flakes.

But last Monday morning it was: Surprise! Surprise! As I carefully separated the sides of the inner wax bag, innocent as a babe at the breast, my peepers nearly popped out of my head. What to my wondering eyes should appear? Dead bugs. Numerous dead bugs. I did not pause to do any entomological research. I saw a great deal of gray stuff, at least two sets of wings, and that was it. I squeezed the bag shut and did my best to reinsert the shattered tab.

I tried not to take it personally. I'm sure no group of slimy men at US Mills in Omaha, Nebraska, sat in a smoke-filled room and said, "Let's be sure this bug-infested box reaches the Kahn woman in Berkeley." There was certainly nothing unusual about the box that would draw me to it. It had the same photograph of the perfect bowl of raisin bran placed next to a bunch of grapes (the from-the-vine-came-the-raisin motif) that I have looked at for the past seven hundred and thirty mornings. It had the same reassuring statement on the cover: "A Whole Grain and Fruit Cereal. No Preservatives or Artificial Coloring Added." They could, of course, have marked this box, "Dead Bugs Added for Extra Energy," but that would have spoiled the effect.

As I marched up to the Co-op Market, I felt doomed. I couldn't help taking this as an omen, some sign that Something was out to get me. Just as ancient soothsayers read their fortune in the bones of the dead, I have this funny tendency to tell my fortune by the wings in my cereal box. And this was looking like a four-wing week. You know what I mean?

Approaching the Co-op, I felt a little sadistic glee at the thought of "sharing" my surprise with the store's employees. Thus I was rather disappointed when I dashed up to the clerk and said, "There are dead bugs in my raisin bran. Wanna see?" She said, "Ugh," and called out, "Monica, get the manager!"

I had expected that Co-op clerks, like seasoned operating room nurses, would remain emotionlessly clinical in the face of unscheduled material in the merchandise. We all read about things like rat hairs in the foods we eat. Surely an occasional smiling rat face shows up. Don't the Co-op clerks, as part of their professional responsibilities, have to see it? Was it necessary for her to say something as emotive as "ugh"?

The manager, thank God, had more of the spirit of scientific inquiry. "Dead bugs in my cereal," I said. "I bought it here. Wanna see?" Her response: a cool, crisp, "Sure." Slowly, I unraveled the wax bag and opened it up—just a crack. Then, suddenly, a bug flew out! (We'll call this novel *One Flew Over the Co-op's Nest*.) Imagine it, this critter stowed away and survived the journey from Omaha to Berkeley. The manager and I shrieked. "That's enough," she said and quickly closed the box. When you're a pro like her you can make rapid assessments.

Now, just think of that poor bug from Omaha flying around Berkeley, disoriented as hell, looking for something familiar to sink its mandibles into. Think of it looking for the cornfields, the grain elevators, the towheaded youngsters that say "thank you, ma'm" and "yes, sir." Consider its shock when it discovers that the bowling alley is a fruit store and the funeral home is a shopping "centre." And think of what a time it'll have trying to hitch a ride back home down at Sixth and University: "Santa Cruz," "Mendocino," "Omaha?"

The Co-op manager immediately reassured me that the store would refund my money. "Can't I just trade it in," I asked, "for another box?" She shot me a look of total disgust: "You mean you'll eat that stuff again?" Obviously the woman does not understand the tawdry nature of addiction. She has never roamed the angry streets at dawn, waiting for a store to open so withdrawal symptoms could be quelled. Oh, sure they say it's only psychologically addicting. You try to function in today's high pressure go-go world while lusting for a bowl of Skinner's Raisin Bran, the monkey from Omaha always on your back.

Still, I didn't want to appear weird to the Co-op manager, so

I asked if she'd mind if I opened the new box in the store right in front of her. Naturally, I did not want to be alone at a time like that. In fact, the precious experience of scoring a fresh pound of Skinner's was taking on a new and ominous light. As I eyed the boxes on the shelf, searching for the one with the latest pull date, I realized that now they were all potential Cracker Jacks, a surprise in every package. Just when you thought it was safe to eat breakfast. . . .

I grabbed the one with the January '86 pull date. Holding the box an arm's length away, I carefully lifted the tab to open. The joy was definitely gone. The manager was there with me all the way, but what about the rest of my life when she wouldn't be? I imagined myself dashing upstairs to the bulletin board and posting: "Morning Breakfast Cereal Support Group Forming. Nonsexual. Let's open up together."

I separated the sides of the wax bag, and the manager breathed a sigh of relief. I stared at the upper stratum and inhaled deeply, my nostrils luxuriating in the aroma of raisins, whole wheat, and just a touch of malt flavoring. I longed to get that two percent non-nutritive fiber in my mouth. "January of '86," I proclaimed. "An excellent year."

Our Secret Lives

It was Friday night and something was stirring in the soft, wet core between my legs. Or was it between my ears? My heart throbbed as I entered the car and clutched the stiff, taut stick that held me motionless. Is this what they mean by auto eroticism? Brakes released, no longer clutching, unbound like Prometheus, I headed to the Avenue, looking for action.

Near the corner of Bancroft and Telegraph, I found a large group of bodies, packed closely together, getting high and talking dirty. The punks down near Blondies Pizza Parlor? Nah, you can't talk dirty with a quarter-pounder of mozzarella sliding down your gullet. Besides, kids don't need talk. No, I found myself enveloped in the crush in a shop called The Musical Offering, an outpost of conservative grown-upism in the sugar-coated streets near the University of California's Sather Gate. In this classical music and book shop, a small group of masked women had gathered with a throng of admirers. It was, of course, the Kensington Ladies Erotica Society hostessing a booksigning party for their red-hot paperback, *Ladies Home Erotica*.

Let me tell you, I haven't seen this many over-forty, upper-middle-class, uninhibited people out after dark near Telegraph since Frazier's Danish Modern Home Furnishings closed. The music store was absolutely packed and the irony of having to hump one's way through a crowd of flaming heteros to obtain the autograph of an eroticist was not lost on your faithful correspondent. I plunged right in, however, my hips if not my reputation preceding me.

The Kensington Ladies are a small, literary society from that community between the Berkeley Hills and El Cerrito. They have been meeting monthly (ladies do it monthly?) in their homes for eight years to share a potluck dinner and a potpourri of self-composed erotic fantasies culminating in the production of this book, a collection of "Tales, Recipes, and Other Mischiefs by Older Women." These naughty but respectable wives and mothers have come out of the closet. But only partially. They write under pseudonyms like Sabina Sedgewick and Elvira Pearson and Nell Port—names which suggest the polite Victorian masque of the book. The ladies also wear masks for the public appearances, presumably to protect their husbands, successful older urban professionals. One of the ladies mentioned in an interview that she'd had a better time at her typewriter than she'd had in twenty years of marriage. For a good time, phone IBM.

Grabbing a glass of wine, but unwilling to risk the molestation involved in getting to the bread and cheese table, I began working the crowd. "Why are you here? Did you read the book? How do you like to do it?" There was, as I said, a remarkably uninhibited atmosphere for so established a group. Obviously, the Kensington Ladies have finally "given permission," as the therapists say, to an entire subculture.

"This is definitely *ladies'*, not women's erotica," two working gals from Martinez told me. "We've read a lot of heavier stuff but I think this is great." The husband of one of the authors, a white-haired, kindly patrician, looked overwhelmed but amused. One of the store's clerks walked by him carrying out boxes of erotica over the heads of the crowd to customers requesting car service. "I'm very proud of my wife," said the husband. A balding, preppily dressed, rakish-looking man in his late forties stood in one corner surveying the scene. He'd come from San Jose to see what it was all about. "I write a little erotica myself," he said, checking me (and the woman next to me) out. "Have you seen the man with the plaid beret?" a well-dressed woman in her thirties asked me. Yes, I had noticed the man with the white muttonchop sideburns who was sweating profusely. "He's out for anything he can get," she said, smiling.

I recognized two doctors, partners in a long-established gastroenterology practice, one of whose wives did the charming illustrations for the book. "I hear that man is a maniac with a sigmoidoscope," I said, just to make conversation, to the man standing next to me. The man turned out to be George Young, editorial director of Ten Speed Press, the Berkeley publishing house which put out *Ladies Home Erotica*. Young said the book had gone into its third printing. "You can't believe the submissions we've been getting since this came out," said Young. "We'll be fighting over the slush pile."

With the million-selling *What Color Is Your Parachute?* under its belt, this is not the first time Ten Speed has hit the charts. But with *Ladies* quickly rising among Bay Area paperback bestsellers, it was no wonder that Young and Ten Speed publisher Phil Wood were gloating at the overflow crowd. You could almost hear the words of Robert Duvall in *Network*: "We've got a hit . . . a hit . . . a great-big-titty hit."

Okay, I thought, you've seen the phenomenon, now let's read the book. I'd hesitated to read it for several reasons. One, a review of it I read said something to the effect of: is it literature or isn't it—who cares? That sounded ominous, like the reviewer thought it stank but was too chicken-feminist to say so. Why, I thought, should the Kensington Ladies be sacred cows? True, it was courageous for these women to dare to be erotic and then go exposing their private literary parts in public. True, they are not established professional writers. But can we talk? Is it literature or is it Memorex?

Another reason I hesitated to read it was my fear that as a collection of amateur writing it could be the unintentional *Stuffed Owl* of the 80's. *The Stuffed Owl*, you may recall, was a marvelous anthology of bad verse that gave us such folksy literary giants as Julia Moore, the Sweet Singer of Michigan, authoress of "Steam: The Seamy Side," coiner of couplets like:

That's why I wish again
That I was in Michigan.

One look at the Kensington Ladies, however, told me these were no simple sweet singers. They were obviously very well educated, had traveled the continent and then some, and had lived too long in a high IQ scene to produce mere trash. If this book were a bomb it would be a sophisticated laser of a bomb.

Finally, I hesitated to read it out of pure, bitchy jealousy. Here I'd been talking dirty and wanting to be a famous writer all my life. Believe me, I paid a price for it. From the time I was five years old, kids told me they couldn't play with me because their parents said I had "a dirty mind." When I was thirteen, I sang a parody my sister and I had written to the tune of "Bye Bye Blackbird" to a friend. My pre-liberation ditty was called "Bye Bye Cherry." The friend walked out.

When I was in high school my teacher returned my paper, "Hidden Dirty Puns in the Works of William Shakespeare," with a D and the comment, "this has no place in a high school English class." So after a lifetime of rejection (with the exception of intellectuals who'll always give you a lot of leeway verbally), after a childhood racked by threats of getting my mouth washed out with soap, after trying to get my own sexually explicit articles published, along comes this Sabina Sedgewick. Not only had she managed to gather a support group for talking dirty, she had gotten others started, and provided the catalyst for a successful book to boot. Had I left my capacity for envy of other women in my 1971 feminist CR group? You bet your bigger tits and slimmer ass I hadn't.

Thus it was with a heavy heart that I crawled under my Mexican blanket to read *Ladies Home Erotica*. I had thought it was the kind of book you'd want to read in snatches, so to speak, over time. Instead (and perhaps because I had the flu) I gobbled it all up in one day. In the spirit of the book, I imagined that I was on a cruise ship to Bath for the healing waters, sitting on a deck chaise with a thick, Shetland blanket over me. Yes, this is an under-the-cover book, a pillow book, and why not? Like any other work of literature, it must be measured by objective standards: does it take you to what Johnny Carson has called "the Edge of Wetness?"

Visceral response is, after all, what we ultimately seek from a story—the throbbing heart of suspense, the convulsions of laughter from humor, the tears from tragedy, and the hots from erotica. As a writer who has cast out a gag or two it has given me incredi-

22

ble satisfaction to hear someone say, "you made me laugh out loud." My own Best Moments in Reading in the recent past included the tears I shed during *Terms of Endearment* (the movie left me dry) and the torrents that covered the last thirty pages of *Dinner at the Homesick Restaurant*. We've all read about the healing power of laughter. Now, actual experts are claiming we must cry real tears—onions won't do!—to release those old devil *toxins*. It looks like holding in the juices can lead to neurosis, cancer, or a one-way ticket to Palookaville. Therefore, what better way to judge a volume of erotica than physical response?

The Kensington Ladies, however, set off in search of a new erotica. They had to look at response in terms of social conditioning. They had to ask: Isn't what turns us on related to what we're told should turn us on? Without continuing to subject you to yet another boring, hohum discussion of what is erotica and what is pornography, let me suggest that I'm probably not the only woman who has found herself inexplicably turned-on by some hokey "Playboy adviser" letter like: I was in this restaurant when a waitress suddenly began humping me right there on the counter. To my embarrassment, she undid my fly and ripped out my throbbing member for all to see. . . . As they explain in the introduction to the book, the Kensington Ladies moved from sharing food to *Playboy* to Anais Nin to their own homegrown erotica, written from the female point of view. They evolved only one rule: No victims.

The book is arranged by the topics they had agreed to write about, spiced with actual recipes written in a tongue-in-cheek droolingly sensual style and occasionally broken by verse that serves as a kind of poeticus interruptus. The verse tends to be the weakest part of the book. It ranges from the amusing "Farewell, Fanny," in which a big-assed woman implores her lover to "feel free to choose / another kind / and leave my own / behind," to the totally kinky "Feliny," which has a woman caressing her cat's "soft hollow expanse between her legs."

The phrase "whatever turns you on" came to my mind often as I read through this anthology. Like any collection, the quality was uneven, uneven between authors and within authors. Overwriting, which was part of the Victorian tone, at times worked beautifully, creating a *My Secret Life* kind of intimacy and humor. A good example of this is Rose Solomon's piece "Fever," which includes sentences like "Her tongue traced Corinthian scrolls upon my incredible column." Yet, in another story, Solomon tells you "The unguided head of a penis butted its way toward my safe, wet enclosure." I'm not sure how seriously she wants to be taken here.

Again, Elvira Pearson in "Vegetable Love," a story about eating tomatoes and asparagus as foreplay, moves from the mundane, "She felt his warm hardness against her pubic bone," to the creative breakthrough of: "she sucked in and released the silken, round tomato perched on his sturdy stalk." In this way, the writers struggle with a problem as old as erotica itself: there seem to be as many metaphors to describe sex as ways to do it. But can we get away from the old "macho porn" tradition of cunt-dick-pussy-cock and still keep a straight face? Does the language enhance or detract when we enter a world of tentacles, tendrils, soft hollow expanses, warm, wet, welcoming vaults, swollen penises, and an "auburn bush of Irish heather growing from her crotch?"

I think erotica works best when it is truly uninhibited, outrageous even. Somebody *should* want to ban it. While much of the writing in this book is relatively tame, polite, literate stuff of the should-a-gentleman-offer-a-lady-a-throbbing-member variety, there are many moments when the ladies really start cooking. Particularly outstanding are the sections on "Forbidden Fruit" (real no-nos) and sex-with-strangers fantasies (variants on Erica Jong's "zipless fuck"). To me, these stories were the hottest and the best pieces of writing. Here, we get Sabina Sedgewick's "Schubling Liebling?" a clever fairytale taking a mere prurient fantasy about a fat, long, juicy sausage and weaving an artful structure around it. In the same section we find Rose Solomon's totally outrageous "Pope Innocent XV: Scenes from a Dream." (Although she uses the small "p" her pope speaks Polish when he calls the Vatican.) The story describes a kind of reverse gangbang triggered when a willing pope starts twirling around, revealing the munificence beneath his robes. "He spins faster. The robes rise above his strong, chunky thighs and I behold him—in Excelsis Deo! He *is* Omnipotent, Infallible." Then later, when the pope reclines, "His glorious erection points heavenward . . . some mount it and glide dreamily up and down like glassy-eyed children on a carousel . . . Obediently we file out, leaving him erect and glowing, the everlasting light."

I would have been terribly disappointed if this book were lacking in any power to shock. That would have recalled Norman Mailer's characteristic praise for feminist writers, "those women were writing like tough faggots." I would also have been disappointed if they had merely put out their recipes, which would have been the safe thing to do, food being no-fault sensuality. And the recipes included are charmingly written. Consider Bernadette Vaughan's exhortation to use a savoy cabbage in her Warthog Pie recipe: "You never feel that you've violated a savoy; it gives itself joyfully and without regrets."

I would also have felt this volume were a copout, a mere tease, if it did not include elements of the ordinary, the mundane matters of a *real* woman's life that one never finds in male-oriented erotica. I mean things like references to homemaking, furnishings, children. One story even has a daughter who is writing a manifesto, *Our Barbies, Our Selves.* True, at times this folksy element can cross over into the Sweet Singer's turf, as in the housewifely description, "Like a grooming fish, lodged in his mouth, / I have picked the debris of countless breakfasts / from his teeth." On the other hand, who else but a woman would dare say, "She was proud of her athletic trim body and her small, girlish breasts. She was glad she had put on her luxury underwear." Do men have any idea how many sexual encounters have been lost not because the diaphragm was left in the drawer, but because the beige lace with the rosebuds was there and the white cotton with the underwire was here?

With this book, the ladies stand alongside Lily Pond (who edits *Yellow Silk,* a journal of erotica), sexologist Lonnie Barbach, journalist Nancy Friday, and humorist Cynthia Heimel (*Sex Tips for Girls*), who have all expanded our sexual imagination. The goal is really a very modest one—good, clean, wet fun. This also marks a break with the recent humorless feminist past as women move from small women's confessional and support groups to fat-is-a-feminist-issue weight groups and now, finally, to erotica-for-the-hell-of-it groups. What a revelation: ladies, too, just wanna have fun.

Still, I couldn't help but wonder about the husbands. Thank goodness the book is a success or wouldn't there be just a tiny bit of hell to pay? Aren't those lawyers, doctors, professors, or whatever, bothered by the frequent theme in this book of the lusty vitality of working-class men? There are fantasies about a gardener, a truck driver, a construction worker, a waiter, an escaped convict, etc. There's a vengeance fantasy where a woman whose husband falls asleep over dessert every night begins carrying on with his best friend right under his snoring nose. I suppose this proves it takes a real man not to mind being cuckolded by a typewriter.

Insofar as any theory of this form of literature is presented, it is presented artfully in a story in which a crude-talking Henry Miller character is conned by a lady into giving without getting. He calls her "whore" and "slut" and tells her, "Here, feel my dick, I bet you don't get that every day? I bet you haven't had a good fuck for a long time, not with a real man. What do you say to that, eh?" In this contribution to the war between the sexes, Sabina Sedgewick fights size-queen porn with an indulgent discipline (sans bondage) fantasy. " 'I am not afraid of you,' she continued, 'and I am not a whore.' Obviously, there was no point in telling him that she was president of the League of Women Voters. 'I'm going to tell you what I want.' " What she wants, the story explains, is not to ban sex (or pornography), but to see it from a radically different point of view. And, viewed from a woman's position, it's a whole new ball game.

How many feminists does it take to produce a volume of erotica? Ten worked on this book and they range from gifted writers to one who, as she explains in the biography section, was afraid to write. The charm of the book, however, really does lie in the fact that these are ordinary women, a fact that cannot be entirely separated from the collective writing. As such, we should not expect the slick, Manhattan pro style of a Cynthia Heimel. These are just the ordinary fantasies of the sweet swingers of Kensington, singing homespun songs of desire. And what is it the ladies really want? " 'Kiss them, suck them,' " begs Gwen in a story about sex in a hot tub. "Then she turned over and let him kiss her buttocks and the small of her back." *Let* him kiss her buttocks! Now there's a sentence you won't get from Mailer.

Blow Tech

My friend Bob Marsh, the semiconductor semi-legend, once warned me not to write an article on computer illiteracy. And why should I? Here I sit, with my finger on the trigger of my Macintosh, Macwriting away. It was love at first byte. I heart-heart-heart my Apple-Apple-Apple. Even I, who can barely operate a car, have been forced out of medieval Poland. I have seen the Macfuture and it works.

However, none of this would have been possible had I not mastered a more simple but nonetheless vital technology. I am speaking of the machine that catapulted me into the 20th Century, that most basic tool for clawing one's way up the scale. We can talk about it now: blow dryer literacy.

Like a Japanese general found wandering around a Pacific island long after VJ day, I remained the lone hold-out against the blow dryer until well into the '80s. Now, from my vantage point on the other side of the ever-available stream of hot air, it's hard to recall what I was escaping by avoiding this vital tool. I only know that I had an ongoing vision of my tombstone that read: She died with her hair wet.

You may think it's easy acquiring blow dryer skills. After all, we are talking about two speeds—high and low—and two programs: on and off. What could be more user-friendly? But think again. Could an entire personal drying (PD) revolution come about because of something any idiot could use? And if I couldn't use one, what does that make me, friend?

Consider my plight. Here I am at an age when most women are moving up the career ladder and being lifted by their bra straps into middle management and me without my hair blown. It's like finding a Neanderthal woman incapable of starting fire or a Huguenot unfamiliar with the wheel or a 50's household without a set of pink Melmac dishes. When they wanted to show my generation in the opening scenes of *The Big Chill*, did they portray the characters slaving away over a hot disk drive? No, they showed them in the throes of the PD revolution, each alone in her (his) room unpacking a portable pistol of hot air velocity. When famed auteur and snob Gore Vidal wanted to express his alienation from the YUPsie generation, what did he say about our fearless leader: "The only thing Gary Hart had going for him was his blow dryer."

You see, this is something I'm supposed to know by now. I can't just walk into a bookstore and ask for the blow dryer section. I can't go to a magazine rack and pick up a copy of *MicroBlow* or *PD World* or *Blow Dryer Currents*. I can't find articles about acquiring a personal blow dryer or using my blow dryer to advance my small business in magazines like *Inc* or *Success* or *Money*. The basic message is that without my hair blown into submission I have no business even reading these magazines. By contrast, acquiring computer skills is a piece of cake. You simply walk into the store and choose from the thousands of books on the subject. Anyone who is a computer illiterate in this atmosphere is merely an illiterate.

As I saw it, I had two choices: major research through back issues of *Seventeen* or spill my guts to a hair stylist. Thus I found myself heading up the street in this little college town I live in to a local salon wedged in, as it is, between a shooting gallery hotel and a fashionable new Thai resturant. In a matter of moments I was seated beneath the hot air of a former New Jersey teenager now called Lance of Berkeley. And mighty glad I was that the young woman with the purple mohawk was unavailable.

Lance, who wore his hair in a sort of heavy metal pageboy, turned out to be a second generation Grateful Deadhead, and a swell kid to boot. I started out with small talk to disguise my hidden agenda: a blow dryer literacy make-over. "So what do you miss about New Jersey, the Mafia or the toxic wastes?" I began innocently enough.

"Hockey," said Lance definitively, foreclosing further questioning along this line.

We chatted briefly about how I wanted my hair done. I made some vague comments that I hoped indicated my desire to disguise my midlife feminist interior beneath the facade of a porno movie vixen. "Take about three years off the top," I suggested.

"What hair care products do you use?" asked Lance nonchalantly. Hair care products, I thought, searching carefully for the right answer. "Shampoo!" I blurted out like an A student.

"Shampoo? That's it?" I could tell he wasn't being deliberately snotty, just displaying genuine astonishment. Since the cat was now out of the bag beautyskills-wise, I got right to the point. "Can you give me some tips on blow drying?" I asked. "I just got my first blow dryer."

"What!" screeched Lance, dropping his styling comb and letting the Newark accent work its magic: *"If ya just got one, what wuh ya usin' all these yeahs?"*

"Air . . ." I offered feebly.

"What about when you were in high school, didn't you blow dry your hair then?" he asked, trying to figure out what he was dealing with.

"They didn't have blow dryers then. I'm old, Lance. The blow dryer was not introduced into the culture"—and here I switched my tone to that of a native, offering oral history to an anthropology grad student—"until the late 60's."

"Oh," said Lance, giggling and finally appreciating what he had on his clippers, "that's when I was born."

I then launched into a brief and personal history of the hair care movement as it occurred in my lifetime. I told him how I came into consciousness in the Era of Good Hairclips. Eventually we slid into that dark age when women slept in large brush rollers, waking each morning to tease the hair in the vainglorious hope that Jackie Kennedy would stare back at them in the mirror. Around this time, a primitive form of personal dryer was available, although it lacked the high-tech breakthrough of channeled blowing. These macro devices, I told him, resembled large shower caps stuck in Barbie clothes cases. "Yes, I think I remember seeing them," he said, his mind obviously drifting back to the underdeveloped world of his childhood.

"Then around the dawn of the blow dryer age a lot of us were into a fashion the designers called 'The Natural Look,'" I continued. "This consisted of letting the hair grow, using shampoo, and finishing with exposure to actual air." And, I might have added, I for one continued to roam about in this condition like so much lost data until my file was retrieved. What retrieved it was a visit from my old pal Sierra Carol.

Carol was one of those people who retreated to the high Sierras around fifteen years ago when The Natural Look was absolutely the rage. She built her own house of her own trees—"my Doug Firs," she called them familiarly. She only ate the fruits and vegetables and chickens she grew herself. And when one had the misfortune to return to the city in a car with her, she would start coughing and saying things like, "Look at it. It's like driving into a mushroom cloud."

Imagine then my shock when Carol showed up at my house two months ago with her wild mane now tamed into cantilevered feathers—looking like Farrah Fawcett having just earned an MBA at Stanford (or Snodfart as we say in Berkeley). What had she done, I wondered, jojoba shampoo, an aloe vera massage, deep scalp tissue acupressure? "A blow dryer," she offered. "You can get them at a discount store for seven bucks."

Faster than you can say dress-for-success, I hauled my little frozen-in-the-60's ass over to Save-Less and got my finger on the trigger of a compact, light, 1250 watt "Pistol Power" hair dryer. A month later I began working on my personal computer, and the rest, as they say, is Machistory. The '61 Olympia portable got tossed in the nostalgia bin. Look out, world—I'm ready to network.

Slight problem, though, as I was telling Lance, is that my blow drying skills are way beneath my word processing ability. For want of a good blow dry job, my kingdom could be lost. "So tell me please," I pleaded with this wise young man, this Buddha of the 1250 watts, "what is the secret of this new technology? Why is it when I do it I look like Phyllis Diller after a hard day's hanggliding?"

The secret, he explained with that delightful lack of literal-mindedness that characterizes the techno-relaxed generation, is that you don't use it until your hair is almost *dry*. It's all in the wrist and the timing! Thinking that you use a blow dryer to actually dry the hair is like thinking you can have a meaningful relationship with a *personal* computer. What we're dealing with here is an already dry blower.

Far out. I can access it.

Green Acres

It's a crisp Indian summer day as we travel up the northern California coast. Leaving the rocky cliffs of Highway 1 just past Point Negras Blancas, we head inland on a quiet unmarked dirt road. Here, traveling uphill among the second-growth redwoods, the peeling madrones, and the renegade tan oaks, there are but few signs of civilization—unless you count the CBS News mini-cam focused on the road, the *New York Times* economics reporter in the four-wheel-drive limo, and the permanently encamped crew of *San Francisco Chronicle* staff reporters, agriculture experts, photographers, and people with "contacts." What brings us all here to this remote corner of once logged-over land are the high holy days in northern California. No, it is not Yom Kippur that has these pilgrims riding on the Sabbath. It is harvest time in Mendocino County.

We turn off the road and enter the tiny municipality of Cantaloupe, population usually 47, but at harvest time it swells to a whopping 3,000. We park outside the hardware store, and I notice the window is filled with hundreds of manicure scissors ranging in price from an ordinary Maybelline seven dollar job to the Berlin Alexanderplatz precision instrument which goes for thirty-eight dollars a pair. Have we come upon an epidemic of ingrown toenail, or is something somewhat sinister afoot here? Let's put it more simply: are the somnambulent citizens of Cantaloupe seriously bent on multiple manicures, or are the scissors serving some secret purpose?

32

We know. We know that it is not just harvest time in Mendocino County. We know it is pot harvest time. And we also know that it's not just pot harvest time in Mendocino County, it is—to be as precise as that German cutlery—sinsemilla harvest time, the Chivas Regal of dopedom. We know that these carefully manicured stalks of hemp will eventually bring in a street value of several thousand dollars a plant. We know what the scissors are used for, but we don't let on.

The Cantaloupe Hardware and Cutlery Company is owned by Fred Bunyan, a former logger and longtime area resident. An extremely tall man—just over seven feet—with a large physique, Bunyan is wearing Levi overalls and a plaid flannel shirt. He looks like the very portrait of a backwoodsman except for a red cap that says, "This Bud's For You." Bud, indeed.

"Excuse me, sir," I say. "We—my friend, Biff, here and I—have driven up from the Bay Area to cover events in Mendocino County for our local paper. Can you please tell me why a hardware store in a town of 47 would stock what appears to be several hundred pairs of manicure scissors?"

"We stock 'em 'cause the folks want 'em," he says.

"Yes, but what do they use them for?" I ask, honing in on the real story here.

"Clippin' toenails," says Bunyan.

"Come now, Mr. Bunyan . . ."

"Call me Fred."

"Fred, you don't really expect me to believe that, do you?"

"It was good enough for the *Chronicle* and the *New York Times* and *CBS News*. It's going to be good enough for you, little lady."

"Please don't patronize me, Mr. Bunyan," I say, doing my Gerry Ferraro impression. "Isn't it true that these scissors are used in the production of sinsemilla, the seedless marijuana crop valued at two billion dollars, that has made you and hundreds of other innocent people rich? Isn't it true that, while you don't support the growers, you also don't want to cut off your cash flow? Mr. Bunyan, who else in Cantaloupe buys these hydroponic grow lights—dairy farmers? Who are you stocking these food processors for—tourists?"

He goes to a shelf behind the counter and lifts a large blue object. "Lady, this here's Babe, the blue ax. You open your mouth again, and I'm gonna clear-cut your head off."

I think it is, perhaps, the theatrical but highly effective gesture of baring his teeth as he lifts the ax handle that persuades Biff and me to exit rather rapidly. As we do, I hear Mr. Bunyan say to a companion, "I really kicked ass, didn't I?"

"A *little* ass, Bunyan," I scream as Biff shoves me into the Peugeot and we peel away. We whiz past Ma's Cafe, but not so fast that I don't notice the long line of blurry-eyed hippies smelling faintly like skunk. At the end of town, we pass Stan's Redwood Burl and Used Car Lot, a ragtag collection of polished redwood pieces and refurbished jeeps. On the window of one jeep stands a large sign: We Take Cash and Don't Keep No Records.

Now we're on the road again, turning down the nearly invisible, narrow, winding lane that is our destiny. We're on our way to meet Chip and Scarlet, mom and pop marijuana farmers in the rugged, rocky country somewhere between Point Negras Blancas and Mount Crisco. Biff's Peugeot makes a huge cloud of brown smoke as we tear along the dry road. Suddenly, we come to a clearing, and there, adjacent to a rare 1948 Airstream trailer, stands a tall man with waist-length hair and a beard that could get caught in his fly.

"They don't make hippies like that anymore," I observe.

"It's Chipper!" Biff says buoyantly.

Biff and Chip had gone to Princeton together before coming to San Francisco in the spring of 1966 to collaborate on a book called *Bohemian Subcultures in the Haight Ashbury District*. Prior to that, Chip had been writing a thesis on Victorian poetry and, believe me, it still shows.

Chip and Biff embrace, and Chip shakes my freckled hand, saying "Glory be to God for speckled things." I let it pass.

"A pleasure," I say, shaking his hand warmly.

"Well, things are quiet around here today," he begins, "but you missed all the action yesterday—helicopters, uniforms, dogs, guns. It was unreal, man, like the second coming of the antichrist. They got my whole crop, you know, the Duke's gooks—the guys from CAMP. It was a bummer. Remember the time we dropped acid in San Francisco in 1970 and went to the Princeton reunion? It was like that, man, a real bummer."

Biff embraces Chip again, in the way men now do, patting his back in the time-honored gesture of support. "But it's not too bad, you know," Chip goes on, "because—remember Skip Miller, class of '67? Well, he's with Salomen Brothers now, and he put all my money from last year's crop in a blind trust, so it's like, you know, amazing grace. I can still make it. But Scarlet, she's having a real hard time with this. I tell her to look on the bright side—we didn't get shot, we didn't get busted, it's just a plant. We can always grow more. Hell, we can do it with lights in the garage in Mill Valley."

"Where is Scarlet?" asks Biff.

"Follow me," says Chip.

We walk up a narrow deer path. On the way, Chip stops to pick some wild huckleberries which he tells me are "sacred." We come to another small clearing where the hacked-off stalks and the pungent smell speak of a recent assault. It's hard to believe that just yesterday forty grand's worth of drugs grew here.

In the middle of the clearing, a russet-haired woman is sobbing. "My girls," she's crying, "they raped my girls." Apparently she's referring to the valuable female plants.

"I blame it all on the damn reporters," says Chip. "All the government needs to do is follow their trucks into the woods, and they've got us. I was in the *Chronicle* last week. I'll bet that's how they found me. I never should have said we don't have guns, man; that's why they picked on me. But what I really resent was that in the *Chronicle* story they called me 'Phil.' They shouldn't have done that. I told them I wanted to use the name 'Ashley.'"

At this point, we are rocked by the sound of a helicopter flying low overhead. Then another. The earth is shaking; the sound is deafening. Scarlet lifts her hands to the sky and screams, "As God is my witness, I'll never pick sinsemilla again."

Chip rushes to her side and takes her in his arms. "Frankly, Scarlet, I don't give a damn," he says, kneeling by her side. "We'll start again tomorrow."

Today Is the Worst Day of the Rest of Your Life

Aren't you just sick of those phony, up-beat horoscopes? The fools who write that trash know nothing of the stars. They're just servile flatterers pandering to the hopeless dreams of frustrated millions. But you don't need another yes person leading you down the wrong free-way ramp, do you? Uh-uh. You need me, Ms. Anthrope, the searing seer for the 80's. I don't use primitive tools like paper, pencils and outmoded reference books. My methods are so new, so floppy, so latest-state-of-the-art that I dare not even hint at them, for even as we speak we are being watched. Those who follow my advice will quickly perceive that I have no agenda other than to put you, my seersuckered readers, into instantaneous, push-button touch with irrefutable destiny. Fasten your seat belt; we are about to ride that streetcar named Delusion.

Aries (March 21–April 19)

Isn't it time you stopped banging your head against a brick wall? Now is the time to surrender, give up, sell out, go public—whatever it takes to get yourself off the merry-go-round. These are tough times, Aries, and when the going gets tough, the tough quit.

Don't go for it! All your life people have been telling you you're a creative, dynamic, aggressive person. Not true, and you know it. A ram? You're a hamster, Aries, a weasel at best. Stop trying. Balance your life with the yang of failure.

Look at fellow Aries Diana Ross. Remember that concert in

Central Park? Don't wait until it rains on your parade and you release the angry mob of your subconscious desires. Quit while you're behind, Aries.

Taurus (April 20–May 20)

Earthy, sexy, pillar-of-strength Taurus, right? Bull! Time to stop chewing your cud and seek greener pastures. You can do better. Marital failure is inevitable in the slowmoving Taurean lifestyle. Why just sit there waiting for spousey to ditch you? Consider the upside potential. Tell that crazy fire sign you married that the flame is out. Do not be deterred by the old what-about-the-kids routine. The kids are off in the garage building their own empires and experimenting with booze. Have you seen your kids lately?

Once your mind is made up, there'll be no stopping you. Just take that trip you've always dreamed about, the Greyhound bus to Encino. (Imagination never was your long suit.)

.Look at Barbra Streisand, a true Taurus. Does she let anything—personal loyalty, paranoia, artistic integrity—stop her? Live like her. I'm offering you a hole in the fence, Taur. Take it or you'll regret it the rest of your life. I hear Encino is lovely this time of year.

Gemini (May 21–June 20)

Henry Kissinger is a Gemini. Need I say more? Brilliant, witty, charming, with just a trace of the Strangelovian accent, you attract people. They depend on you, surrender to you, sense your power, but they never quite make you the CEO of their lives. The truth is, they leech your talent. They're using you, Gem. They're sucking you dry. Time to break away from the rat pack.

Now is the time to pursue the career you've always wanted, the one your logic, intellect and talent dictate. You should be a rock star. You were meant to bask in the simulated anguish of rock 'n' roll. And you're almost too old. This is your last chance to form the group, cut the record, plan the tour. Quick, before you and rock 'n' roll are dead. You've got the talent; now all you need is the glove and the sex-change operation.

Cancer (June 21–July 22)

If only we could get you elected, Moonchild, then we'd see what a cancer on the presidency is all about. The sign of the crab is appropriate to your cantankerous, irritable and thoroughly unpleasant nature. I've never met a Cancer I could like.

With both Ann Landers and Amy Vanderbilt born under the sign of Cancer, I can't really give you any advice, can I? I mean, we're talking coals to Newcastle, or perhaps pearls before swine. What good would it do to tell you anything, Cancer? For example, if I said, "Buy Tandem now, it's about to turn around big," would you listen? Noooooo, because those born under the same sign as Dorothy Kilgallen, Princess Di and Merv Griffin are going to dig their own toilets. You're a loser, Cance. Now, Franz Kafka—there was a Cancer. A helluva guy. They don't make 'em like Franz anymore.

Leo (July 23–Aug. 22)

You should be king of the jungle, Leo and instead, you're living like a monkey in a cage. Your Mars is conjunct your ascendant, Leo. Do you know what that means? Do *I* know what that means? Does anyone know anything?

Let's not let these questions deter us from our mission in life— the acquisition of capital. What nobler aim for royalty? But first you must break out of the zoo.

Tomorrow, at 9:00 a.m. Monday morning, I want you to go right up to the boss and give Madame President the farewell raspberry. Do it right—tongue hanging out, thumbs in ears, fingers waggling. We're burning our bridges behind us here. You're a sun sign; be a flamer. It's only money.

Once you're released from captivity, it's time for the start-up. What kind of company? Find a need and fill it, Leo. Take the talking cigarette, for example. The world is waiting for this life-saving device. Or the self-cleansing navel. We now have decaffeinated coffee and non-alcoholic wine. What about no-pain-killer aspirin? Get in on the ground floor on this one, Lee. Out of the cage and into the garage, pronto.

Virgo (Aug. 23–Sept. 22)

Enter the virgin. In a world filled with the fly-by-night and the impromptu, your steadfast refusal to try anything new is a kind of monument to denial. But in your own way, Virg, you too are a slut. Ruled by Mercury, you'll do anything for money, short of selling your own mother. And there's where you're missing the boat.

Your mother is your greatest asset and you have failed to exploit her in the best sense of the word. She could yield much better rates than T-bills if you had the right marketing concept. Surely a person born under the same sign as Lyndon Baines Johnson, Michael Jackson and Pontius Pilate can network this and come up with the right venture utilizing the resource that keeps on giving.

Won't you devote a few moments of your time—the same amount you spend, say, flossing your teeth or cleaning the crumbs from between the boards of the picnic table—to consider a business plan for Virgo's Mother, Inc.? Maybe a slightly more upscale name could be found, like Virgomatic or Mommatech. You're the one with the eye for details. Let's make it pay off.

Libra (Sept. 23–Oct. 22)

OK, Lib, now is not the time to tip the scales. This is going to be hard on a mover and a shaker like you. People will come up to you with all sorts of advice like "Buy!" "Sell!" "Buy then sell!" "Sell to buy!"—but I don't want you to let this verbal tickling of your mental armpits affect you. Stand fast. Your day will come—but not in the next six or seven years.

You are a flirt but flirting could be dangerous at this time. If anyone so much as approaches you at a party, I want you to start screaming at the top of your lungs, "Get your hands off me!" I don't care who it is—Dustin H., Bob Redford, Alan Alda. Just scream, "Hands off!" Other opportunities will arise. If I am wrong, you can always phone Redford and beg him to take you back. If you are a man, this will be even more interesting.

Scorpio (Oct. 23–Nov. 21)

The moon is in Uranus, Scorp, what more can I say? This just isn't your day. Death, disease and pestilence are your provinces and when's the last time anyone got excited about pestilence around here? Other famous Scorpios include Bela Lugosi, Grace Slick, the late Mohammed Reza Pahlavi and Gore Vidal. Let's face it, you're a creep, Scorp honey. No wonder no one wants to play with you.

As to your much touted sexual prowess—a mere remembrance of things past. Have you looked in the mirror lately? You're an anaerobic disaster. Wake up. This is the 80's. Move, or accumulate hideous cellulite that will render you a pariah. I suggest you do it all at once. Jog with Heavyhands to the nearest Jazzercise salon. Follow that with a few hours on Nautilus using the heavy weights and then do a quick 50 laps. And, please, don't give me that I'm-going-to-die-anyway crap. You call yourself a Californian? Move it or move back to New York.

Sagittarius (Nov. 22–Dec. 21)

A human from the waist up, a horse from the waist down, you're a real shocker in the sack, Saj, but don't let it go to your head. Anybody can impress a Libra. Their scale swings both ways.

You are a powerful leader because of your willingness to murder your opponents ruthlessly. A trained archer, you go for the jugular and frequently hit it. And your verbal barbs are often as deadly. William F. Buckley, Jonathan Swift and Ms. Anthrope herself are fellow Sagittarians. Now do you understand why everyone wants to punch out your lights?

It's obvious that yours is the sign for venture capitalists. Now is the time for you to invest in every project that crosses your desk. You simply cannot lose. Don't listen to those negative nellies who say there's a bear trap ahead. What do they know? You can't trust anybody but yourself. Go get 'em, killer.

Capricorn (Dec. 22–Jan. 20)

You're not playing with a full deck, Capricorn, but who cares? Richard Nixon was a Capricorn but did that stop him? Your type has the remarkable ability to take a licking and keep on ticking—with the regrettable exception of the late Capricorn, Elvis Presley. His mistake, of course, was entrusting his life to that Scorpian, Dr. Nick. Had he hooked up with a Gemini healer he'd have been out of diapers and alive on uppers today.

One bit of advice, Cap. As you rise in the upper echelons of the organization, ditch those friends you no longer need. They're dead weight. They'll only drag you down. Loyalty to insignificant others could be costly at a time like this. With your jovial personality and ability to mix drinks, you'll never be lonely. You can always buy new friends.

Aquarius (Jan. 21–Feb. 19)

It still is the age of Aquarius but not the way you thought it would be. It's time to shed those hippie-dippy ideas from your childhood. Remember when you were the last kid on the block to cut your hair? Now it's time to cut out the drugs. I know you thought giving up LSD and marijuana was enough. Sorry, Aqua babe, but a case of Remy Martin a month and a pound of French roast is still drug abuse in my book. Time to come down from the clouds and go straight. I suggest you call Cognac-Enders and go on a really healthy diet.

I want you to eat, drink and smoke nothing for one week. Then, slowly add prunes, beet tops and bone marrow to your diet. I've seen more than one flaky Aquarian turn into a hotshot on this program.

Pisces (Feb. 20–Mar. 20)

You've been acting like a carp, Pisces. I want you to think shark or, better yet, barracuda. Stop your daydreaming. Consult your lawyers immediately. Use your imagination, Pice, and your jaws.

Speaking of swimming, isn't it time you got your own pool? Better yet, why not create your own personalized pool environment? What better way to entertain your old friends and show them how much you can spend. It's the socially responsible thing to do. I think you should go absolutely deluxe on this—waterfalls, slides, floating bars, wet bars, gay bars, behind bars—the works. You're a complete, ultimate kind of fish, Pisces. You earned it, now flaunt it or sink.

Fame

When dance fans flock to see the Lar Lubovitch Dance Company "where
classical ballet and the avant-garde meet," they will see a company
remarkable not only in its creative achievements but because, as
the *New York Times* has said, for fifteen years "the company has
managed to survive in large measure off its earned income which
constitutes a whopping 86 percent of its yearly budget." In a
profession which relies heavily on private endowment (meaning
the ritual asskissing of rich patrons) this level of self-sufficiency is
astounding. Much of it can be attributed to the energy of Lar Lubovitch himself, and it is because of him that I will be there watching his flowing dancers (many of whom have been with the company since he founded it in 1968). I will be there also because Lar
was a friend of mine—a really special friend.

I met him the week before we both started high school—a
critical time. I suppose it's not every girl who's lucky enough to get
someone who will become a world-class talent to choreograph her
rough transition into adolescence, but I found mine. Lar taught me
how to dress, act, and socialize. He saved me from the throes of an
undeserved "bad rep" and transformed me from a lower-class Italian girl (my fashion image from the old neighborhood) into a
pearl-necklaced, middle-class, Jewish princess. Anyone who
thinks Jewish princesses are a myth didn't go to my incredibly
competitive Chicago high school, where girls could choose from
two roles then—princess or slut. Although my parents were un-

able to provide me with all the necessary indulgences for true princesshood, the image saved me a lot grief. And Lar supplied the emotional support in long conversations that frequently ran from midnight to 4:00 a.m. Of course, it was a two-way street. He was also looking for someone to depend on beyond the screaming voices of his own parents.

In concerts, the Lubovitch company performs a new dance of Lar's, "Big Shoulders," inspired by the architecture of our native town—the one which Carl Sandburg called "the city of the Big Shoulders." I look for reminders in this dance, memories of the adventures we had romping among those historic buildings in the middle of the night. With Lar, I had full license for fantasy—a welcome respite from the conformist pressures of the Eisenhower era, pressures which seemed out of phase with the chaos of my own family life. At night, we would become the characters in the Tennessee Williams movies we adored. I'd be Anna Magnani, hiding the rose tattoo on my breast, and Lar would be Marlon Brando in his snakeskin jacket. "Wild things leave skins behind them." We would cheer each other on with our highest praise: "You break every rule."

We would ride the buses and the El on those chilly nights, talking to strangers in affected accents. I could do a passable Katherine Hepburn and would accost some stranger, point to Lar (who in my mind was now Montgomery Clift), and say, "Suddenly last summer, Sebastian went away. There was debris, debris everywhere." Sometimes Lar would physically move me from one seat to another because "the composition isn't right." All the while, the train would be whizzing by those buildings—the jewels of Frank Lloyd Wright, Sullivan and Adler, Mies van der Rohe; I didn't recognize the names, but I'll never forget the details. Lar would point them out—a sculpted ledge, an elegant cornice, a lion's face carved above a third floor window. I was sure that no one but us saw these things—we, the dancing prince and princess, beyond any parental consciousness, in the dead of night.

By day I had to share Lar with the real Jewish princesses who fought to be his dance partners. He never studied dance. No boy who wanted to remain alive at my high school could have. In fact, Lar had no notion of being a dancer at that time; he was a painter. Still, he was in excellent physical shape because he joined the school gymnastics team. And at weddings and parties a group would always form around Lar and clap and beg him to do the "kazatski," the kicking Russian folk dance. Then, some girl whom I invariably hated, one of those pampered, ponytailed darlings whose parents made sure she was home by midnight, would grab Lar's hand and share the spotlight with him as they jitterbugged to Little Richard or Frankie Lymon or Elvis. I was far too awkward to ever dance with him in public. Alone, he tried to teach me, but he always laughed too much.

Lar was in charge of our high school theatricals, of course. They would be produced by, directed by, written by, choreographed by, and, frequently, starred in by Lar Lubovitch. They were always wonderful rousing shows about love, God, clowns, and America. He'd usually write in some cameo role for me—frequently a comedy part where I would be a little girl in a big straw hat with a lollipop. I could consult on music because I had a good memory for lyrics. In our junior year, I got us on a local TV show called *Musical Charades* where we would play against teams from other high schools, guessing songs and acting out the lyrics to our teammates (no kidding). We won every week for thirteen weeks until the show went off the air. It was my one contribution to our careers in show biz.

We wrote to each other from college—mostly witty poems in which we tried to outdo each other in the free use of obscenity. He came to my school once to choreograph a show I wrote, a musical comedy adapted from Albert Camus' *The Stranger*. Not a great idea; it was my last fling in the performing arts. But not Lar's. Suddenly that summer, he dropped out of the painting program at the University of Iowa and went to study dance in Germany. At nineteen he had found his metier.

He moved to New York and earned a dance scholarship to Juilliard. There he would meet and study with such dance luminaries as Antony Tudor, Jose Limon, and Louis Horst. With a friend in the Big Apple, I decided it was time for me to shed "these little town blues" and moved East. My flight to New York at nineteen was my first time on an airplane. Lar and I shared a section of the plane with a man who was vice president for International Telephone and Telegraph. As we landed, Mr. IT&T said of the city at night, "Doesn't it look like diamonds on a jeweler's velvet?" He offered us a ride into town in his chauffeur-driven Caddy limo. The radio played a hit song of the time, Jay and the Americans singing "Only in America, land of opportunity . . . Yi-Yi-Yi."

The friendship didn't quite work in New York. Adulthood was closing in with the increasing pressures to mate, find work, stop fooling around. The fantasy life took on more of an air of escape than enrichment. We would stage mock fights in front of the window of his apartment for the benefit of the hundreds of windows that looked on. I was Gittel Gitlitz, aspiring actress and poetess (the name came from Gitlitz's, a favorite deli). He was (and here the name was invented) Lar Lubovitch, aspiring choreographer. Behind the scenes we had real, brutal fights. We talked a lot then of feeling "desperate." Meanwhile Lar was rising in the dance world and would soon perform with Pearl Lang, Donald McKayle, Sophie Maslow, Glen Tetley, Anna Sokolow, and Rebecca Harkness. I was writing hundreds of poems which I buried in a drawer, studying literature, and doing a thesis on my heroine, Emily Dickinson.

It was painful to face up to the fact that our friendship was just not helping either of us anymore. One day I told him, in essence, that I was going to California and didn't think we should see each other until we grew up.

Eight years later, we got back in touch. He visited me at my apartment on Vine Street when his company was touring California. He was still dancing then and when we sat out in the sun he took his shoes off. I gasped when I saw his toes. There were muscles where I never knew muscles could exist. They were almost freakish.

In some ways it was easy to talk. In others, it wasn't. He had become something of a celebrity—world acclaim, featured on the TV series *Dance in America*, and soon he would appear on the cover of *Dance Magazine*. He was now a decidedly more private person, much more protective of himself. But the need for a friend was still there and the bond of humor still worked in our favor. When I asked him once how he felt about all he'd accomplished, he said, "The greatest moment in my career was when I saw a bum sleeping in the doorway of my building in New York, resting his face on *Dance Magazine*, his cheek on mine in the picture."

Through the years now we've kept in touch. Occasionally I will get a letter from Palermo or China or the Gopher Campus Motor Lodge in Minneapolis, Minnesota, and Lar will describe the vicissitudes of life on the road. Or he will visit, and Uncle Lar will pick up my daughters and spin them around with an ease that obviously thrills them. Or we will visit his New York loft (home and dance studio), seen by millions as Dustin Hoffman and Bill Murray's apartment in *Tootsie*.

My husband happened to be staying at Lar's while on a business trip the night Baryshnikov came by to watch the company rehearse. Some nervous dancer offered Baryshnikov a beer and began to fumble around looking for a glass. At that point, Misha the Magnificent pointed to my husband who was chugging his Michelob from the bottle and said, "I will drink it redneck style—like him."

It's nice to have a link with greatness. Nicer still to have the kind of friend you can call at any time and say, "I'm depressed." I made such a call to Lar a few weeks ago. He responded by saying, "I am too. Right before our New York opening one of my lead dancers suffered a serious injury onstage and had to be rushed to the hospital in an ambulance." "What should we do now?" I asked him. "Let's go ride around on the El," he said.

Doctors and Other Common Health Problems

A Nurse's Guide to Doctors

By training, I am a nurse but in real life I am also a person. The same thing can be said for doctors, with two important differences—they're not nurses and they make more money. Some people (not me, of course) seem to resent that.

It really isn't fair of us to begrudge doctors their salaries. They work long hours, take great risks and, more and more, must suffer having the government and insurance companies dictate how they practice. Two recent surveys on doctors' incomes (one by the nationwide Roth Young Personnel Service and another by the American Medical Association) place the average annual net for all physicians at about $99,500. Now Lee Iacocca makes a much a higher salary than that, and when was the last time he gave you something for pain?

It's not fair to blame escalating health care costs on doctors alone; by and large, they aren't the ones who are profiting. (Speaking of profiting, don't blame us nurses either—as everyone knows, we're underpaid Angels in White.) But as the embodiment of the health care system, doctors come in for both our gratitude and our anger at how this system serves us. Perhaps if we understood how to use our physicians better, we'd be less angry and resentful. In pursuit of this goal—from my vantage point as a nurse and a real person—I'd like to offer a user's guide to doctors.

We'd all be much better off if we remembered one simple fact: Doctors are a lot like personal computers. As with PCs, much disappointment stems from unrealistic expectations of what the machine/person can do. Also, in both cases you can thoughtlessly throw away money hoping to buy "the best" without any real sense of what you want from it. For example, you do not need a highly specialized computer to balance your checkbook and file your recipes. Nor do you need a brain surgeon to repair a bunion (or *hallux valgus*, as we say in the nurse biz). I've had a bunion repaired and, believe me, any idiot can do it. In fact, an idiot did mine.

The garbage in/garbage out rule also applies to doctors. That is, if you feed a bunch of garbled, unrealistic messages to your doctor he will probably send you home the same wretched junk heap you were when you came in. I know how he feels. I had to take a medical history on just such a garbagewoman myself recently. Let's call her Mrs. T (no relation to Mr. T).

Me: What seems to be the problem today?

Mrs. T: Well, I've got a horrible headache, a pain in my chest, all my joints ache, I can't sleep at night, I've been constipated for 14 years, my husband just left me and I want to be tested for hypoglycemia.

Me: What is the problem that's bothering you most today?

Mrs. T: The buzzing in my ears.

Me: Did you say ringing in your ears?

Mrs. T: No, I said *buzzing*. Ringing, I've had all my life. But today it's buzzing.

What we've got here is the kind of patient who immediately gets dismissed as having "a positive review of systems." This means that when questioned about potential problems (e.g., "Do you have headaches, earaches, chest pain, stomach pain, etc.?") Mrs. T will respond positively for all of them.

Another secret code doctors use for this kind of patient is "positive for phosphorescent stools." This means that when asked "Do your stools glow in the dark?" she will respond "yes." These patients get categorized as "crocks," and most doctors will decide there is no helping them. Therefore, even though you may have come to the doctor because everything *is*, in fact, wrong with you, it's probably best not to mention it all on the first visit. You'll overload his system, poor baby, and then, you see, he cannot compute.

You've probably noticed—sharp social observer that you are—that when I describe these situations, the patient is a woman and the doctor is a man. There are several reasons for this.

First, most patients actually are women. That's because men usually don't come whimpering to their doctors with every little thing. They prefer to wait until they're unconscious and meet the doctor only when it's absolutely necessary (e.g., after the coronary bypass is over, and he's explaining how it really shouldn't affect a person's sex life—much). Second, most doctors actually are men. Although more and more women are entering medical school, they haven't caught up yet. Also, should Hollywood call and want to buy the rights to the Mrs. T story, I think the film would work best with Diane Keaton as Mrs. T and Nick Nolte as her doctor.

Finally, nurses are generally women because, as we all know, men look silly in knee-length white polyester.

No amount of medical wisdom on my part seems to have helped in my personal quest for an MDeity. My experiences as a nurse have not encouraged me to see physicians as inherently user-friendly creatures. Worse yet, the behind-the-scenes view has not encouraged user confidence. Once you've heard a surgeon say "whoops" over an anesthetized patient, you're kind of reluctant to take on the patient role.

The last time I tried to find a personal physician was when I was in nursing school. For educational purposes, I'll tell the whole story exactly as it happened—except for the names, which have been changed to protect the guilty.

We were studying the neck, and I was practicing examining my own when I felt a large lump down near my collarbone. I showed it to my instructor and she said, "You better show that to your doctor."

I didn't have one, of course, but my daughter did. She had a wonderful pediatrician. For some reason, all pediatricians are wonderful—a fact that is, unfortunately, lost on children, who are naive enough to assume that *everybody* should be wonderful to them. To us adults, who've been kicked around a bit, pediatricians are a medical tease: I-may-be-wonderful-but-I'll-never-be-yours. So, although my daughter's doctor was forthright, honest, intelligent, warm, supportive and, oddly enough, a woman, the most I could hope for from her was a referral to a doctor who sees grown-ups. She recommended her neighbor, Marvin the internist.

Now Marvin is probably a hell of a fellow—the kind of guy who comes running into a hospital staff party with an IV bottle full of Wild Turkey. He's the kind of neighbor you want to run into over by the garbage cans and chat with about new movies and loud dogs up the street. But over my dead or, in this case, live body? I'm not so sure.

Marvin had an impressive office. His interior decorator, Lance of Princeton, had papered an entire wall with Marvin's academic degrees. It put me in mind of a doctor I used to work with who once confided: "I'm doing OK with this white coat act of mine." I might have been in a better position to appreciate how long and dedicated an academic career Marvin had if only I could have read Latin.

I explained to him that I was there because I was worried about a lump on my neck, but that I also wanted a personal physician. As an internist, would he be able to deal with all of me—ear, nose, throat, body and soul?

"Hey, no problem," Marvin said, and led me to an examining room. He felt my neck and said, "Don't worry. Just a little thyroid nodule." He then went on to check my heart and lungs. Assuring me that I was in great shape, he was about to leave the room when I asked if he was going to take my Pap smear.

"Oh, did you need one?"

"It's been a couple years. Aren't you supposed to get them regularly to prevent cervical cancer from developing?"

"Well, don't you have a gynecologist?"

"But Marvin, I thought you could treat all of me?"

By then it had dawned on me that Marvin had that uncomfortable oh-no-I-have-examine-her-*down-there* look, but we had reached the point of no return. He got his nurse (his defense witness for the rape case) and began to set me up for a pelvic exam. I should have been clued in to the fact that Marvin didn't do pelvics very often when he got out a white-on-white linen tablecloth instead of a disposable paper drape to cover my legs. When it was over, he raced out of the room saying, "I'll phone you in a few days." Sure, Marvin, I've heard that one before.

But a few days later, Marvin—in sharp contrast to the guy with the gold chains in the fern bar—actually did call. "Don't worry about your neck," he said, 'but your Pap smear is abnormal. A gynecologist! And step on it!"

Panicked, I soon found myself in the stirrups of Shaun Le Flesh, hip gynecologist. "God, your cervix looks great," Shaun said, with the enthusiasm of someone discovering the Michelangelos in the Sistine Chapel. "But sit up for a moment. What's that great big lump on your neck?"

"Oh, that's nothing. My internist isn't worried about it."

"Well, *I'm* worried about it," he said, wrapping his fingers around my neck and doing a fine Boston Strangler impression.

To make a long story longer, my neck-lump odyssey next took me to the offices of Dr. Brad Harvardgrad, Ace Endocrinologist. Harvardgrad did a number of expensive, latest-in-med-tech tests which proved that I did, indeed, have a lump on my neck. He sent me on to Dr. Stitch Longing, surgeon. The lump had to come out, Longing told me listlessly. It could be The Big C. I got a second opinion from Dr. Hans Shackey, who said, "Don't take it out. Even if it's cancer you can learn to live with it. Thyroid cancers never kill. Well—almost never."

I went back to Longing for the operation. Before the surgery, he did a complete physical. While examining my breasts—which he did with the delicacy of a checker on the assembly line of a pillow factory—he said, "Tsk, tsk—lumpy." This wasn't just some one-night stand making an idle comment. This was a surgeon! A man who cuts! Believe me, I was glad to get out of there with anything left below my eyebrows.

The net effect of the whole experience was that I lost one benign neck lump, gained one small scar and still—after five doctors—had no personal physician. It reminded me that however powerless I may feel nurses are at times, it's nothing compared to the powerlessness you feel as a patient.

One reason encounters with medicine are so unpleasant is the inherent conflict of interest in the patient role. What you want to hear is, "You're really OK and you're going to get better." But medical training puts the doctor in alliance with your worst fears. Unlike a computer, which is merely there to do what you tell it, a doctor has a mind of his own—and it's a mind trained to find what's wrong. Professors of medicine will always question a novice by asking, "What are your findings, Doctor?"

Nurses, on the other hand, are trained to look at the social and psychological meaning of disease. We become the patient's ally and advocate, holding her hand while the doctor does cruel and unusual things. When we perform unpleasant procedures it's usually because "the doctor ordered it." Don't blame me—I'm just following orders.

Nurses' training emphasizes empathy, encourages identification with the patient. Doctors' training encourages objectivity, the kind of scientific distance that allows for an unbiased investigation of a specimen (i.e. patient). We're trained to give back rubs. He's trained to do sigmoidoscopy.

I recall a horrifying moment when I saw a young man transformed into a doctor right before my eyes. He was a fourth-year medical student I had known years before, when we had been idealistic volunteers together at a neighborhood free clinic. Running into each other one day at the medical center where we both were working, we spoke nostalgically of the old days and our vows to "serve the people." Then he went into the examining room to see his patient, a woman with a serious but as yet undiagnosed illness.

A few minutes later, he emerged from the room with a look of wild glee on his face. He rushed up to me and said, "I found a mass!" Then he proceeded to literally skip down the hall chanting, "I found a mass! I found a mass! I found a mass!"

The patient has a bit of a conflict with all this finding business. After all, for her the product in question is none other than her body, her self. This means she hopes the doctor won't *find* anything. On the other hand, people usually go to the doctor because something is bothering them and they want it found and treated.

Where, then, do you jump into the medical system for help?

As a nurse-practitioner, I frequently see people who tell me "I hate to go to the doctor's." I usually respond, "That's fine because I'm a nurse." And indeed, some people now see nurse-practitioners or physician's assistants for their first contact with the health care system. If you're sick of self-care and can't find an N.P., however, you probably need to find a physician.

Generally speaking, your personal physician should be a generalist—a general practitioner, family physician or internist. Some people call these initial or basic providers of health care "primary care providers." To me, that sounds a little ominous—like if primary comes, can secondary or tertiary be far behind? And why not skip the middleman?

But primary care is the place to be, unless you know *exactly* what specialist you need (see my directory below). The advantage is that you can get nose-to-toes one-stop service without the expense or the dehumanization of seeing a separate skin man, lung man, and foot man. Then your primary provider can tell you if you really need a specialist or if the buck stops there. The trick, obviously, is finding a first-care provider you can trust.

When it comes down to it, what you really want is an unambitious doctor who watched too much *Marcus Welby* or *Dr. Kildare* when he was growing up. Most people who go through a long, grueling, and expensive medical training come to expect a reward for it—more money, social status, the chance to growl at nurses. But general practice and family practice doctors frequently claim they just want to be nice and help people feel better. Some even see nurses as colleagues—a real sign of degeneracy.

For these reasons, GPs and FPs are generally regarded by their peers as "jerks." Last year, these jerks (according to the AMA survey) actually saw their net income decline to a measly average of $71,900.

No doubt about it—a jerk is what you want.

Know Your Specialists

Often it is necessary for your primary care physician or nurse-practitioner—assuming you've been lucky enough to find one—to send you to a specialist. Specialists are people with lengthy training who perform procedures nobody else can do. It has been observed that their lengthy training often neglects the area of communications skills.

Obviously, it's a waste of their time and your money to see them inappropriately. Worse, it could be hazardous to your health. There is a glut of specialists in some areas, and studies have shown that rather than lowering health care costs, specialist gluts tend to increase the number of procedures performed. This means that if you walk into the wrong office, faster than you can say "earache" someone will have your gallbladder in his hands.

So to avoid unnecessary procedures, you need to know your specialists. Here's a quick guide to the major ones and their domains.

ALLERGIST—He tries to find out what's causing your chronic sniffles and wheezes. Usually he tests you with many tiny shots. You have to ask yourself what's worse, your symptoms or the treatment.

ANESTHESIOLOGIST—He sees you when you're sleeping. He knows when you're awake. For this (according to the Roth Young Personnel Survey) he is the highest paid physician, with a median net of $150,200.

CARDIOLOGIST—Curer *du coeur*. He benefits from our virtues and our vices, scraping the over-enthusiastic jogger off the ground and seeing the end result of a diet of buttered cigarettes.

DERMATOLOGIST—Envied by other doctors because of the relative ease of his practice. Nobody ever gets called at 3:00 a.m. to perform an emergency zitectomy.

ENDOCRINOLOGIST—If your glands secrete 'em, he can treat 'em.

56

GASTROENTEROLOGIST—He can find your ulcer, your cancer, or your alcoholic liver but mostly what he gets is a lot of gas.

HEMATOLOGIST—Not quite a Draculologist, he helps diagnose and treat blood diseases and cancer.

INDUSTRIAL MEDICINE SPECIALIST—After a long career of eating asbestos, you go to see him and he tells you why you don't feel so good.

INTERNIST—An expert in the area sometimes known as "infernal medicine." He is a diagnostic detective, supposedly more sophisticated than a general practitioner.

NEPHROLOGIST—This is the guy with the kidney-shaped offices. Not to be confused with the "cash-for-kidneys" transplant ghouls.

NEUROLOGIST—See him when there's something wrong with your brain or nervous system. When it's all in your head he can take it out; but can't he do anything for Rodney Dangerfield?

OBSTETRICIAN AND GYNECOLOGIST—A (usually) male midwife.

ONCOLOGIST—Don't ask.

OPTHALMOLOGIST—Eye spy.

ORTHOPEDIST—Bones are his business. As one recently remarked to me, "One more jogger's knee and I'll have a Mercedes."

ORORHINOLARYNGOLOGIST—Ear, nose, and throat to you, but if you can say the word the visit's free. Be highly suspicious if he asks you to strip.

PEDIATRICIAN—The wonderful doctor who lets your children spit in his face.

PLASTIC AND RECONSTRUCTIVE SURGEON—The ultimate make-over artist. See him for everything from a nose job to a suction lipectomy (or "sucking fat" as this procedure is quaintly called).

PSYCHIATRIST—This is the guy in the black negligee who's hanging upside down from the chandelier laughing. Confide your deepest problems to him.

PULMONARY DISEASE SPECIALIST—A pack a day brings business his way.

RADIOLOGIST—The man with X-ray vision. According to the AMA survey, his income was up 17 percent in 1982 to an average net of $136,800.

RHEUMATOLOGIST—See him when the joint is jumping.

SURGEON—Comes in two kinds: conservative and aggressive. Conservative here does not mean a right-winger; it means a guy not eager to cut. Aggressive means he's standing at the door of his office waving a machete and smiling. Vote conservative.

UROLOGIST— A man's gynecologist.

Cold Comfort

Writing about health around here is a little like stepping into a cowboy bar and shouting, "Who's man enough to take me?" *Everyone* I know in California assumes the role of health expert, and we live in a virtual supermarket of competing systems of healing. You've got— just to name a few—your western medicine, your eastern medicine, your native American healers, your acupuncturists, megavitaminists, and irridologists. Most people try to hedge their bets by popping a couple vitamins, eating a little garlic, and hoarding a few prescription drugs when the opportunity presents itself. But what actually happens when you get sick?

I don't mean *sick* sick—Killer Disease sick. I mean the kind of thing that will happen to the average adult 2.5 times this winter. I am talking about the times when you go to bed feeling great thinking that tomorrow's the day you're going to wake up, jog ten miles before breakfast, eat a plate of fresh-picked wheat and raw liver, then go out there and begin that relentless climb to the top, but instead you wake up with that little sandpaper feeling in the back of your throat. You're too tired to jog. You begin to sneeze and decide to go heavy on the vitamin C. You spring for the rose hips, but by midafternoon even you can't stand the adenoidal twang to your voice. By evening the slight drip from your nose has advanced to a flash flood. Determined to lick this thing, so to speak, you behave sensibly. You go home and get into bed. You decide to do some light reading but a youth wasted on the study of literary criticism renders you unfit for most trash. Fortunately, you do have *Shelley*, the autobiography of Shelley Winters.

You lie down under the comforting blankets and think: if I just get a good night's sleep I can lick this thing. However, you soon become aware of the impossibility of sleeping. For one thing, somewhere up in your sinuses nasty little tiny elves are laughing and spilling buckets of mucus. The faster you blow, the harder they pour. Soon your poor nose begins to ache and chafe.

Okay, you say, I'll forget my nose. People can live very nicely without noses (Gentiles have been doing it for years). So, you decide to limit your breathing to your mouth. It's then that you become aware of a dry gagging sensation at the back of your throat. I will not cough, you pledge, but the tiny elves are back. This time they're swinging on your uvula, that obscene little flap hanging at the back of your throat. They'll never break my will, you vow. I will not cough. But the elves are going wild now, yanking that uvula first leftward, then rightward—heave, ho—heave, ho! Cough, you sonofabitch, cough.

More elves come. They're down in your chest now, swabbing those little tree-like branches in your lungs with yet another bucket brigade. You, with your steel will, can no longer stop it and you let go with a violent crescendo of coughing. When the quaking stops you see your night stretched out before you like an endless line of telephone poles . . . a sitcom, a cop show, two newses, and when you hear that "Heeeeeeeeeere's Johnny" you know you're on a one-way ticket to Zombieville. The sleep cure will not work without sleep.

The next day you attempt to tough it out and go about your business. Just a little cold you tell yourself, old *coldus commonitis*. Just in case, you take massive doses of vitamin C and try to remember what it was that Linus Pauling won the Nobel Prize for. Maybe it was in literature—*Lord of the Lies* or something.

Your friends and colleagues wait patiently, albeit holding their breath, as you finish each paroxysm of coughing. Each one of them is an expert and will tell you with an authoritative pointing of the index finger and a generous waiving of the customary fees what you *should* be doing.

"Warm vinegar and honey every two hours. My grandmother did it and it always works."

"The bourbon cure. It may not work, but halfway into it you won't care."

"I have a friend who does biofeedback . . ."

"Continuous pressure between the 4th and 5th toes, right along the uvula meridian."

"How about a little snort? Things go better with coke."

That night your insignificant other not only refuses to participate in "the sex cure" but he takes half the blankets and goes to sleep on the couch. Abandoned, coughing, red-nosed, you make the following vow: if I get out of this alive, I'll douse myself with Jontue and find some working-class stud at Brennan's Irish Bar. You know, the kind that won't let a little tuberculosis spoil a good time.

The next day a friend at work who is also a psychic reader offers the following devastating insight: you're not just sick, you're depressed. Absolutely, you agree, but I'm too sick to do anything about it.

Wrong. Colds are caused by denying your sadness, she tells you. You've been wanting to cry but you've blocked your mucus. The mucus has to come out so you get the cold. See? The cure, of course, is "to get in touch with your feelings," which presumably means to cry your mucus out.

That night you resolve to take the cure. You ask your partner to leave with something succinct like "since you're incapable of being supportive, go to hell." The children, if you have them, go to your ex's or the sitters. They, who reserve the right to scream and cry over anything from a missing Barbie shoe to the suggestion that they clean their room, are appalled at the idea of mom crying. Also, an article you read maybe in *Redbook* suggested that crying in front of the children leaves subacute emotional scars. Rather than paying the future emotional cleaning bill you get them out of the house.

Finally you are alone and free to express your emotions. Okay. Now cry, you sonofabitch, cry. But the tears won't come. Your nose is still running like Niagara, but emotionally it's a Grand Coulee situation. In an effort to free your tears, you get out the old schmaltzy records. First, there's Julie London having an asthma attack and wheezing, "Cry Me A River." Nothing. Not one little tear is making a break for it. Frank. How about Frank? Can he scooby dooby do it? You listen to . . . "Only the Lonely."

Hey, look out Jack—no tears. Smokey. Smokey'll yank 'em out with . . . "The Tracks of My Tears."

Not a track mark in sight. Since the old songs won't seem to get you there you try a little Stanislavsky. Method acting. You draw on personal experience. You dredge it all up now—the funeral fantasy, the unrequited love, the rejection slips. . . . Pretty soon it's Gush City. Boy were you blocked. Once those flood gates are opened it's three hours before the last tissue is saturated. You should've bought stock in Crown Zellerbach.

You begin to regret going the cry-it-out route. You should've gone with the Norman Cousins' healing with laughter method. More fun.

The next morning you wake up feeling lousier than ever. Your nose is a disaster area and your eyes are virtually swollen shut. You begin to wonder if there isn't something *really* wrong with you. You get out *The Overeducated Person's Guide to Complete Total Absolute Wellness* and look up lupus, osteoporosis, and sarcoma but none of your symptoms fit. You probably have something really weird. You must get help. Looks like this is a case for young Doctor Killjoy.

Killjoy's receptionist says he can squeeze you in next month. By then I'll be dead, you think, and you decide to exaggerate a little as your self-advocacy workshop taught you. "This is an emergency and if I am not seen today I will contact my lawyer and make sure the malpractice settlement is included in my will."

In an hour Killjoy has you stretched out on the table and is fast at work invading every area of your body. "Throat's a little red but nothing to write home about. Eyes are kind of puffy—you been crying? Ears are fine. No otitis media. Lymph glands? Within normal limits," he says moronically exploring your armpits. (You: I will not laugh. I will not laugh.)

"Your lungs are clear so forget pneumonia and bronchitis. Now if you'll just roll over and bend your knees I'll do the rectal."

Whoa, Killjoy! Just a minute. And you try to recall whether you've ever read about any connection between the rectum and the common cold. Outside of an old joke about an opera singer who was just clearing her throat, you fail to see the potential yield on this procedure. You explain your reluctance.

"Good. You're questioning me. That shows you're thinking," says Killjoy, showing he's hip. "However, suppose you leave here and later it turns out you have a massive hemorrhoid. You sue me for malpractice and there goes my vacation in Puerta Vallarta not to mention the kids' orthodontist. You see, I've got to practice defensively. Now, bend and spread."

The indignities over with, you are now invited to sit opposite Killjoy's framed academic This Is Your Life as he pronounces the verdict: "Your lack of fever combined with the symptoms of runny nose, cough, tightness in the chest, and sore throat lead me to conclude that you have a viral upper respiratory infection. In short you have the common cold and will be fine in a few days. Thank you very much. By the way, we now accept Visa and Mastercard."

Not so fast, white-coat-man, you think. Although his hand is on the doorknob, you assert yourself and say, "Well, can't you give me anything? I have a very busy week."

"Sure, I could give you some combination of antihistamines and decongestants that might make you feel a little better. But these things only help relieve the symptoms and have no effect on the outcome. In fact, there's some evidence that antihistamines may prolong a cold."

"What about antibiotics?"

"Useless on viruses."

"Well, how did I get this in the first place?"

Dr. Killjoy gives you a slightly annoyed look, but he gives up on the knob and returns to the chair. "The cold is spread by airborne droplets from others who have the germ. Most people will get two or three colds per year except preschool children [who are pre-people anyway]. They get an average of six to twelve colds a year. That means parents of young children will have more like six colds themselves. You wanna stay well? You take The Pill. Haw. Haw. Haw."

"But I'm a very careful, healthy person. Why did I get sick now?"

"We don't know why the incidence of common colds goes up

in the winter months but typically colds occur in three waves. The first is in the fall shortly after school starts. The second wave is in the middle of winter and the third wave is in the spring. So you've just caught a wave, as the surfers say. Haw. Haw. Haw."

"Does the cold weather give you colds?" you ask undeterred.

"There are several theories on this. One is that people spend more time indoors in winter making it easier for the infection to spread. Another is that the lack of humidity caused by overheated houses dries the respiratory passages making them more suscepti-ble to infection. Finally, there is the observation that outbreaks of colds follow sharp changes in the weather. But nobody has ever proven anything other than that over ninety different strains of vi-ruses cause what we call the common cold syndrome. Therefore, exposure to one confers no immunity to another."

"This is all very grim news, Dr. Killjoy. But don't you have any suggestions for what I can do?"

"Sure. First you place a gun to the temporal lobe. Haw. Haw. Haw. Seriously, a lot of humidity and maybe some chicken soup ought to do it."

"Oh, come on now, does that really work?"

"There's actually evidence that it does. Several years ago there was a study on the use of chicken soup done at Tel Aviv Univer-sity." (You: Haw. Haw. Haw.)

"Seriously, there is something in the chicken soup. I think it's the electrolytes. I don't know. Anyway, call me if you develop ear pain, fever, lots of yellow-green sputum, or an inability to pay your bill." And laying his finger aside of his nose, Dr. Killjoy dis-appeared among the viral-infested corridors of his office.

Chicken soup. I've got to have the chicken soup, you think. But how? Sick as you are, you look in your cookbooks—*Sushi Si, Pasta No!, Nouvelle Riche*, and *The Joy of Hunan*. You can't find chicken soup anywhere.

Relax! Your quest is over, my gentle but highly contagious reader. Before you turn the next ink-smeared page, I will reveal to you the secrets of boubies past—the ancient art of making matzoh ball soup as passed down to me by the wise women of medieval Poland and western Chicago.

The induction into the cult of matzoh balling is one that has intrigued feminine healers through the centuries from the cauldrons of Europe to the tupperworn kitchens of suburbia. It is rumored that the first thing Arthur Miller's mother did upon learning that her boy was about to marry sex goddess Marilyn Monroe was to teach the actress how to prepare the soup. Upon tasting her first matzoh ball, Monroe is reported to have said, "It's delicious. What do they do with the rest of the animal?"

Just so there is no confusion as to which part of the soup is what, here is a step-by-schlep guide to the making of the soup.

1. Throw a chicken into a pot. (You can, of course, merely place the chicken in the pot or gently lower it into a crock or flip the bird to the cauldron. Whichever method you choose, the chicken should be clean, free of feathers, and, certainly, dead.)

2. Add vegetables. Tradition dictates an onion (peeling it may also combine the crying cure with the soup cure), a few sliced carrots, and a few stalks of celery with the leaves (the real voodoo's in the leaves). Now, my mother always sent me out for something she called "a parsley and a parsnip" but this may just be the Bialystok regional variant. You can use the vegetables as a chance to "go creative," throwing in a little basil to make it trendier, a little red pepper to give it some third world power, a little garlic just to show you're hip, or some file to show you've been to K-Paul's.

3. Cover with water. Tap ordinaire will do. Perrier would be decidedly *goyish* and really jack up the price. And no sherry, please. Here you would be getting into the area of sacrilege.

4. Add salt, boil, then lower to simmer until done. How long will this take? Opinions vary but a good guide is the chicken himself (*sic*sist). Orthodox doneness means when you yank on the leg, the bone not only comes off but crumbles in your hand. Conservative doneness has the meat still adhering to the bone. Reformed doneness means that the chicken is still a bloody mess. Consult your clergyman on the ancient question of how done is done.

5. Remove the chicken. Make the matzoh balls. The best way to make the matzoh balls is to prepare the mixture according to the directions on the matzoh meal box. Combine the eggs, water, shortening, matzoh meal, and salt. (Ancient wisdom dictates you add a hair from the beard of the Rabbi of Danzig. Although I'm sure the real cure lies here—especially since the town is now called

Gdansk—we'll skip this step.) Let the mixture stand twenty minutes, then start shaping the matzoh balls. Drop your balls in the soup and cook until firm.

Within three to six days after consuming the soup, you will be a little, if not completely, better. If the soup doesn't work then you will know for certain that you have the uncommon cold. If this is the case, I want you to march promptly back to Dr. Killjoy's and demand massive quantities of dangerous drugs.

Going with the Flow

About once a month I get a strong urge to write about menstrual periods. Usually I wait a few days and then I forget what all the fuss was about. This month, however, I have decided to go with the flow and tell all. Not that this will be anything new for women readers. I believe it was Aristotle who said, "The real challenge in life is to write something about periods that men can stand to read."

Not exactly cocktail party conversation, you say. And, of course, I must ask myself: why risk a reputation for tact and delicacy by going public with a subject that's been taboo since ancient times? I suppose it's because I suspect that there are men who wonder what the *real* story is on cramps, premenstrual tension, fertility awareness, cyclic variation in sexual desire, and a number of other problems usually thought to be women's matters. I asked a man friend if he thought that men were simply too shy to ask about these things. "Shy?" he said. "I think more like revolted."

It was a boy, in fact, who first broke the news, euphemistically called "the facts of life," to me. It was in the fifth grade and his name was David Jacobs. I remember him well because I'd had the hots for him since kindergarten. On that fateful day, we were sitting in the assembly hall watching the annual Christmas pageant. (Where were you in '52?) As I was sitting there resenting the fact that I had once again failed to land the part of the Virgin Mary, David turned to me and said, "You know girls bleed once a month for their whole life."

"You're crazy."

"I'm not. You get this thing called a period when you're around twelve and you bleed."

"Bleed where?"

"Down there," he said, pointing between the legs of his nubby corduroy pants.

"That's the most horrible thing I've ever heard."

"You ask your mother."

"Just girls?"

"Just girls."

So, I asked my mother. She giggled and said, "That David Jacobs is a moron. Don't sit next to him."

A few days later she handed me a pamphlet called "Growing Up and Liking It." It was produced by Walt Disney for the Kotex Corporation. It was probably the way most girls in the 50's learned about menstruation (or ministration as I called it for years). I vaguely remember a picture of a girl who looked like Snow White standing in the shower with a look of horror on her face. Then a creature—maybe Bambi—was sent out to the drugstore for a box of Kotex.

I still couldn't believe it but one day when I was eleven it happened to me. I told my mother and she slapped me across the face—an old eastern European superstition, I learned later, to make sure the blood still comes to your cheeks.

Somewhere, I got the idea (cultural sieve that I was) that my "monthly" was a dark secret. I lived in fear of any revealing signs of it. (You'll notice that tampon ads frequently feature a confident girl in white shorts.) I could talk to my girlfriends about "a visit from my Aunt Mary" but somehow got the quiet message that you *never* mention it to boys, not even hip ones like David Jacobs.

Some girls couldn't keep it a secret. For them "the curse" really was a curse. They suffered from terrible pain called "cramps" every month. They claimed they could hardly do anything at this time, especially PE. Like most girls who only had mild twinges, I joined in the almost universal opinion that these prima donnas were a bunch of crocks. Medical opinion concurred. *Current Diagnosis and Treatment*, a medical reference book widely used by physicians, described cramps this way: "The pain is *always* secondary to an emotional problem" (emphasis mine). The text then explained, "In women with insight who are cooperative and want to be cured, the prognosis is good. Very little can be done for the patient who prefers to use menstrual symptoms as a monthly refuge from responsibility and participation."

Around 1980, a theory of menstrual pain emerged. It was thought to be caused by excess secretion in the uterus of a chemical called prostaglandin. A whole group of drugs that were traditionally used to treat arthritis and that were functionally anti-prostaglandins miraculously stopped the pain. One of those quiet little revolutions took place. From 1980 on, *Current Diagnosis and Treatment* dropped all discussion of menstrual cramps as a psychological problem. Today's edition describes a straightforward physical entity and its treatment. However, there probably are still women out there doubled up on some analyst's couch, trying to answer the musical question, "Zo, ven did you first hate being a vomen?"

The big new sign of the crazed bitch is a condition called Premenstrual Syndrome (PMS). *The Journal of the American Medical Association* has called PMS "the women's health problem of the 80's." PMS is the "in" problem because it occurs primarily among women in their 30's. Thus, it hits the babyboomers, which makes it marketable. You'll find articles on PMS stuffed between the cigarette ads and the sexual enhancement suggestions in almost every women's mag.

What is it? It's pretty much everything that can go wrong from the time a woman ovulates in the middle of her cycle until "Aunt Mary" pays her a visit. The symptoms are physical (fluid retention, headaches, fatigue) as well as emotional (depression, anxiety, feeling out of control). PMS has been used successfully in England as a kind of insanity defense leading to the acquittal of some women who killed during this time. Feminists are in a quandary—wanting to support PMS sufferers but not wanting to legitimize an excuse for not hiring women because they may be unstable seven or more days every month.

The causes and the treatment of PMS are under debate. A popular theory, advanced by Dr. Katherina Dalton in England, is that PMS is caused by a deficiency of one female hormone, progesterone, and that it can be cured by hormone replacement. Most doctors in the United States feel this is unproven but they're not sure what to do. At a recent discussion of PMS at Alta Bates Hospital, a prominent endrocrinologist suggested (half seriously) that "these women might want to consider locking themselves in a room with a good supply of Valiums for several days."

On the bright side, PMS may be useful as an adjunct to natural birth control or fertility awareness. This method combines observing body signs and temperature to determine when ovulation takes place and when you can safely have sex without contraceptives. Fertility awareness is well described in many books, such as Margaret Nofzinger's *A Cooperative Method of Natural Birth Control*. Since the safest time is after ovulation, PMS combined with temperature readings can allow for carefree contraceptive-free sex. Unfortunately, there is a tendency among some women, as reported in the literature, to note a decrease in desire at this time. Libido (that little sonofagun) seems to be the strongest around the time of ovulation. This is wonderful news for carrying on the race but a real drag if you're merely looking for a good time.

For a woman trying to conceive, the appearance of menstrual bleeding is a bitter disappointment. But for the millions who use *chance*—the world's most popular birth control method—the sight of the blood is a welcome reprieve from unwanted responsibility. Perhaps many of you are right at this moment saying silent prayers of thanks: Hail Aunt Mary full of grace . . .

Shelf Help

You don't mind dyin'
if you've got a natural sense of rhythm . . .
　　　　　　　　—LENNY BRUCE

It is 3:00 a.m., and you can't sleep. You shift positions. You rub your face. You scratch your back. Nervously, you slip your fingers along the side of your neck. It's still there—the lump. It's not getting bigger, but it's not going away. A lump that won't go away . . . isn't that, you think, one of the Ten Commandments of cancer? And hey—wait a minute—yes, down on your leg: sure enough, it's a sore that won't heal. Strike two. By now you are in a deep fetal position and feel a tightening in your throat. You cough. That would be your persistent cough. Strike three.

You are not alone. You are one of millions of modern Americans having a religious experience. And, if anxiety is our religion, then worry is our form of prayer. But how to cope? You can go through your black book and phone one of the friends you haven't previously burned out on 3:00 a.m. anxiety attack phone calls. (No, better to save them for when you're actually spitting blood.) If you're lucky enough to have an entire cheesecake in the refrigerator, you can eat the entire cheesecake but—no such luck. You can always go to a hospital emergency room, wait several hours, risk making an ass of yourself, and end up with a stiff tab for the pleasure. Or you can do what millions of people in angst-filled chambers across the land are doing—reach for the good book, the prayer book, the self-help medical book.

Armed with this shelf help, you soon realize your lump is a calcified lymph gland, your sore reoccurs because you pick it, and your cough is caused by *globus hystericus*, a neurotic feeling of a lump in the throat. You will live. You will dance again. You will wake up on other nights, turn other pages, label other symptoms and, by labeling, end them—to sleep, perchance to dream.

I have been reading upon the midnight when in pain since my girlhood. I can trace the stages of my life recalling what self-help book I kept near my bed. First, it was Dr. Morris Fishbein's *Home Medical Advisor*, biblical in both size and scope. You would start out trying to find one sympton in the book, and end up worrying about five or six new ones you didn't know about until Dr. Fishbein brought them to your attention. This was followed by *Growing Up and Liking It*, something my mother gave me because she couldn't explain the facts of life without giggling. Next came my adolescent obsession with finding a label for my insanity. My two favorites at that point were *A Primer of Freudian Psychology* and my older sister's abnormal psych text. These gave me the tools I needed to lie awake for hours debating whether I was schizophrenic, psychotic, or merely neurotic.

As soon as I was on my own, I spent my would-be sleeping hours poring over *The Egg and Sperm Handbook: How to Take the Worry Out of Being Close*, an early booklet on contraception. Then, finally, came the book that would carry me through the next decade, *Our Bodies, Our Selves*, the ultimate self-help book written by ordinary women and originally distributed for free. Then I got pregnant—for many people a time for an orgy of self-help reading—and my particular bible at that time was *Spiritual Midwifery*, the only book that really describes childbirth in all its mind-altering weirdness.

If you support your local bookstore, you probably know that they have an extensive "health" section (with the possible exception of toney new bookstores, which seem to regard cuisine and belle lettres as more important than self-diagnosis and treatment). You will also notice that at least two-thirds of these health books are geared towards women "and the men who love them." There are several reasons for this. Women comprise two-thirds of the patient population in doctors' offices. Women are traditionally the guardians of the family health, expected to nurse the sick and tend to routine doctor visits. Worrying about your body is also viewed as wimpy, a sign of weakness, something a real man only does when he is on his way to a triple bypass. And, finally, let's face it— there's something about bleeding every month that forces you to pay attention.

With this in mind, stand by for the next avalanche of self-help books. They will be about menopause. With the bulk of the baby-boom book-buying public pushing forty, redefining and refining the older woman has become big business. Check the bestseller list for the latest offering from Queen Midas, Jane Fonda's *Women Coming of Age*. Ms. Fonda's main contribution here, perhaps, is taking the subject out of the bathroom bookshelf and laying it, in an attractive format, on the coffee table. (I have long suspected that men purchased Fonda's *Work-Out Book* for their female partners with the ulterior motive of access to the softcore photos of Barbarella stretching her hamstrings.)

A less glamorous but very valuable book on "preparing for the second half of life" is *Menopause, Naturally*. It was written by Dr. Sadja Greenwood (formerly Goldsmith), who has long been an almost cultlike figure among women's health groupies. She is certainly my idol and a role model for me as a health care provider. I benefited from her instruction when I worked with the women's health collective as well as when I studied to be a nurse-practitioner and, later, when I worked with her at Planned Parenthood. She's always exhibited a rare combination of compassion, common sense, and technical expertise. Plus she is a lovely woman—beautiful at fifty-three (but not in the Joan Collins unattainable sense) and admirable in having overcome her own bout with serious disease. As she explains in the introduction to her book, "A patient for the first time, I understood the fear of disease, the power of modern medical treatment, and the awesome side effects they create. My reaction was to try my utmost to get healthy and stay that way."

The title, *Menopause, Naturally*, is a pun on several levels. It reminds you of the underlying fact that menopause is a natural phase of life, not a disease. Greenwood's approach is an affirmation of the progress women have made since the dread Dr. Robert Wilson's 1966 bestseller on menopause, *Forever Feminine*, which advocated hormonal treatment for all. Here is an example of Wilson's attitude:

"It is on the next lower rung of the social scale that the most pitiful causes of menopausal negativism are usually found. In the vast social and spiritual wasteland below the comfortable suburban strata, in the drabness of the lower middle class. . . . Typically, such a woman, shackled to a dull commonplace man, lacks that margin of imagination, cultural interest, and developed taste that helps upper-class women to fight back against menopausal despair . . . such women generally flock together in small groups of three and four. Not that they have anything to share but their boredom and trivial gossip . . ."

Compare this to Dr. Greenwood's observation: "Recent research indicates that people with close-knit ties to family, friends, religious, or social groups have lower mortality rates from all diseases than people who are socially isolated. It has been postulated in this regard that one reason women live longer than men may be related to their greater interest in social and family ties."

Menopause, Naturally explains the ways in which drugs like cigarettes, alcohol, coffee, and marijuana may affect a woman physiologically and make her more symptomatic at menopause (i.e., more hot flashes, night sweats, and erratic bleeding). It also includes valuable, clearly explained information to help a woman decide such crucial issues as when hysterectomy and estrogen replacement are necessary. Since Greenwood is on the gynecology faculty at the University of California and a student of Eastern medicine, she tends to see all sides of the story. Thus, she observes about women facing hysterectomy: "Many fear the idea of losing a part of their body, entering a hospital with its relative impersonality, and experiencing pain, weakness, and possible complications from surgery. Others see drama in the hospital atmosphere and enjoy the special attention and the mind-altering drugs they receive."

Greenwood is a strong advocate of use-it-or-lose-it, not only when it comes to exercise, but also sexual activity. She quotes Rosetta Reitz saying, "The nutty thing about being an older woman as far as sex is concerned is that most women don't feel old when it comes to sex." Then, Greenwood points out that "a recent study of women after the menopause revealed that those who continued to have intercourse, or to masturbate, showed fewer signs of vaginal aging than sexually inactive women." There is also a break with the fraternal order here as Greenwood questions the medical practice of routinely removing a woman's ovaries (a procedure called "castration") along with her uterus during a hysterectomy. Although doctors have argued they can replace the hormones put out by the ovaries with pills, Greenwood points out that they cannot easily replace the androgens necessary for sexual function. "Recent research indicates that androgens are secreted in small amounts even by women in their eighties," she reports, and urges women to question the practice of needlessly removing the ovaries.

With such information, *Menopause, Naturally* rises above self-help and moves into the area of *informed consent*. If I have one main bone to pick with the megatrend towards medical self-care (aside from the dreadful writing in most of these books), it is the over-emphasis on the self which has led to an epidemic of responsibility. People no longer believe in germs and disease. They believe in unhealthy lifestyles, in lack of exercise, in the wrong diet or attitude—in short, in a cruel, unrealistic, and condemning self-control.

When I spoke to Greenwood about her book, I expressed my concern that too many of the new books on aging were nauseatingly upbeat. This is not how I am experiencing midlife. I am finding it a confusing time, somewhere between the attractiveness and energy of youth and the dignity of age. I'm not Joan Collins in *Dynasty*, but I'm not Shirley Booth in *Come Back Little Sheba* either. I'm a pioneer, trying to find a new road, and, frankly, I'm scared. After all, I am on a continuum towards what poet Philip Larkin described this way:

Only one ship is seeking us, a black-
Sailed unfamiliar . . .

Signs of aging are my first glimpse of this inevitability. As such, I feel I need all the help I can get—self and others.

I've Known Dentists

In one week I was transformed from a lively, productive human being to a whimpering mass of dental pain. That a small area in the mouth can take over one hundred percent of your life is testimony to the excruciating nature of such pain. My friend Don tells me that dental pain was the leading cause of suicide in the Middle Ages. Now, however, through the magic of modern odontic science, the need for suicide can be delayed for weeks, years even.

My dental problems probably originated in the early part of my life. It's true that, like the high school science experiment, I kept my teeth in a glass of Coca-Cola for about eighteen years. This led to the dubious achievement of having the most root canals of anyone ever seen by any of my dentists from here to New York. A "root canal," for those of you unfamiliar with the procedure, is an operation in which a dentist drills a hole in the tooth and then sticks long toothpicks into it in a bizarre attempt to reach your brain. Once the brain is reached, the hole is plugged up, and you are reminded, as you pay three hundred dollars for this privilege, how lucky you are that the tooth (although no longer viable) has been saved.

I, however, have these phantom teeth. They take a lobbing and keep on throbbing. They rise from the dead to haunt me with new waves of pain. This week I learned the silver points in my old root canals had corroded, causing inflammation, infection, and

swelling. I walked around all week looking like the bride of Quas-
imodo. My right side sprouted jowls as if some hideous Richard
Nixon buried deep inside me was struggling to get out.

With teeth like mine, you don't need a religion. You get it all—
guilt, suffering, retribution, absolution, certain knowledge of
your own inner corruption—the whole *mishbawkha* in a neatly
self-contained system between your nose and your chin.

The dentist, that funhouse-mirror face behind the gigantic
hypodermic of Novocaine, becomes your high priest. Believe me,
I've known dentists. This time it was one of those enlightened
modern guys who wants to *share*. When he pulled out the corroded
piece of silver, he insisted on holding it up to show me, as if he'd
just delivered my baby: "Congratulations, Mrs. Kahn, it's something disgusting." He wrapped it in its little blanket of gauze and
got a new silver point to demonstrate just what a gross mess I'd
been walking around with. Of course, all the while, I was trying
to talk with this big metal clamp forcing my mouth open—unable
to say, "Don't show me anything. I don't give a shit. Let me out
of here."

The dental chair, that strange platform of torture somewhere
between the gynecologist's stirrups and the executioner's hot seat,
still remains the last frontier of the human imagination. If you
can—through the magic of your own brain—get out of there
while your wide-mouthed body remains trapped behind, then you
have achieved true power over your life. Thus, I began my search
for nirvana at age six in the office of Dr. Samuel Aberman, DDS.

Dr. Aberman's office was medieval to say the least. He used
no Novocaine, no painkillers. It was just the good doctor, the large
oak cabinet where the implements of torture were stored, and one
child and her imagination—me. Dr. Aberman was a tall, gaunt,
unsmiling man who, in his bifocals and black three-piece suits, resembled Calvin Coolidge dressed up as an undertaker. The office
offered little for the mind to play with—there weren't even acous-
tical panels on the ceiling so you could count the holes. There was,
however, an excellent view of the parking lot sixteen floors below.
This opened up limitless possibilities. You could count the moving
red dots or the blue dots or the toy green cars down there. Occasionally, a convertible would appear, and then you could simply

fly out the window and land in the driver's seat. Why—you could even be driving the car over Dr. Samuel Aberman himself!

Years later, when I was receiving Novocaine from the enlightened hands of Dr. Arthur Weitz, DDS, it occurred to me that Dr. Aberman really was a sadist. But the full potential for dental incompetence didn't hit home until I was beneath the drill of Seymour Horowitz, DDS&M. I only visited Dr. Horowitz once, but that was enough. As I recall, Dr. Horowitz had just finished the long, slow injection of Novocaine. You know, the old this-will-sting-a-bit-yeeeeeooowww! routine. While waiting for the anesthetic effect, Dr. H. took advantage of my inability to respond by treating me to a lecture on what a lovely boy his son Myron was and wouldn't a nice girl like me (whose parents had paid cash in advance) love to meet a fine boy like Myron? Before I could say, "All this and Myron too?" Seymour Horowitz placed the drill on my tooth full blast. To call what happened next "pain" is a monument to the inadequacy of language. I didn't just see stars; I saw previously undiscovered solar systems, new red blazing galaxies, screaming life on other planets. The last words I heard before I literally ran out of there was Myron Horowitz's father saying, "Ooops! Wrong tooth."

For a while, in New York, I had a lovely woman dentist, Dr. Rosie Sheik. Dr. Sheik (a strange designation for a woman) had small, patient hands, and a pleasant singsong middle-Eastern accent. It is a tribute to her skills that I remember little else of our time together. Although I think I did imagine my way out of her office by picturing Dr. Sheik as she would have been in her native country—in flimsy purple gauze harem pants, belly dancing for sultans.

Next stop: the Berkeley dental pad of Dr. Don Rico, DDS. Well I remember the day the Don (as I thought of him) got his nitrous tank. It was like a dream come true. One no longer needed imagination; let your nitrous do the walking. A few deep breaths and an out-of-body experience was available to any dummy. Unfortunately, not everyone reacts that way. My husband, for example, was told that the nitrous oxide would make him philosophical. He realized after inhaling it that hating the dentist was the cornerstone of his belief system and proceeded to act this out by throwing up on the doctor.

Finally, my voyage through the wonderful world of dentistry led me to the offices of Painless Ralph. Painless has it all—Novocaine, nitrous, a pleasant manner, and a great view of the Berkeley Hills. In his office, I can soar with the hawks while Ralph reminds me that my teeth look great but my gums are shot.

This last visit, sad to say, I was beyond Ralph. He had to refer me to an oral surgeon. The oral surgeon is doing his best—he's put the toothpicks to my brain, he's explained everything, he's only left me in the office staring at the four walls and the dead plant for brief periods of time. But the pain continues. Finally, I was prescribed some Percodan, which is, I believe, socially responsible heroin. It took away the pain but it made me throw up, so I flushed it. And this now is my life—pain interrupted by boredom. Only through the greatest effort of the will can I get myself to the window to look at the large speckled birds in the backyard and wonder where they are going and can I fly with them.

Yuppies and
Still More
Relationship Problems

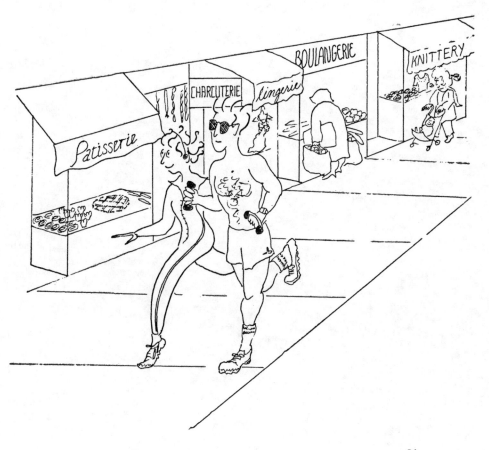

Yuppie!

Where would I be without my children? Just another relentless hack striving to be the Fran Lebowitz of the West Coast, the Erma Bombeck of the East Bay, the Harriet Tubman of the repressed emotion, the Marie Curie of the undiscovered phrase . . . I could go on. However, I have not flirted with your attention merely to discuss my would-be brilliant career. If you can make the commitment to get through this essay you will see that I am into really serious matters here. Going beyond the usual chitchat about life, death, and human sexuality, I wish to address the problem experts are calling "the plague of the baby boom generation."

I am not referring to herpes or AIDS, for only fundamentalists see meaning in these cruel diseases. I am speaking of the menace that is stalking our streets, threatening to ruin our neighborhoods, overtake our towns, and wreak havoc with the economy. Lock up your daughters, for this menace lurks on every corner. We who have survived the hippies, the yippies, and even the junkies wonder: will we survive the ultimate? I am speaking, of course, of the YUPs, the Young Urban Professionals. Like mutant rats, they multiply without even reproducing.

Let us observe a typical yuppie couple as they go through their day. By using the case study method we can, perhaps, come to a precise definition of this disorder with an eye towards its amelioration (at least it could be the basis for a grant proposal to fund a

Yuppie Abatement District). I will also discuss my own yuppie avoidance technique as well as present a modest proposal for de-yupping the neighborhoods.

Enter your basic cohabiting couple, Dirk and Bree. She, the former Barbara "Babs" Wellington, a Milwaukee, Wisconsin deb who came out at the 1968 Blatz Cotillion. He, the evolution of Richard "Little Dickie" Miller originally from Proctown, New Jersey. Both are 32.2 years old. They have a combined education of 39.4 years, a combined weight of 265 pounds, and a combined income before taxes of 77,500 dollars and 23 cents. This last bit of data is the key to appreciating the YUP's potential to wreak havoc. They're young, they're restless, and they gotta spend.

The YUP is investment wise (some would beg to disagree) but cashflow foolish. While agonizing with their brokers over the right options deal, they treat their roll of twenties like goodtime coupons at the county fair. Would your average YUP take the time to comparison shop for the cheapest croissant in the area? Noooo—not even if the *Bay Other* did the foot and mouth work for them and published it as Superlist #8885: Best Bets for Bay Area Bites: Beyond the Valley of the Bagels. No, not even if you pointed them towards Bite My Buns, the cheap new boulangerie in East Oakland, would they go out of their way to appreciate the savings. Says Dirk: "My hourly rate is far too high to waste my time bargain hunting."

Instead, Dirk and Bree continue to stop off at their neighborhood place, Arnie Seligman's Little Touch of the 6th Arrondissement, where the buttery, curved rolls go for $1.75 a pop. Does the haute bucks for hot rolls bother Dirk and Bree? "No, to us as a busy, and, I might add, highly productive working couple, the convenience is everything," responds Bree.

Convenience is only one of the gods these yuppies worship. It is part of a triad of "ences" essential to this cult. The other two are Indulgence and Obedience. To see how the three "ences" operate, let us look at a day in the life of Dirk and Bree.

It is 6:00 a.m. at the Lower Piedmont Highlands condo that Dirk and Bree like to call their own personal convenience station. For the moment, all is silence as the first light of day breaks in on the silver gray and musk blue decor that forms the sleep section concept of the condo. (By their willingness to pay $129,500 for what is essentially a two-room apartment, these YUPs and countless others like them have made their mark on local real estate prices.)

The silence is broken by the quiet strains of a lite rock sound. It is none other than the late, anorexic tragedian, Karen Carpenter, singing "You Light Up My Life" on the clock radio. "Ugh," says Dirk, opening one eye. "Turn that disgusting music off."

"She's dead, you know," mutters Bree.

"Tell me about it," he says, and cuddles up to Bree for warmth.

Dirk and Bree go on sleeping, for the clock is on snooze alarm, and they are exhausted from the lengthy but civil discussion they had the night before about their relationship.

"I really think we need to talk about where we're going," Bree had implored.

"Why do we have to? Why can't we just enjoy where we are?" Dirk had retorted.

"But what about the future? You know we won't be 32.2 forever."

"Your problem, Bree, is that you can't live for today . . ."

"Oh, forget it, Dirk. Pass me the diaphragm and just shut up."

"Do you really need to use *that thing?*"

"Then you do want to talk about the future . . ."

The snooze alarm allows the couple that extra ten minutes of shut-eye. But at precisely 6:10 a.m. the shriek alarm sounds—a noise so piercing that even the most determined slouch is driven to fast-track upscale behavior by its high decibel scream. The invention is part of a last-ditch effort to Japanify the American worker.

While Bree puts on the video cassette for Jane Fonda's Morning Stretch Out, Dirk starts the Signore Cafe for that first cup of cappuccino. The machine is the latest in low tech from Kitchomatic, a new neighborhood necessities shop. Then it's into those his-and-hers workout suits that come from another cute little shop called Hung for Health.

Worked up and tanked out, they get in the BMW and drive to the Rockridge BART station. Here they kiss bye-bye (or ciao-ciao, as they say). He heads to San Francisco and she's off to Oakland. Dirk is a Level Two Junior Manager for a prominent San Francisco firm. His department: Human Resources. His specialty: Sensitivity Enhanced Personnel Displacement. Bree is an attorney with a large law firm in new old Victorian Oakland. Her department: real estate litigation. Her specialty: how to set up a dummy receivership and what to do when the Hong Kong money backs out.

We won't go into the gruesome details of how Dirk and Bree spend their work day. For this is the obedience part of their lives, that time when they delay gratification so that they may have the cash to carry out their real mission in life: indulgence. They have learned to embrace the work ethic. Each spent brief periods of time unemployed. During those times they made the following pact with the Great Spirit: get me a professional job and I'll do whatever they ask. Not that their work isn't reasonably high in salary, status, and decision-making opportunities; it just isn't fun. Suffice it to say that several hours, a light lunch, a few snacks, and innumerable office flirtations later, they emerge from their commute. Once back home, they change into their jogging clothes for The Run.

Dirk and Bree are into running, self-care, and a high zinc diet. For now. Being *into* something is an essential part of Yupritude. Have you ever noticed that the official greeting of the Yupsie generation is: "What are you into?" Not the traditional "How are you?" or the Hebrewfied "So what's new?" or even the hipsters' "Hey, what's happening?" but "What are you into these days?" or "Are you still into (fill in the blank)?" The *blank* here ranges from Yoga to jogging to practicing law to snorting cocaine to eating vegetarian to living with Fred (or Mary). The underlying assumption is that one goes in and out of things, that there is no constancy or stability but an endless series of flirtations with life, a deep cultural promiscuity.

After The Run, it is time for dinner. Bree and Dirk either eat out (2.3 dinners a week), buy gourmet fast foods (2.3 dinners a week), or cook at home (2.3 dinners a week). The other .1 meals are taken furtively at McDonald's. Since it is Friday, it's time to kick off Le Weekend with a $22.50 or more per person dinner. They head towards their favorite new place on Berkeley's restaurant row, "Little La Cienega" as they say in the real estate ads.

They enter the Cafe Tres Tres. The maitre d', who studied at the Inspector Clouseau School of Heel Clicking and Wine Sniffing, invites them to have a drink at the bar while they wait for a table. Here Bree and Dirk have a chance to encounter their drug of choice, the grape—the Pinot of Noir, the Cabernet of Sauvignon, the light, little Gewurztraminer.

At last their chance to beat the other couples comes, and they are seated. While the poor suckers who are standing and starving look hostilely at their table, the waiter brings Bree and Dirk the first course. On a spotless white plate sit three perfect local fresh walnuts covered with virgin olive oil (who actually does the checking on the olive?) and sprinkled with fresh basil (grown on the premises) and prosciutto bits. The main course is stunning: a paillard of local quail (grabbed from an East Bay regional park that very morning), basted in a sauce of cream, butter, Sonoma goat cheese, and other imported cholesteroids. It is accompanied by a ragout of garlic topped with five millimeters of *creme fraiche* and garnished with wild neighborhood sorrel grass and nasturtium leaves. "Sensational," says Bree. "Outstanding," adds Dirk. Dessert, of course, is their favorite, the Tres Tres's own creation—Chocolate Adolescence. This is a cake made from five pounds of Venezuelan chocolate and equal parts of Amaretto, Grand Marnier and—a nouvelle touch—Diet Shasta. All proceeds from the sale of the cake go to the No Nukes of the North Political Action Committee.

After dinner they consider a walk, but appreciating the fact that they make the ideal crime victims (i.e., loaded with cash and scared shitless), they unlock the BMW and head home.

"Don't you think we should talk about our relationship?" says Bree as they get out of the car.

"Not this again," says Dirk.

"But you never want to talk," she returns.

"Can't we talk about investing in the vineyard instead?"

"You mean you think it's a good idea?" she asks him.

"Of course I do, Bunnynose," he tells her, switching to pet names.

"Wild Thing, I think I love you," she says. "Get over here."

The diversion of diversifying worked for Dirk. This time.

Some Saturday mornings they will get in the car for a country weekend—Bed and Breakfast, antique furniture, fresh air, exercise, and cookies and milk served in bed. All this for only $150 per night (tip included). This particular Saturday morning ushers in the acquisition phase of the YUP's indulgences. This is the day Dirk and Bree take to the streets to act out the psychopathology of the YUP. One hears a lot these days about the disease of agoraphobia—fear of public places, literally fear of the marketplace. It is a disease that imposes untold sorrow and limitation on the agoraphobic individual but, fortunately, no price to society. The YUP, on the other hand, suffers from severe agoraphilia, love of the marketplace, adoration of the Macy's, intercourse with boutiques. While it's a fun leisure time activity for the yuppies, we all pay a higher price for the way they squander their surplus income. And the demand for stores that service the needs of the YUPs radically alters our neighborhoods. We complain as we lose our local service shops, our hardware stores and shoe repair shops, our bourbony taverns for blurry-eyed old-timers. These essential services are replaced by sofabed emporiums, new wavish T-shirt zones, friendly neighborhood high technica, and food specialty shops of every description (with appropriate names of endearment).

To fuel these maniacal shopping sprees, the neighborhood becomes infested with sweet stations, gelatos, chocolate heavens, French bakeries, honey heavy yogurt stands, Italian bakeries, gourmet jelly beans, etc. As the poet said: I have seen the best minds of my generation destroyed by sugar, hypoglycemic hysterical naked / dragging themselves through the bourgeois streets at noon for an angry chocolate chip fix . . .

Others of this generation, including myself, the would-be Margaret Mead of the Lifestyle set (see my forthcoming *Coming of Age in Sonoma*), consider it a matter of personal honor to avoid these trendy shops (except when the physiologic need for pasta pesto becomes unbearable). To get around the inflated prices, we search out thrift shops, flea markets, and garage sales looking for YUP discards—cheap Cuisinarts, sturdy preppie clothes, last year's captain's beds.

We also indulge in a unique form of reverse snobbism in which we boast of knowing "old neighborhood type places" to shop. I certainly know of a few, and it is my intention to share them with you. Perhaps we can even begin to compile a Community Guide for YUPfree Shopping (send your suggestions to World Without YUPs Project). Here are some examples:

Archetypical of the lost-among-the-groovies shops is University Plumbing and Hardware, virtually next door to North Berkeley's YUP-infested Cheese Board (the Board's success comes through no fault of the politically correct collective who staff it). The hardware shop, however, sees one customer per every two hundred that enter the Board. Is it because we can live without keys but not Camembert? Is it the old-timey patriotic posters on the hardware shop's walls in marked contrast to the Board's constant reminders of impending nuclear doom? I asked Mrs. Benton, who has owned the store since 1957, how she manages to stay in business. "It's getting harder every day. The landlord has no conscience," she says, referring to her recent 400 percent rent increase. You'd better see this one fast.

For a truly YUPless hunk of meat, try Natural Foods on Grove Street. When the butcher there put in wood walls, a few plants, and organic grain bins, they thought business would pick up. But somehow the combination of meat and natural foods just doesn't seem to work in Berkeley. There's something about buying a carob-covered spirulina bar from a guy in a bloody apron that just drives the YUPs out. As a result, the place is never busy, the service is friendly, and the bulletin board offers an intimate glimpse of the "chemically sensitive" subculture.

Another place you won't find a YUP is Value Village Thrift Shop. You also won't find many values there as the worldwide demand for schlock has driven prices to record levels. Whereas once you could furnish an entire house in Early VV, they now charge $69.96 for a half-broken bed (the previous owner's entire used Kleenex collection is thrown in gratis). There is still, however, the two buck cashmere sweater or the collector's Bauer bowl to be found if you have the time to sift through the rubble. Dirk and Bree actually admit that in their unemployed phase even they shopped the Village.

I could go on but, in regard to my own YUP avoidance techniques, I have finally come to see it as another case of the vanity of human wishes. As the lowriders so eloquently put it: You know, homies, you can run but you can't hide. You simply cannot escape the YUPs unless you are prepared to live in the country, the suburbs, or the non-gourmet ghettoes. What then can we do to keep our communities from being overrun by these high-paid hordes?

We can contain these chic high-rollers, but they cannot be stopped on the planning commission level. No, even if you maintain the pristine purity of your own neighborhood, they'll just set up their sushi bars and their pate pits and their gallerias and their Victorian commons and their atriums somewhere else close by. I maintain that there is only one way to stop them: get them pregnant.

Children, it turns out, are the cross to hold before the vampire of YUPula. Of course, they can keep up the act for a while. They even have books to help them like *The Whole Birth Catalogue*. (You couldn't make this stuff up!) Sure, you can be a pregnant YUP, a birthing YUP, a newborn father's support group YUP. But you cannot, I maintain, be a terrible-twos-parent-and-in-midlife-crisis YUP. We need to remind these people of their responsibility to commit themselves to the sanitarium of carrying on the race.

Why do kids spoil the YUPs' thing? In the first place, they co-opt indulgence opportunities (buy me this and buy me that). They flaunt the obedience ethic—they won't even clean their damn rooms. Furthermore, they know of no convenience beyond their own. Think about it. They rub their jammy hands on the unbleached raw silk sofa. They spit up on the Wilkes Bashford navy cableknit sweaters. That lovely little well-arranged bowl of fruit on the table—they eat the fruit!

Children consume free time and thereby interfere with the joy of consuming. The last laugh comes as they snort all that surplus income right under the parenting YUP's nose. They have their own adorable little demands that can take up that surplus in no time. Without this income and the time and lust for shopping, what is the YUP? Just a working slob, a mom or dad, an older generation, someone who's wedded to the one commitment from which you can never get a divorce. You notice that nobody asks, "Are you still into being Ringo's mother?"

So drop your neighborhood preservation ordinances. Leave the developers alone. Stop forcing rent controls on the poor landlords. Just keep telling those YUPs about how your little Sasha or Sagebrush lights up your life. Don't mention ear infections, childcare, school board meetings, neighboring ten-year-olds who use drugs, orthodontists, and cries of "I'm thirsty. Bring me an orange juice . . . on ice . . . in the Miss Piggy glass" in the middle of the night.

Kids are the answer to urban density. Do us all a favor: get a YUP off birth control.

The Yuppie Saga Continues . . .

Baguettelles:
Sweet and Sour

O h, Mai!" gasped Bree Wellington as she sat up in bed to assess the damages. Had she merely failed to meet her dear friend, Mai Blender, at the City Cafe—as indeed she had—that would have been bad enough. But no, she had to go and get seduced on the Strawberry Canyon fire trail—picked up in midjog like a galloping trollop. It was the kind of cheap fantasy you'd expect from a Kensington housewife.

Like Tina Turner, Bree never did anything nice and easy. Lying next to her in the antique brass bed in the Claremont Hotel was none other than Neal Blender. Neal just happened to be the ex-husband of the friend she'd failed to meet that very afternoon. Why had she been persuaded to follow his Porsche from the parking lot at the Space Sciences lab, throwing caution and a parking ticket to the Grizzly Peak winds, and proceed to his bayview room at the Claremont? How could she explain her lack of control? Was it his direct approach, straight out of a made-for-TV movie: "Hey, babe, how 'bout it?" Was it her frustration with her boyfriend, Dirk, who was ready to make a commitment to *her* but not to having a baby? Or was it that old devil moon in his eyes?

Some questions are best left to the experts. Meanwhile, Neal Blender was stirring. With his thickly hairy chest and his gold jewelry, he seemed far less naked than Bree. He opened his eyes, looked up at her with a dopey grin, and said, "Five cents to ride again."

Bree grabbed the floral top sheet that matched the "Iris" pattern of the wallpaper and, wrapping it around herself, got out of bed. "I'm getting out of here," she shouted, searching for her jogging clothes, which Neal had tossed about the room unceremoniously a few short hours ago. "What's the matter, baby?" asked Blender, forced out of his post-coital haze.

"I am not a baby, let alone your baby," she sneered, pulling up her jogging shorts. She grabbed Blender's hand to look at his Rolex. "Six-thirty!" she cried. "I'm ruined. I can't go back to my office. How am I going to explain this to everybody?"

"Tell 'em you got a load of this," Neal said, standing up.

"That's it. I'm leaving," she exclaimed, and grabbed her sweatshirt and car keys. She headed for the door, but Neal, still naked, blocked her way.

"Listen," he began, "we had a terrific time. Once you think it over, you'll know that. I'm heading back to LA in the morning, but I'll be back up here soon. I'm taking some of the profits out of my LA ventures—the Cafe Sycophant, which I think makes the Hard Rock look like a dump, and the Malibu Wolf where all the great chefs of Oakland were trained. I'm going to open up my new restaurant here in Berkeley. It'll be like nothing this town has ever seen—somewhere between Narsai's and the Emergency Food Project. We'll have it all under one roof: pate, gumbo, mu shu pork, kreplach. And I'm going to invent a new dish just for you— melted cheese on unleavened bread. I'll call it "Matzo Brie Wellington." If that ain't love, baby—I mean, *Big Mama*—then you don't know it when you see it." With that he opened the door and bowed, adding, "Farewell, my lovely."

There was something to be said for a person who could remain poised while naked. "I'll think about it," she said and headed toward the elevator.

In the parking lot, she found her car, distinguished from the other products of the Bavarian Motor Works by its half bumper-sticker that read "for a better America." She'd torn off the "Mondale-Ferraro" part three days ago, immediately after walking out of the little booth that resembled a 25 cent porno viewing space or a urinal. There she had committed the private act required for good citizenship.

She entered the bumper-to-bumper Friday night traffic on Tunnel Road. It was pointless to go back to her law office in downtown Oakland, although she'd left her clothes there. To get into the City Center Building at night, she'd have to ring for old Steve, the security guard. She could just see herself standing there in her shorts while he breathed bourbon at her and laughed, asking, "What you been up to, baby?"

No, better to head home and face Dirk, poor thing. He was probably worried sick. Didn't they have reservations for tonight at the Chez? *Tres* YUP, of course, but it was their anniversary. The remembrance of that fateful day in 1980 when they met at the dismal Carter-Mondale victory party made her shudder. The mood had been grim that night as the Democrats lost it, and a petulant Dirk approached her and said, "Take me hostage."

Dirk, dear, sweet Dirk. How could she possibly leave him for an egomaniacal jerk like Neal Blender? She must not tell about this afternoon. Telling is cruel. She would say she'd gotten lost taking what she thought was a road off the fire trail. It was terrifying— lost in Strawberry Canyon, wandering around all afternoon with nothing to live on but eucalyptus acorns, trying to find her way home by the sound of the Campanile bells. *It started out as a fun run but turned into a marathon in hell.* Surely she couldn't have made up a story like that.

Exiting at Redwood Road, she looked up at the starry sky, drew the line at the heavens, and headed towards the Piedmont highlands. Her favorite song came on the radio and she turned it up. You've heard of sing along with Mitch? This was whine along with Cyndi as Bree joined in for, "They just wanna, they just, just wannna—ooow, girls just wanna have fun."

As she drove into the Bay Gauche driveway, she saw that the sign was still up. It showed a young man in a tuxedo holding a wine glass, and it was captioned, "If we lived here, lover, we'd be home now." Underneath that it said, "West of the moon and east of the Bay—Bay Gauche: luxury, maximum security, condominiums for today's easy livin' young adults. Studios from $129,500. Terms available." Two years, Bree thought, and they still haven't sold them all. That was Dirk's latest ploy. "We can't have a kid until we buy a house; we can't buy a house until we sell the condo—and the market's slow right now." Were there many others among the potentially unborn, she wondered, whose right to life depended on the condo market?

As she turned her key in the door, Bree thought she heard someone saying, "Here she comes." The lights were out. Maybe, she thought—just maybe—she could get away with this after all. But no sooner had she flicked on the switch than her entire life flashed before her. There was everyone she knew, all her friends, dressed to kill and standing there shouting, "Surprise!"

All the people from Bay Gauche were there—Scott Fishbein and Nan Corleone from Unit A, Leroy Mannikan and Meo Myo (the fashion designer), Dr. Fred Nuddleman and his brother, Norm, Jan and Michael Vincent and their new baby, Megan, and Lou and Les ("the gay guys," as everyone called them). There was Mai Blender with a faint air of amused irony about her. She was with her new boyfriend, Rod Rodriguez, and her son, Che, who was wearing an Iron Maiden T-shirt. There were her bosses, Bill and Mary Sharkey and Sid Goniff. And there was Dirk in his tuxedo staring at her jogging clothes, her uncharacteristically messy hair, and her vague look of satisfaction.

On the table in the dining room was a platter of tiny roast birds, a wooden board covered with labeled cheeses, a basket of baguettes both sweet and sour, a large bowl of crab and pasta salad, and a chocolate cake shaped like a heart which had the words "Happy Anniversary" spelled out on it in raspberries. "Light the candles," someone said, and, without taking his wounded eyes off her, Dirk reached out over the cake and touched his match to the four tiny pink candles. Right on cue, the crowd began chanting, "Four more years, four more years . . ."

Ask Ms. Popsych

Once upon a time when the world was organized you knew where to go for help. If you had a problem, you went to the designated wise person of your choice. However, today's modern guy or gal who believes in nothing still has the need for counsel. How many times have you faced a crisis with no one to turn to? Why, just the other day, I was in the middle of making some pesto when I discovered that I had no basil. What did I do? I broke down and cried, that's what, because I—alone in the world, incapable of believing in anything—had plenty of pine nuts but no one to turn to.

How often have you faced a similar crisis and shouted, "Get me a rabbi, quick!" only to realize you didn't know a single rabbi in town? And, even if you did, you're not sure you can ask a rabbi the kind of intimate things you need to know, like just where does chlamydia come from and where can you find fresh basil at 11:30 at night? And if you can find it, what does that say about the world we live in?

Oh yes, sure, there's therapy. Great if you happen to be in the middle of it but useless for those little spur of the moment crises that occur to Normal People. Normal People, by definition, are able to function through the most dreadful lives and situations. Quiet desperation? No problem. But every once in a while some little trigger goes off and then—boom boom—your Normal is temporarily transformed into a raving lunatic. I undergo these lit-

96

tle outbursts regularly. Perfectly normal; but difficult to endure alone.

Well, fear no more the heat of the sun or the furious winter's rages. I, Ms. Popsych, have emerged from the depths of my own severe depression to serve the people. Armed only with my women's magazines and my clippings of feature articles on "relationships" (say it with sarcasm if you must), I am here to provide succor and glib aid to the truly needy (and those too cheap to spring for professional help). Let me make your lonely life a little brighter and forget my own miserable existence, my own problems that I am incapable of solving, by losing myself in your poor, pathetic struggle.

Along this line, we hear from the following readers with current state-of-the-relationship problems:

Dear Ms. Popsych,
I met Armando while Trick or Treating for UNICEF. A few people foisted candy upon us. We shared a Baby Ruth, some Malt Balls, and sucked on some unidentified wrapped candy until the creamy nugget melted. Well, one thing led to another and before I knew it we were at my place doing what comes naturally. In the morning Armando turned into a different man. He called me terrible names. He ate all my toast and jam. He broke my piggybank and stole all the contents and said, "you're nothing to me" three times. I ask you, Ms. Popsych, can this one night stand be saved?
Sincerely,
All Day Sucker

Dear Sucker,
No.

Cordially,
Ms. Popsych

Dear Ms. Popsych,
I went to a party at my friend Steve's and met this real nice girl there. We had a wonderful time together. She was kind, loving, and fun to be with (a little kookie maybe?). I told her I would call the next day but when I went to the phone I got scared. I tried all

day but I just couldn't dial (or in this case pushbutton). I have been hurt in the past and I can't go through that again although I also can't stop thinking about her. What should I do?

Morning After Pill

Dear Pill,

I want you to put the phone on the floor. Then I want you to get down on your hands and knees and dial (or whatever) her number and beg her to forgive you. How long has it been since that night? A week? Two? If I know that girl—if she's anything like me—she's probably sitting by that phone wishing and hoping and dreaming and praying that you'll call. In fact, she's probably a wreck. Hasn't eaten in days. Afraid to order out a pizza for fear of tying up the line.

So you've been hurt in the past. If you don't mind my saying so: welcome to the club. That's the way it is in Grownupsville. You might as well know (I hope I'm not the first to tell you) it's potentially one big hurt from here to retirement. You haven't got time to waste, brooding over every little individual episode. Do what other grown-ups do—drink, jog, use drugs, overwork—anything to numb you up a bit. You simply cannot waste time feeling bad.

What if nuclear war breaks out? Who knows but it isn't happening right now? How do we know for sure that some trigger-happy world leader (and is there a sane one in the bunch?—I mean, by objective standards) isn't saying right at this very moment, "Oh, well, what the fuck." So you see there isn't a minute to lose. Run to her. You need each other. Love is the only good thing left.

Cordially,
Ms. Popsych

Dear Ms. Popsych,

I was on my vacation, playing the slots in Vegas, when this guy approached me. He kept asking me to come up to his room for a drink. (Drink. Ha. Ha.) Said his name was Ed. Said he was in government. I said no, but now I wonder. He said, "Show me a good time and I'll give you Health and Human Services." I said, "Get lost." He said, "What do you want? EPA? Interior?" I said, "Beat it." "Beat it?" he said, "for beat it you can have Energy." Finally, I began to walk away. Then he said, "I can get you the Vice-

Presidency. How 'bout it, Honey? It'll only take five minutes." Well, I didn't beat around the bush. "Stick it in a socket," I said and left. But now I wonder: did I do wrong? Do you think I should write to him and ask him to reconsider?

Bush League Bimbo

Dear Bimbo,

There are certainly better ways for a woman to rise than through performing sexual favors. And there are worse. You blew it, honey. What's five minutes of holding your nose compared to the chance to influence policy? If you believe in The Cause you would have made this sacrifice for the millions of people you could have helped. Think of what it would have meant to the country to have a woman under Reagan. You could have left the Me Generation and joined the Meese Generation. But no. You were too high and mighty for a little *quim pro quo*. Thanks a lot. Viva La Causa!

Cordially,
Ms. Popsych

Had enough? Please send your questions no matter how trivial or significant (but not too dirty!) to Ms. Popsych, Berkeley, CA. I promise to give your problem my undivided attention—left and right brain. I can't wait to hear from you and if I don't I'll just have to keep on making this stuff up myself.

Ask Ms. Popsych

Pre Pie Pan Syndrome

Dear Ms. Popsych,
Are you for real? I mean, you don't expect anyone to believe in you, do you? You just make up those letters, don't you? The other day I was having an argument with my lover who thinks you are real. But you're not, are you? I think you're a big phony. I dare you to print this.

Undoubtedly,
Virginia Skepticemia

Dear Virginia,

I know the rumors you've heard. The whole Bay Area's just one small town. People are always spreading rumors: this one's gay, that one's having an affair, this one's not for real. You believe this baloney?

Baby, I'm for real. Sure, I've heard the rumors too. I've heard people's insinuendos that I make the letters up. That's because they can't believe how truly weird our modern society has become. In a Ronald and Nancy kind of world, who needs fiction? Of course, the Ohlone Indians didn't have a Big Chief Popsych because they lived in harmony with nature. But look around you. The times are out of joint. People are out of joints. It's a dirty job, but some sharp little cookie's got to do it.

Yes, Virginia, there is a Ms. Popsych. She lives in the hearts and minds of boys and girls over thirty and under forty with relationship problems and generalized angst everywhere.

Cordially,
Ms. Popsych

Dear Ms. Popsych,

My husband is so jealous you wouldn't believe it. Get this. Last week the boss took me out to Fat Apple's Cafe for breakfast. When my husband Phil (his real name) heard about it, he hit the ceiling. He called me "bitch" and a lot of other names I know you wouldn't care to print. The very next day, he took me to Fat Apple's, and while we waited to order, Phil kept saying, "How could you have done this to me? You know how much I love this place." Then he ordered an entire pie—a la mode, no less—and proceeded to eat the whole thing before my very eyes. He would only pause briefly and look at me with Dreyer's Vanilla ice cream running down his beard, and say, "How does it feel?" At the end of the meal, he lifted the near-empty pan and licked it. It was absolutely the most disgusting thing I have ever seen. I hate to spill my guts about this to a perfect stranger, but I don't know who else to tell it to. What is going on, Ms. P?

Pied Piper

Dear Pied,

You've got yourself one sicko hombre there, Mrs. Piper. Fortunately, you've come to the right place. Ms. Popsych is more than able to recognize the symptoms of infantilism, hedonism, sexism, and anti-socialism that your husband has demonstrated.

Problem: inability to cope with reality.

Code name: Peter Pan Syndrome.

In your husband's case, we are dealing with a particularly recalcitrant form of the disease, a uniquely American variant that was described at a conference I attended at Esalen last summer. The variant, known among professionals as Peter Pie Pan Syndrome, consists of a mad, sick, insane escape into the pre-androgynous state represented by the pie. The gooey filling surrounded by a tough crust is an apt metaphor for the male condition.

There is, however, hope. Remember, the tough crust can still be crunched and chewed to bits, but it won't be easy. What you need is both a deprogrammer and a pie-er. You need someone dressed in your likeness who will throw pies at your husband while shouting, "Wake up, Phil, the party's over."

May I recommend Lois the Pie Queen combined with Sam the Drag Queen? And, by the way, what were those names Phil called you? We'll print anything. We have nothing to fear because we're in touch with our feelings. I hope you can reach Phil before Gravenstein season.

Cordially,
Ms. Popsych

Dear Ms. Popsych,

I feel as if I am about to lose my mind. I know I'm getting close to it because last week I lost my car keys.

This is kind of hard to talk about. So, Ms. Popsych, how are you? Que pasa? What's happening? Are you having a nice summer? OK, OK, I know. Get to the point.

The thing is this: my lady and I are having a little sexual problem. It seems that at certain times, when I approach her to make love, she just gets up and starts singing and dancing. Sometimes she will even play the banjo, which is particularly disheartening to me because, you see, she doesn't know how to play the banjo. She was first flautist in her high school marching band, but to my knowledge, she has never studied a string instrument and, believe me, it shows.

I am not one of those machismo maniacs you read about. I can take "no" for an answer. I can accept the fact that women have frequent headaches. "Not tonight, Manny," is part of reality as far as I'm concerned. But this singing and dancing is truly bizarre.

I have racked my brains and browsed the racks of numerous bookstores trying to understand what is happening. Could this be the famous End of Sex I have been reading about? I also remember some years ago reading in a book by Ishmael Reed about a dance movement that swept the country in the past. I believe he called it the Jes Grew movement. Do you think that is the answer? Is my lady suffering from Jes Grew?

Immanuel Who Can't Stop
the Music

Dear Immanuel Can't,

Mr. Reed is a deep thinker, but he has not kept up with the latest gynecological research. You have come to the right place. It was obvious to me as soon as I read your letter that your lady is suffering from PMS—Pre-Minstrel Syndrome. This affliction, which has only now come to the attention of the sexist, capitalist, arrhythmic health establishment, most commonly affects women between the ages of 25 and 45. In the late forties, the high kicks of the pre-minstrel sufferer are relieved by the hot flashes of menopause. The syndrome was first described by Dr. Katrina Bones of the University of Southwestern Arkansas at Arkadelphia. The good doctor was struck by the number of patients who cakewalked into the exam room chanting, "Dr. Bones, Dr. Bones . . ."

At this time there is a debate in the medical community as to the proper treatment for PMS. Some, who believe the condition is hormonal, advocate the use of natural estrogens derived from Mexican yams. Others feel this is unproven and a further ripoff of our neighbors to the south. They feel the symptoms are best controlled through the use of B vitamins and the music of Neil Diamond. Advocates of the Diamond theory maintain that after several hours of Neil-therapy, the patient is completely free of all sense of rhythm.

The important thing to remember about PMS is that it is not a disease and should not be used as an excuse for keeping women out of executive or missionary positions. You can help your lady by offering support and studying the music of Stephen Foster. There are some who believe that men also suffer from PMS but are generally not in touch with their feelings and therefore are inhibited from acting it out. It was, however, the case of a man, the late Al Jolson, that first led to the discovery of pre-minstrel syndrome.

Cordially,
Ms. Popsych

Confidential to The Lady from Hong Kong: I was absolutely thrilled to get a letter from such a faraway place with such a strange-sounding name. Your problems are beyond me. But say, could you send me some jade earrings and a couple of suits?

Ms. Popsych regrets that she cannot answer all your letters due to space limitations and the severe space cases that have been writing. However, I remain eager to hear from those of you who can articulate a problem in three hundred words or less. The first ten letter writers will receive a copy of my helpful pamphlet, "How to Talk to Your Teenager About Not Stealing Your Drugs."

Gone With the Wimp

*Q: How many New Sensitive Males (NSMs) does
it take to screw in a light bulb?*
A: One but only if you ask him to stick it in.

Pity the NSM. He has worked so hard to educate himself, to be correct, to purify even the slightest sleazy thought. Now he finds himself the object of ridicule, not only from his unrepentant brothers (*Real Men Don't Eat Quiche*), but, worse yet, from the very sisters he has tried so hard to understand and empathize with. There are even some women who doubt his absolute sincerity, who consider his proclamations of feminist principles yet another subterfuge to get under the covers—a kind of missionary impossible, Clint Eastwood in Alan Alda's clothing. My feeling (and I know you care about my feelings) is that NSMs are not made; their sensitivity is born out of pain. Frequently there is a history of unrequited love, performance anxiety, or a deep longing to be morally superior that few women are sensitive enough to understand. It is this callous streak in women that drives the NSM mad. He can't tolerate cruelty or ambiguity. He has gone to great lengths to please, to be correct, and now feels hurt by what he perceives as the double message women seem to be sending.

This quest for miso and macho in one man was driven home to me some years ago while driving home from a feminist conference with a woman who called herself Shanti Litvok (not her real name). Shanti, a sensitive soul if ever there was one, had done time in every ashram from here to Delhi. Yet it turns out she had finally achieved Perfect Bliss with a simple flesh and blood man, an artist, a sculptor who possessed "magic fingers." Not only could he cook up a mean bowl of tofu but he would often pause in the middle to grab Shanti, throw her over his shoulder, and carry her up to the bedroom. "You know," she said, pausing to cast a glance towards Mecca, "sometimes you really need that male energy."

Of course, not every man is capable of achieving such sex-role centeredness (SRC). Thus we have at one extreme the NSM, the man who has sought through pain and guilt, or sheer lack of humor, to drive all assertiveness from his behavior. His quest is for real moral macho, and like all martyrs, he fails to understand why his effort is not appreciated, or better yet, rewarded. Then, at the other extreme, we have the Norm Nuddlemans of the world.

I recently met Norm in front of Peet's coffee shop on a cool morning. He was wearing a sleeveless sweatshirt cut off at the midriff, revealing a well-trained physique and a lintfree umbilicus. A mutual acquaintance introduced us. He was drinking black French Roast. I was pouring cream and sugar in my Mocha Java.

"Are you Jewish?" he asked as he sat down next to me on the bench outside. Two dogs were actually going at it, right in the middle of Vine Street, unacknowledged by the sophisticated crowd who make their morning pilgrimage here for caffeine and chatter.

"No, I just talk with my hands for exercise," I said accidentally swooshing a little java onto his Frye boots. "It's a little workout I learned at Jane Fonda's, Fairfax." I paused for laughter. There was none. I considered "Jane Fonda's, Hestor Street?" but let it pass.

"Of course I'm Jewish. Isn't everybody?"

"Well I am," he said. "And let me tell you I've had quite a time with the Jewish women in this town. A bunch of bitches. What do they want? Why are they such bitches? I'll tell you what they want. They want wimps. You know what I mean. You see these wimps everywhere . . . with their beards and their glasses. . . ." He sneered contemptuously from under his shaving cuts. "They're all wimps. Did you happen to see an article in the paper recently, written by a rabbi, that talked about how Jewish men and women don't marry each other anymore? I've tried to relate to these women, I really have . . ."

Who did he think he was explaining this to, his mother?

"So now I only go out with Peruvians or Persians."

Take that, Ma. Lord knows he's tried. But why only these two groups? Is it alliteration? What's wrong with an occasional Chilean or how about a Korean forchrissakes? And what ever happened to Scandinavians? Weren't they all the rage a few years back? When did they get out of line? One Britt Eklund too many and the thrill is gone.

"But you," he said to me a full three minutes after we met, "why are you so different?"

I suppose the fact that I hadn't uttered the words "Beat it, schmuck" did place me one step beyond. But this was getting interesting. How did he know I was so wonderful?

"So what do you do besides being married?" he said eyeballing the simple gold band that usually marks me as an Untouchable at parties. *Do?* In what sense did he mean "do"? As in: Do you do coke? Or: What do you do for a living? Or: Do you *do* anything on the side?

"You know, Norm, behind all these women you find so hostile there's probably some story of pain, some reason for their anger. Some are not even interested in men. Many have been damaged."

"Damaged! I'm the one who's been damaged. And the wimps are the ones who let them get away with this. But you're so different, so wonderful . . ." he said moving in closer.

"Look here," I said getting up to leave (this was getting embarrassing), "I've got to go do the laundry. That's what I do, Norm. But I have to tell you if you knew me for six minutes more you'd probably think I was a bitch too."

"No, not you," he called after me; then added, "Wimps . . . they're all wimps."   —

A few weeks later, I was sitting out in front of Peet's again when he walked by accompanied by a tall, lithe, dark-haired woman. Belizean perhaps?

"What's my name?" he shot out like it was a quiz.

"Norman Nuddleman," I responded with the instinct of an A

student. "Right," he shouted giving me the index finger.

He and the Belizean faded out in a trail of pink buds down Walnut Street. I thought about his defensiveness and considered smashing a quiche in his face. I also considered his plight.

Is there no end in sight to the battle of the sexes? Must it be wimps and tough guys and bitches to the bitter end? Can't we declare a truce? Perhaps women in search of men could send clearer messages. How about: Make Love and Breakfast. And men in search of women must work on their sex-role centeredness. It will be necessary for these men to undergo A Sex-role Self-Assessment (ASSA). PART ONE: Are you a tough guy? Hey, loosen up. See, this is easy. No mess, no fuss, and godforbid, no therapy. Just *loosen up*, let yourself go, the camera's not running and John Wayne is dead. Now, for the hard part. PART TWO: complete the following test.

The Test: Are You an NSM?

1. Do you watch football? (Score 10 points if you said no; 5 if you watched only when the 49ers were champions because you thought Joe Montana had NSM role model potential.)

2. Are you now or have you ever been married? (Score 10 points if you said no. NSMs don't marry; they prefer to struggle with a relationship until they're really sure.)

3. If you were married and had children would you change diapers? (Score 10 points if you said yes; 5 if you said only the pee-pee ones.)

4. Are you comfortable with words like "flow," "vagina," "tampons," "areola," and "placenta?" (Give yourself 2 points for each word you're comfortable with.)

5. How about "pussy?" (Deduct 10 points.)

6. Are you able to hug and kiss other men? (Give yourself 5 points for hugging, 5 more for kissing, but 0 if you find it an erotic experience. NSMs aren't latent or blatant. The otherwise totally sensitive NSM feels absolutely nothing in this situation. They really don't.)

7. What drugs do you use? (Score 10 points if you said herb tea. Deduct 10 if you said cocaine. Deduct 20 if you said Wild Turkey.)

108

8. What do you do for exercise? (Score 10 points for dance, Jazzercise, or co-ed volleyball; 5 points for jogging, skiing, or swimming. If you play team sports with men only or lift weights give yourself one point because you care about your body.)

9. Do you believe in God? (10 points if you answered: Do you?)

10. You hear a woman call another woman "girl." What do you do? (5 points if you correct her; 10 points if you know it's wrong but say nothing.)

11. Would you work as a nurse, secretary, or day-care teacher? (10 points if you said yes; 5 points if you said you'd be afraid to take these jobs away from women.)

12. A guy on your construction crew asks if you want to take in an adult cinema and have a couple of beers. What do you do? (10 points if you explain that pornography exploits and perverts normal sexual feelings; 5 points if you shanghai him and force him to attend a Men's Awareness Workshop; 0 if you go along with it but are totally disgusted by the experience. Deduct 10 if you dig the blonde with the cute ass.)

SCORING: Need I say it? NSMs are *not* into scoring. But for the rest of you here's the breakdown:

0–40 HE MAN. Move to Oklahoma or seek professional help.

40–80 NORMAL. If you don't have a mate it's time to look elsewhere for answers. Your breath, your clothes, perhaps arch supports would help. You may be one of those people who actually *needs* a Mercedes.

80+ NSM. Is it lonely at the top?

Sense of Place

That's Not Funny!

I have this recurring nightmare: I am standing in front of the University of California, and I have just told a bad joke. A crowd surrounds me and begins to jostle me. Finally someone shouts, "To the Tower!" "Yes," the crowd shouts, "take her to the Tower." A woman named Madame DeFarge places a blindfold over my eyes and binds my hands. With a Ronald Colman accent, she says, "'Tis a far, far worse joke you've told than you have ever told before."

She leads me through Sproul Plaza where throngs are alternately cheering and booing. A missile hits me on the forehead. I recognize the succinct splat of a ripe tomato. Another object pounds me on the rear end. The plaza reeks of rotten vegetables. "Aye, citizen," I hear a voice say, "another bad joker. There was three led through here last week. None came back." I wait for Mario Savio to come roaring through the crowd on a white Buick Le Sabre, shouting, "In the name of Free Speech, release this woman." But—damn that Cinderella complex—no savior comes.

Finally we arrive at the Dark Tower. The elevator is cleared of tourists. The operator doesn't even want my dime. We get out at the top and climb the stairs for that last mile. Each footstep echoes with the clank of eternity. At last we enter the bell chamber. I feel the wind blowing my hair. I can hear the shouts from the crowd below, "Sentence her! Sentence her!"

I contemplate my crime: was the joke *bad* bad or just not funny? Am I evil or inept? Was it my timing or my mortal soul?

"Any last requests?" the Madame asks.

"Yeah, could you send out to Arinell Pizza for a slice of Neapolitan with extra oregano?" I ask meekly.

"Sure, sure. Anything else?"

"Well, I wouldn't mind a cappuccino from the Cafe Med . . . extra foamy . . . with lots of chocolate and cinnamon. And, since we're not counting calories here, could you pick up a chocolate pastry with sprinkles and a pink rose?"

"No problem."

"Sentence her! Sentence her!" the mob is shouting.

"Is there anything else you'd like to say before we carry out the sentence?" she asks me.

"Yeah, did you hear the one about the guy who's half-black, half-Japanese?"

"What?" she asks incredulously.

". . . Every December 7th he attacks Pearl Bailey."

"Turn on the juice!" she cries.

At that moment the chimer begins a rousing version of *Hava Nagila* on the Campanile bells.

And there I am, stuck in the tower for all eternity with *Hava Nagila* being pounded into my brain. *Ha va na ra na na* . . .

You see, Dr. Lobestein, I tell my therapist, the dream began two months ago after I attended a dinner party. It was a small group, and the conversation was lively. We were telling jokes and I decided to share, as we say, the following joke I'd heard making the rounds:

Q. How many Berkeley dykes (lesbians/radical feminists) does it take to screw in a lightbulb?

A. (stern voice) That's not funny! . . . And a man at the party starched up and said, "I really feel uncomfortable with your telling jokes like that. When I hear you say that I just hear 'Jew.' Next thing you know, you'll be telling Jewish jokes or black jokes."

He was right, of course. Waiting in the wings was: Did you hear about the Jew with the erection who walked into a plate glass window? (He broke his nose.)

There was a deadly silence at the dinner table as the man and I stared at each other. I felt my cheeks burning. Guilt? Anger? Embarrassment? All of the above.

114

I started to think of what to say to back my way out of this—"Some of my best friends are dykes." Or, "Culturally, I'm a Berkeley dyke" and, "What do these labels mean, anyway? I mean, you never know when Ms. Right will come along." Or, "I'd hire one." Or, "I wouldn't mind if my sister married one." No, the party was over. Best to shut up.

Since then, I've been on a quest, searching for our regional humor and trying to understand the rules that govern jokes or joking here. Most people I talked to believe the issue of politically correct humor is a hot topic. And even though it may seem obvious that the common enemy is a former actor who calls his wife Mommy and arms repressive governments, we all seem to spend an inordinate amount of time correcting one another.

So watch your step. Unlike San Francisco where "anything goes" in the name of comedy one can imagine a sign on the freeway reading: Berkeley Exit; Abandon All Jokes Ye Who Enter Here. Some claim there are entire feminist hiss squads lining Alcatraz Avenue. The university itself is seemingly surrounded by a human chain of sour academics. (Have you heard about the new Berkeley Wine? [Whiningly]: I get it but it's just not funny.) *Ne plus ultra* Marxist spies sit monitoring KPFA broadcasts, their Stalinist fingers glued to the phone ready to dial-a-threat when the dogma barks up the wrong tree. Bored Again Jews lie in wait, determined to Smash the Stereotype by pointing to their unsurgically tiny noses and their inability to see the humor in anything. Angry Chicanos stare out of low-slung Chevys, mad-dogging the gringos with a look that could kill. Nonpassive Asians blast out letters to newspapers objecting to Jewish princesss jokes: "I for one, resent the acronym JAP." Blacks have stopped seeing the humor in white liberals who asks, "Hey, Bro, when the hell are you people going to start rioting again? Power to the People in your own neighborhood."

I discover as I talk to folks from these parts that humor is no laughing matter. It calls into question our values, our identity, our very soul. The joke, casually told at a party, can become the trigger for laughter, an inherently pleasant physiological experience, shared relaxation. But it can also be seen as an act of aggression, hostility, even cruelty. Figuring I'd better think this thing out before I am found to be guilty again of Attempted Humor, I have committed the ultimate Berkeley joke: I have interviewed professors, comedians, therapists, and Ordinary People, asking them to talk to me in deadly earnestness about humor. I have also subjected myself to several painful scenes of public humiliation that pass for stand-up comedy in the East Bay.

I present here only a selection of the interviews with absolutely no claims of scientific sampling or objective journalism. What I have chosen are those things that may be of particular interest to people who want to understand East Bay humor and how it reflects what we are.

"Despite its frivolous nature, humor is very serious. It's the most profound indicator of relationships and identity," says Dr. Stanley Brandes, UC Berkeley professor of anthropology. Although he would surely detest the designation, Brandes is the closest thing to a professor of humor on the Berkeley campus. An "Iberian culture scholar," he nonetheless teaches a graduate seminar on humor which "becomes more and more like a therapy session" with students arguing and explaining how one person's humor affects another. (Brandes describes himself as a person who's not funny but has a good sense of humor: He illustrates this by botching the several jokes he tries to tell me. When I ask him specifically about *local* humor he laughs and says that although he's lived here since 1964 he has no idea what's going on in this town. He attributes this to the "bubble of academia.")

"I distinguish between jokes and joking," says Brandes. "Jokes are stories, narrative forms, which include material of a cultural nature, so jokes don't translate well from one language or culture to another. For example, Berkeley jokes might be unintelligible in New York.

"Jokes involve a special psychological relationship between the narrator and the audience. The narrator is on the line. She's a performer and must do a good job to invoke the intended response, which is laughter. The audience must demonstrate understanding of the joke. It's a test of their specialized cultural knowledge. If the joke fails the situation becomes a power play. Who takes the blame? Either the narrator didn't tell it right or the audience might not understand it."

For local joke-tellers, a failure may result from an audience wanting to demonstrate its moral superiority by not approving of the joke and by blaming the narrator for being stupid or insensitive or corrupt—decadent, in short. This is particularly likely to happen with certain kinds of social humor such as ethnic jokes. These are jokes, Brandes points out, that are intended to create group identity. This can be done by telling jokes within a group (i.e. Jews telling Jewish jokes) or telling jokes about outsiders (Gentiles telling Jewish jokes, workers telling manager jokes, etc.). A good example of this kind of humor is the way LA Latino comic Paul Rodriguez opens his stand-up act: "I tell people that I'm Mexican because there are so many Arabs in this neighborhood. And they look like Mexicans. They're short. We're short. They're brown. We're brown. They've got money . . . we're brown." Since the audience is mostly white, there is yet another level of group identity besides the ethnic and economic one highlighted in the joke.

Brandes sees an "extreme sensitivity to sexist humor" in the East Bay. "People fight with jokes here; it's a means of warfare, instruction . . . a way to teach a moral lesson." He observes that in his seminar, women are beginning to fight back against jokes that offend or repulse them with what he called "anti-male jokes." When I asked him to give me an example of this, he attempted to tell me the following joke:

Q: Why are girls so bad at math?

A: (Holding pointed index fingers two inches apart) Because boys keep trying to convince them this is eight inches.

(Brandes version: Why is it men tell you they have eight inches when all they have is this?)

"That's progress for you," my friend Sharon observed about this phenomenon. "We've gone from penis envy to penis derision."

While UC linguist George Lakoff sees the practice of telling jokes as a form of East Coast one-ups-manship (or in the case of the above joke one-down-womanship), Brandes feels it is the practice of joking that really separates East from West. "Joking is spontaneous humor that occurs as part of normal conversation as opposed to jokes which are separate stories. Westerners find New Yorkers brash or unpleasant or aggressive because they joke so much with one another. They use insults as a means of uniting. The idea is: I feel so close to you I can tease you. California teasing is lighthearted, mellow. New Yorkers see this as saccharine, uninteresting, phoney. They'll say Californians are friendly but superficial."

I ask Brandes if there are people with no sense of humor. He says there are, but points out that it is an individual rather than a cultural trait; all cultures have humor. The humorless individual "has a punitive superego," Brandes says. "He can't relax. You're talking about someone who's constantly on guard, a highly controlled individual. Laughter is a physiological release. That's why it's been used therapeutically to treat disease. But this release is frightening to the controlled individual. He can't enjoy it without feeling guilty."

Are humorless people less intelligent or more inclined to be feeling rather than thinking people? "No, it's not a matter of being unintelligent, although to produce humor requires a high level of intelligence. It requires a delicate knowledge of one's self and society and the cognitive incongruities that jokes rest upon."

Darryl Henriques has been creating humor in the Bay Area since he and some friends formed the East Bay Sharks performing group in the late '60s, a landmark troupe for leftist humor. More recently he has performed a solo act which he describes as "not so much stand-up comedy as trying to exorcise the demons of reality. My material is based on everything that freaks me out and outrages me and makes me wonder what I'm doing on this planet."

Henriques lives in San Francisco now, but continues to work mostly in the East Bay as a performer and as a member of North Berkeley's Cheese Board Collective. He feels more likely to be accepted here, particularly among those he calls "the old hip people."

"Most of the comedy in the San Francisco clubs is done for a very young audience and has nothing to do with anything. It's the antithesis of hip, it's anti-conscious humor. It's entertainment that sucks up to the prevailing consciousness and mores. In that way, comedy in San Francisco is more like Kansas. People who come to my shows at Berkeley's Freight and Salvage or the Julia Morgan Theater are willing to laugh at anything. But I won't promote politically regressive humor, humor that stereotypes people. I will make jokes about nationalities because nations are sources of problems."

Henriques states that he doesn't tell racist or sexist jokes even privately among his friends. He says he finds most of them not funny. "They're based on a combination of ignorance and insecurity." Nevertheless, even he has been called before the tribunal for his humor. Henriques, himself a Sephardic Jew from Jamaica, was talking on KPFA one night with a Yiddish accent. A listener phoned in and called him a "fuckin' Nazi." How does he feel about the way he and others have been scrutinized by these listeners? "People listening to KPFA are afflicted with terminal seriousness. They're leftwing puritans. You've got to think a certain way, be careful of what you say. It's the dregs of the Stalinist movement."

Although he considers himself a feminist, Henriques has also been attacked by women who took offense at routines in which he tried to parody sexism. "I guess that explains why we hate women only half as much as we hate ourselves," a Bible reader muses in one such sketch. "They're lucky we let them hang around." In another routine, a macho wimp goes to bed with boxing gloves to control masturbation. "Women booed at these routines because they took the parody literally," says Henriques.

Do we have a situation here in the East Bay of parody's lost? Says Henriques: "Parody and satire don't exist in our culture. *Saturday Night Live* overdid parody. They made fun of everything."

I ask what Henriques like to make fun of. I'm surprised to hear him say "the anti-nuclear movement" since he participates in it. "I'll make fun of any group of people who take things too seriously—something needs to be relieved there. I've offended people here. That's why I'm not more popular. I also make fun of the boutique culture—Carmel-by-the-campus, the place where you can buy anything you don't need. There's a contradiction in Berkeley between being concerned with making the world a better place yet having a lifestyle which is a glorification of consumption and personal comfort. Although the Cheese Board gives a lot of money to support weapons protests I still identify with the animals that have to produce this food we sell."

I ask Henriques whether his humor, particularly his comments about environmental pollution through his character Joe Carcinogenie, isn't a kind of gallows humor. "Sure, it's like laughing at death. The whole place is polluted. My perception of the United States is that most people don't even know we've been colonized by the corporations.

"To me the greatest irony still remains the Jewish notion of the Chosen People. You'd think some rabbi would get hip and say, 'Guess what? Ya know, I think, judging from the experiences we've been having (for the last couple thousand years), maybe we're not the Chosen People. Or maybe we've been chosen for something that's not that hot.'"

I asked Meryl McNew, director of the Berkeley Women's Center (a free feminist therapy referral service) and organizer of the Jewish Feminist Conference, her feelings about Jewish jokes and lesbian jokes. "My friends and I laugh at the most politically incorrect jokes—ethnic and lesbian jokes. To me humor has always been a survival tool, but I guess it does depend on who's telling a joke. People of a target group can say them to each other, and allies can. For example, a Jewish joke might seem anti-Semitic from one non-Jew but not so from another who's an ally. I define an ally as someone who's willing to do the work to make my oppression less hurtful."

Laura Pilnick is a feminist therapist. She disagrees with the stereotype of the humorless feminist. "A lot of humor is closeted. It comes from pain like much of black humor, and we don't want to share it with others who don't sympathize. Sometimes a friend will warn me by saying, 'Want to hear a really repressive, sexist, racist joke?' I feel selective about humor. I wouldn't like a Jewish Princess joke from a non-Jew or a straight male telling lesbian jokes. The audience of a joke is important to me. I'm not comfortable with a straight woman telling lesbian jokes to other straight people. It's too bad people have to be corrected, but there is sexual and ethnic humor which isn't oppressive." She offers the following joke as an example: "What's the difference between being black and being gay? When you're black you don't have to tell your parents."

Whoopi Goldberg—once a performer with the Blake Street Hawkeyes—is black, Jewish, an ex-welfare mother, and an ex-junkie whose father is gay. She was also trained as a Shakespearean actor. If all of that doesn't give her a license to kill with comedy in Berkeley, I don't know what will. Goldberg's humor comes from her experience as a member of every "target group" imaginable. She talks about the characters she portrays as if they are her children, saying "My junkie does this," or "my wheelchair lady does that," or "my old Jewish woman thinks about . . ." "I try to do as many ethnic groups as possible," Goldberg says. "I don't slur people, but I do whatever is in character." While she doesn't get hissed, women do tell her to do more feminist humor. "You can look at me and tell I'm a woman. Every day I make some progress, I'm a credit to my race, my sex, etc. I feel no kinship to any one group, and it pisses me off when people tell me I should be doing this or that. Why don't they go out there and do it?

"I'm working on a piece now where this woman goes into a gay men's dining place, and it's all beautiful—mauve walls, plants, space, real silverware, paintings . . . Then she goes to a lesbian place, and it's all brick. It's got deerheads, ya know, plastic forks and spoons. And she's trying to figure out: what's the difference? What does it mean?

"I want people not to take themselves so fuckin' seriously. Why are there all these factions? Gay men. Lesbians for gay men. Pseudo-lesbians for pseudo-gay men. It's as bad as going from colored to Negro to black to Afro-American. You need to call me something—call me by my name.

"Is it because people want to be accepted? Into what? I just read this book, *The Mayor of Castro Street*. I'm from New York so I didn't know the history of gay folks here. It kills me to see how people are broken into separatist groups. When I hear lesbians say I want to go somewhere where there are no men or when gay men say I only want to be around other gay men . . . anytime I hear that I immediately think: Germany, South, Scottsboro. I try to put humor into looking at this separatism so people might hear this paradox.

"You can say anything in Berkeley and at least someone will get it. Berkeley people let you try out new material. They don't hassle me. When I played in San Diego and LA, I was picketed by the KKK and the Nazis. I do a thing about abortion, about a fifteen-year-old surfer girl, a valley girl, who gets pregnant. The Right to Life people spent $2000 on a mailing to get people to picket my show.

"I moved to Berkeley, near Herrick Hospital, and I woke up one morning to see these anti-abortion people picketing in front of the hospital, so I went out and passed out coat hangers.

"Then I got pregnant and went to the Feminist Health Clinic in Oakland for an abortion. They segregated me from my partner—it's his baby too—and made me listen to this rap about how men did this to you, so we've got to stick together. I ask the woman there for a towel to scream into. She says, 'Oh, come now, you can handle this. You're a woman.' The doctor starts and I wail. She tells me, 'Shut up. You're scaring everybody.' Is this how feminists treat each other? I don't want to be one—not if they won't give you a towel to scream in or let you hold your partner's hand. So I do a thing about this in my act. Every woman in the audience knows what I mean.

"My junkie tells a story about Blee T (the blacksploitation version of E.T.). He doesn't land in the suburbs, he lands in West Oakland. It's about the ugly side of Oakland which scared me coming from New York. Harlem's a paradise compared to some of the places I've seen in Oakland . . . We live in a paradox here. On one hand it's real groovy and radical and cosmopolitan. On the other hand, there are these people living in the streets . . .

"I guess I just see humor in what happens to me in daily life. Like I went to this gynecologist and he gets out a rubber glove and blows it up. He shows it to me and says, 'Moo.'

"Or here in Berkeley I meet these people who used to be hippies. I met this guy, he shows me a picture of him five years ago . . . hair down to his ankles, round glasses, eighteen women every minute. Now he's a fundamentalist. Why? 'I was smoking this joint and the smoke blew into a cross and I saw Jesus Christ.'

"One day I was down in lower Sproul and I saw this street lady and this street man dancing to the drummers. She was shaking all over, twirling and posing, and all of a sudden her underwear fell down to her feet. They were these *huge* white pants— boxer shorts. And you know, everything froze—traffic stopped, birds froze, and I started to laugh. I have no class. I laugh at this stuff. I see people slip, I laugh. Everybody turned around. It was politically incorrect not to be cool when underwear falls down.

"What I've noticed about the comedy clubs in San Francisco is that you don't see many blacks doing comedy. There are a whole lot of black comics, and it bothers me that I have to put it in this kind of perspective. Why aren't there more Chicano comics, Chinese comics? It pisses me off that I have to think in these terms.

"With my humor I want to give a lot to people. I want to piss 'em off but I want to give 'em a lot of love and teach them about people who may be a little different from them, people they may be scared of."

"The truth is the funniest thing around," says lesbian humorist Karen Ripley. We are sitting at the sunny window table of the Brick Hut Cafe on Adeline Street near the Oakland border. When she is not doing her stand-up act or appearing with her clown troupe, the Foolish Company, to support her comedy habit Ripley works as a waitress. She tells me she likes to poke fun at the ads she reads like, "Gestalt, Reichian, reflexology bodyworker who does swami sandbox healing at a drop-in center." As she is talking, I notice over her shoulder there is a bulletin board where a distinctive poster advertises a talk on feminism and animal rights.

"There are a lot of angry women, angry lesbians in Berkeley. Defensive lesbians will get mad at straights telling lesbian jokes, but those who accept their lesbianism probably don't get that mad. It depends on the delivery. Like I saw Bobby Slayton do a routine where he began, 'I was arrested by a gay cop. How did I know? He put the handcuffs on himself.' OK, that's kind of cute. But then he went on and did half an hour of these jokes, making these really angry, hostile expressions. That scared me. If you're gay, you start to get angry. It's like you think: stop picking on me. You're getting too close to home, and I'm not that evolved."

Ripley tells me about the brutal side of stand-up comedy in San Francisco where young, white boys heckle her by shouting, "Get off the stage, dyke." I ask if she's gotten into trouble for joking on this side of the Bay. She says she's been criticized for doing alcoholics. A recovering alcoholic herself, she feels this is a strong part of her comedy. "Humor is just the flip side of pain and sorrow. Tragedy is one of the funniest things—once we've passed through it. I try to come from my heart and not make fun of anybody else's pain, but I've been playing it too safe. I'm hoping to take more risks. I saw Robin Williams last week. He can get away with anything . . . he does jokes about Blacks, Chicanos, disabled, tit jokes. Whenever the energy went down, he would grab for his crotch. All the men comedians did that. A woman finally came on and said, "I just want you all to know I'm not going to grab my dick tonight."

"On the other hand, once I saw Jane Dornacker come on stage with a dildo hanging between her legs. Some people might get really defensive about that because there are many women in the community who take their dildoes very seriously. But, as a woman, she can get away with it . . ."

Ripley is telling me about some of her routines . . . the San Francisco Gay Bridge, the lesbians' maternity shop (zip front overalls, support combat boots), and as we are talking, a drunk man staggers into the cafe. He is stumbling around with an open bottle of Thunderbird in his hand. Ripley says, "Now there's Berkeley humor." Another waitress comes up, obviously familiar with him, and says in a firm voice, "Washington, you'll have to leave." He heads towards the door in what seems like slow motion, and stops by a wooden room divider that is covered with plants. On one side a mother sits on a bench nursing her baby. On the other side, a well-mannered man is eating breakfast. A string quartet is playing Mozart on the sound system. Washington pauses, then staggers. He falls back on the room divider which sways back and forth. Someone in the restaurant screams as several plants come crashing down, narrowly missing the nursing mother and the man eating breakfast. Oblivious, Washington departs and takes a seat on the curb outside.

"That's Berkeley," says Ripley. "That's really slapstick, clowning. I might make fun of him as an alcoholic. But as a starving black man . . . I don't know . . ."

So you see, Dr. Lobestein, I hoped that by understanding how performers consider the effects of their humor, I might find appropriate guidelines for social joking so I wouldn't make mistakes anymore. But I still feel like the man in the cafe, swaying back and forth between wanting to say whatever pops into my head and also not wanting to hurt anyone. Even a recovering sexist like Paul Krassner is worried. "As a performer I try to maintain a balance between a couple of conflicting values," he said in a recent interview, "one, that irreverence is my only sacred cow; and the other, that the victim should not be the target of my humor."

My friend Dobbie, a Jungian, likes the Freudian definition of humor: "the energy that comes from releasing repressions which leads to laughter." Dobbie says, "The more you live with repression, the crazier you get. I'd rather have racism and sexism come out through humor than in other ways. Then you can have a serious conversation about it."

"OK, Alice, let's work on your repression," Dr. Lobestein says. "I want you to go back to the dream where Madame Defarge is about to sentence you for telling your bad jokes. I want you to tell Madame Defarge exactly what you're feeling."

"Listen, you french-fried bitch—I'm speaking to Madame Defarge of course, not to you, Dr. Lobestein—where do you come off telling me what to say. I've suffered. I've been in touch with my pain. But laughing makes me feel good and making someone else laugh feels even better. If I take the risk of telling a joke and it flops, you can vote with your laughs. You know, Defarge, life is not a sit com. There are real divisions, paradoxes, ironies in our community. Ask Darryl Henriques, or Whoopi Goldberg, or Karen Ripley. Speak out if you're offended, but don't gag the jokers."

"Good, Alice, that's the spirit," my therapist says. "What does Defarge do?"

"She throws me my Adidas and says, 'Get the hell out of here.' I jog off into a golden sunset as the throngs in Sproul Plaza sing a rousing version of *Camptown ladies sing this song/do da, do da* . . ."

"Alice, that's very interesting," Dr. Lobestein says with her thick Viennese accent. "Can you tell me why the song *Camptown Ladies* came into your head at that exact moment?"

"Well, I'm not certain I understand all the layers of meaning here, but I believe it's because I'm *gwine to run all night / gwine to run all day* . . ."

Season's Greetings

Months and days I've wasted
Doing some useless thing—
How few the hours that have been well spent
Viewing the flowers in spring!
—FUJIWARA NO OKIKAZE (910 AD)

Around the time most of the American landscape was frozen, I noticed the first bud opening. This is the time that my street becomes transformed into a small paradise by the budding of the Japanese plum trees. First you notice a purplish glow like an aura around the branches in January. Then the whole block goes vaguely purple. Next you see a few buds have popped open—a deep, electric pink. Soon it's all pinked out. You'd call it gaudy if it weren't natural. Like the smell of a gardenia, you want to put it down but your nose says: don't stop now!

As I breathe in the deep incense smell of the plum trees in early February, I am reminded that your fate—yes, even your fate—doesn't await you. If, like I do, you come from that cold country out there, you may wonder: why me? Why did I get out? And I can picture a girl who was once me, frozen hopelessly on those snowy streets. Could I have reached out to her and said: "Someday you will live on a street of pink blossoms and feel warmth in the dead of winter"—would she have believed me?

126

It's been unnaturally warm and dry these past weeks. Perhaps a good wind will kick up and then we can see what the Japanese called *hanafubuki*—the flower snowstorm. By this time all the buds on all the pink plum trees will be open and their sharp incense smell will be gone. The white bud plums will open, and the pink flowers will fade to a washed-out mauve. Then, when the wind starts blowing, it will begin to snow: pale, pink, soft petal snow. Somewhere a wind chime will blow and the fog will thicken. A few raindrops will come and then a torrent. Soon the gutters will be full of wet pink flower petals.

The tree I am speaking of is called *prunus blireiana*, a hybrid of *prunus cerasifera 'Atropurpurea'* (the purple-leaf cherry plum) and *prunus mum* (the Japanese flowering plum). She bears no fruit, *p. blireiana*. "Tell them, dear, that if eyes were made for seeing/then beauty is its own excuse for being." These are the trees that reduce you to quoting Emerson. They are the ones with the knobby trunks. "That's not a disease," says Emile Labadie, retired chairman of the Horticulture Department at Merritt College. "That's the way they should look."

Who had the good grace to put the plum trees in here? Seeking their history in the East Bay, I phoned the bureaucrats who push trees instead of paper. Joe Brown is Berkeley's forestry supervisor, and he has been watching the trees since 1948. He and his staff of fourteen (up from three two years ago) maintain the plums and the 30,000 other trees counted in Berkeley's last tree survey.

Brown believes the first *p. blireiana* "were planted by real estate companies. They were probably planted in the late 30's and early 40's. I think at one time they had a scenic drive of flowering peaches and plums. The peaches all died off. I'm not sure about it, though, because nobody can find the records from those days. They got destroyed somehow." He says Berkeley is not planting plums anymore or replanting ones that die. The original plants were "finger-size when they were put in, hybrids grafted to a wild root stock. They're nice trees, although a lot of them die from aphids or caterpillars or insects since we can't use insecticide anymore. But a lot of them survive on their own."

Surprisingly little is known of the history of the plums in the area either by horticulturists or officials. The city of Oakland continues to plant these popular trees in various neighborhoods. Jim Ryugo, the "tree czar" of Oakland, describes his position as administrative analyst responsible for tree planting in Oakland. The trees are his business. I ask him if he feels they are special. Maybe it's just me. Maybe you have to be raised in Chicago to feel that *prunus blireiana* is one of the greatest gifts these East Bay streets have to offer. "It's a good tree. It has its place," says Ryugo. "They're special because they mark the beginning of spring and are a reminder that we have this wonderful climate."

Running along these streets in late February, you will come to areas that seem literally carpeted with piles of wet pink petals. The plums have their own early, dramatic, and quick spring. It's the first of many springs in the East Bay. They are followed in quick succession in the lush green hills by the profusion of wild sorrel grass with its bright yellow flowers and sour stems that kids love to suck. Next comes the spring of the garden flowers: geraniums, narcissuses, azaleas, pansies, daisies, and the spectacular rhododendrons. Then comes the spring of the wisteria hanging low and pungent in the doorway. Then the spring of the irises . . . then roses . . . then it's all over. The hills start going brown. The fog is in. When the rest of the country is in full bloom and green and celebrates surviving another year, we are starting to die.

Sadly Last Summer

In my whole lousy childhood we never went on a vacation; never went on a trip— I mean nowhere, *nada,* nothing. I believe my parents spent a lot of time in steerage thinking: once these tootsies hit Ellis Island I ain't travelin' no more. They kept their word. As a result, I never left the city—in this case Chicago—not even for one tiny minute until I was well into my teens.

How urban was I? Let's put it this way: seeing a cow in its natural habitat may not mean much to you, Jack, but at fifteen it blew my mind. I mean there were no *bars* around it. The effect of these formative experiences is that today I am one of those adults who, once past Vallejo or San Jo or Novato, will start pointing and shouting, "Cows! Chickens! Horsey! Sheep! Oh-my-god *llamas!*"

Summer was the cruelest time in my childhood. That's when other families on my block packed arcane cultural objects like thermoses and picnic hampers and fishing rods and inner tubes and took off for lakes and rivers and places I could only imagine. They had cars, gleaming liberators that could carry them out from the concrete to where the corn grew. We had no car; not because we couldn't afford one but because we were weird. I could count on one hand the times I sat in a private automobile during the first six years of my life. Each time was a magic voyage. You got in and in seconds you were far, far away. Beam me out, Scotty.

But no trips for me. When the other kids left, my summer loomed like a Sahara: a dry, cruel, still place I had to cross alone.

Someday called September life would return. My girlfriend Nancy would bring me a comb that said "Newport News." Or the Robinson twins would bring me a wallet with an etching of an Indian that said "The Dells." Uncle Leo would send me a tiny crate of gumball oranges: Greetings from Sunny California.

Other kids would come back from camp—we were too weird for that too—talking about "bug juice" and campfires and singing rah-rah songs like "Good morning campers, zip zip zip" and "Boom boom ain't it great to be crazy." I felt like a total freak, definitely un-American. Nobody but a freak spent her summers sitting in front of the TV with a bowl of Minute Rice watching Dennis O'Keefe comedies or Michael O'Shea detective films or the Dead End Kids with Mugs MacGinnis snapping his hat on poor Glimpey's head. I am probably the world's leading expert on a whole genre of B-minus movies, shown on daytime TVcirca 1953, that I like to think of as The Minute Rice Film Festival.

These early experiences did not prepare me for California, where nature and travel are essential to the culture. Citified people like myself generally assume one of two postures towards our reverse hickism. One is the who-needs-it defense. This is the cigarette in the mouth "but there's no the-a-tre in the wilderness" stance. Personally, I shun this "boom boom ain't it great to be unhealthy" attitude. I take more of the I'm a wimp in wonderland position. No one can live here very long without developing a sense of inferiority to the prevailing nature-macho.

"Whadya do last weekend?"

"Oh, I carried a forty-pound pack and walked straight up Whitney. It thundered the whole weekend. I got bit by a rattler and a bear stole all our freeze-dried quiche lorraine."

"So how was it?"

"Fabulous. Oh, yeah, I went into labor on the way down and we had a lovely baby girl—Indigo Bunting."

Clearly, the Queen of the Minute Rice Festival is not entirely at home in this no-kvetching world. But even I can see I've come a long way, baby, from that first fateful day in the wilds of New Jersey. Now I know New Jersey is not *the* wilderness area that comes to mind when a Westcoaster contemplates an outing. But when I was living in Manhattan my college roommates asked if I wanted to go hiking in New Jersey. In those halcyon days before we knew the entire place was reeking toxic slime, I thought of New Jersey only as green trees across the river. Sure, I'd love to go to the country called New Jersey.

Oddly enough, when we piled out of the VW bug, we were in a strange place that could have been Mars for all I knew. The others, twenty summers' experience behind them, assumed an at-ease stance once they got on the trail. They began telling tales of Camp Kowabunga: the time the boys snuck into the girls' tent; the day somebody peed in the bug juice; the scary campfire stories about One-Eyed Ralph, the ghost of Lake Winabagel. Soon they were all singing "The Bear Went Over the Mountain." I could have figured out the words. But I was too busy being terrified. It was the first time in my life that I went for a walk in a place without street signs. Without street signs we'd never find our way back to civilization, which in this case meant a place with pastrami, subways, and mental hospitals.

Other urban aliens report the first time in the woods for them was dominated by a more gut-level terror. You see, there is only one law we learn in the concrete jungle: go poo-poo in the toilet. Naturally the absence of such facilities is an awesome prospect for the uninitiated. But I didn't have this problem because I wasn't leaving anything behind me. No sir. There wasn't going to be so much as one fingernail of mine left for someone to do voodoo on. That's how urban I was.

My mother, when finally forced to commune with the trees, had a different response. It was, perhaps, one that logically followed from a lifetime in Chicago. At age 60 she lost her urban virginity by being taken to a trail in Tilden Park. Wide-eyed, she looked around and said, "Ya know, you could kill someone and leave the body up here and they'd never find it."

With a background like this, imagine how thrilling it is to live in a place that allows easy access to wonders beyond my B movie dreams. I don't mean just mountains and ocean but even little things like egrets near the freeway or redwoods in the backyard. Still, the discontinuity is great. In *The Misfits* Monroe asks Gable, "What do you do in the country?" "Just live," he says. While it's always wonderful to walk along a pretty trail or swim in a clear river or scoop up sand in an abalone shell, I've often wondered: could someone like me ever *live* in the country?

My stranger in paradise status came home again this summer. We were on our annual visit to friends who moved to Plumas County in the Sierra ten years ago. They are part of a group of Bay Area emigrants we see each summer. Usually I listen with envy to stories of their cow's fresh milk and their children growing up knowing which berries to gather and their ten-minute walks to deserted creeks where you can pan for gold.

This year things were different. There was talk among these country folk of moving back. There is trouble in paradise in the form of continuing unemployment and no growth. They see their friends in the city advancing. The women (many of whom have graduate degrees) are sick of chauffeuring the kids and working part-time jobs for four dollars an hour. One Quincy, California resident put it this way: "I don't think I'll be here past Christmas. Quincy's a great place to come for a vacation. I've been here twelve years. The vacation is over."

I felt an odd relief when he said it, like maybe the grass wasn't entirely greener when you had to earn a living in it. While the nature is spectactular and the air is purer I could never quite see myself fitting into rural culture. I had that out-of-place feeling the day we all went to Buck's Lake near Quincy. Buck's Lake is a pretty little reservoir surrounded by souped-up dirt bikes, custom vans, loud portable sound systems, and beer, beer everywhere.

I had to ask myself: what was I doing at a Buck's Lake? Even the name—was that some kind of joke? Buck's Lake. Stud's Point. Testosterone Creek. On this day Buck's Lake was the scene of a tragic, impotent boat incident.

Some guy, a friend of my friends, kept buzzing the shore in his little motorboat. It had a great big engine that said "Chrysler" and an American flag decal. He'd buzz the shore and laugh and wave. Suddenly he was being towed in. The engine had died.

One by one he went up to *everyone* on the shore to explain his shame, his failure, his horsepower interruptus. Even I was not spared. "I don't know what went wrong," he said. "It worked great at home. It was ready all week—then we took it up here, and it just died on me in the middle of the lake."

I had no idea why he was telling *me* this. Didn't he know I was weird? Couldn't he tell I'd just practically stepped off the boat from Poland myself? The *meshuggener*! I mean, couldn't he see the babushka on my head and the shawl on my shoulders? So I looked at him sympathetically and placed my hand on his and said, "Next time—buy Japanese."

And so, as the sun slowly sets on the summer of '83, it is time to say sayonara to Buck's Lake, aloha to the limp machine in Eden, farewell to the rice-laden regrets of my childhood. It's good to taste the fresh, fresh baguettes of home.

The Way We Wear

Hello Darlings! Alicia La Schlep here, your East Bay fashion maveneuse, with my spring fashion report. In a moment, we'll talk about the meaning of ties in men's lives, but first the big news: women are still wearing clothes! This, despite the success last year of the flasher look. The look, as popularized in the movie *Flash-in-the-Pants Dance*, consists of slit skirts, torn sweatshirts, and ripped T-shirts—the molested look. Share the fantasy? Not this La Schlep.

The year past also brought us those misty, pastel-colored memories of the way we weren't—the 50's look. There were tops and trousers of Bermuda Pink, Dawn Gray, Buttercup Yellow, Foam Green, and Turquoise Blue. Like, real gone, Daddy-o. Like, I Like Ike, but I Love Lucy. And, like hey—better pink and black than red and dead.

Speaking of which, they dug up the ghost of poor Marilyn to sell jewelry, perfume, makeup, and tight sweaters and skirts. But it's a rearview, skinny, plunging backline we're getting; not the real full-hipped Mammary Monroe. Still, now that pointed-toe high heels are back I ask you: can the big breasted look be far behind? (Or, can the big behind look be far abreast?) Why, if we can put missiles in West Germany, we can certainly put them back on milady's chest.

The continued ability of designers to get us to submit to being branded with their names has encouraged me to come up with my own La Schlep line. Designed especially for the East Bay, it's a kind of preppie Marlon Brando meets L.L. Bean Bohemian look. Each item will bear the La Schlep insignia—a horse trouncing a human being. It's the La Schlep look: bold, dominant, but yearning to be stepped on. If all goes well, I'll branch into toiletries. There'll be my perfume for women, Eau d'Emeryville—the smell that won't go away; and Chapped, the cologne for men who keep their legs together. Finally, we hope to move into the designer food field, starting with the Berkeley pinge-burge chocolate line. For this I have created the Ex-Lax truffle.

To learn the latest on fashion, I read the *San Francisco Chronicle* series on the Japanese look—bold, daring, but yearning to trounce IBM. Then I looked through *Vogue* and *Bazaar* at the futuristic look, the manstyled look, the layered look, the asymmetrical look—bold, daring, but yearning to spend money.

This is not *us*, I thought. We are not slaves to fashion like those West Bay prostitutes. I try to find *our* look in that bastion of fashion, the Cafe Med, where I land the window seat. I sit there taking notes and staring (I mean really *gaping*) at people, but no one minds because they assume I'm just another psychotic poet— Cassandra La Schlep.

But then, the Med is simply too, too Olde Berkeley, isn't it? I try to think of a more neutral place to look for looks and decide to take a woman-in-the-street approach (that's *in*, not *of*, Darlings). I venture forth to find the People at the cultural crossroads, Ratto's, in the heart of Olde Oakland.

It's been said that anybody who's Anybody in Oakland comes to Pasta Day (Wednesday lunch) at Ratto's. Well, let's just see who's here, and what clothes they're schlurping pesto on.

I approach a man and a woman who stand out as well-dressed, white, urban professionals (Wuppies?). They are both marketing representatives for AT&T. She describes her look as "corporate chic" and then adds, "I'm just kidding about the chic." She is wearing a blue suit, white shirt, bow tie, and black pumps. "That's how I usually dress, and it's how he dresses too." He nods in agreement and comments on the East Bay look. "There's the business look from San Francisco and the influence of Berkeley, so you have the school look, a casual look. There is also a heavy black in-

135

fluence which is more high fashion, a lot of sweater vests, tighter clothes usually."

She explains, "When I first started working in the corporate world, I dressed more like this. I wanted to look just like everybody else and everybody else was men. Now I'm trying to get a more feminine look, maybe pearls or silk blouses rather than cotton button-downs. When you get a little more comfortable with what you're doing, then you can branch out." He says, "The big change for me this year was throwing away my wing-tips. Now I wear loafers, more comfortable shoes." Both agreed that with increasing job security, they can afford to take these "chances" with their looks.

At the next table sit three little lawyers. An unwelcome Goldilocks, I invade their space. Two are wearing suits and ties and neatly trimmed moustaches. The third is a large man who made a striking entrance in a bright red down jacket and a motorcycle helmet. He, counselor number 3, is the most articulate: "Clothes serve two functions: they keep me from getting cold, and they keep me from getting arrested for indecent exposure. Any other level of concentration on it has to be justified either because you wear a uniform (I wear one in court—the same as they're wearing) or because you've got nothing else to do with your life. But I'll admit, I'm nuts on the subject."

Counselor number 2 says, "Clothes also serve the function of creating self-esteem in people who don't have any other way to do it. There's no Oakland look," he adds, "except maybe that it's different from Berkeley—fewer knapsacks." Counselor number 1 then points to number 3 and says, "He's got the biker look, the Hell's Angels look."

Says number 3: "I rode my motorcycle today and I've got a beard but no long hair or tattoos. And I've never dated anyone that wore a shirt that said: Property of Chris Peoples." Then he goes into his summation. "Your question [Is there an East Bay look?] begins with the assumption that there is a look and that we care. In my case, these assumptions are fallacious. I was never in fashion to begin with, and I never gave a damn about it from the time I wore a uniform in grammar school. When I worked in San Francisco, I had to wear my uniform every day, a three-piece suit. Now I only have to wear it when I see a client or when I go to court."

I move on to another table in the large, sunny room and introduce myself to Lee and Mary Maclaine, a retired couple who moved to Union City from upstate New York two years ago. They've been married 34 years and obviously enjoy each other's company. This is their first time ever in downtown Oakland, and they seem happy to share their observations. They tell me they've really been noticing the way people are dressed.

"This place is fascinating," says Lee Maclaine. "I was just about to comment to Mary that there's a real good mix of working class and professional." He points to different people in the food line and comments on their clothes. "There's the sport look—this gentleman here with the blue blazer and beige slacks. It's a real *in* look. Then next to him there's a fellow with a cowboy-like attire. And then I see someone wearing clothes that we would wear Back East. It surprises us to see someone on a day as beautiful as this wearing heavy stuff like that blue parka," says Maclaine, who stands out in the fifty degree chill in a shortsleeved shirt. "He's got on a jacket that I'd wear back home on a day when it's twenty below."

Mrs. Maclaine comments that she likes the change this past year towards more skirts for women. "I like it because it's more feminine and looks a lot neater," she says. Mr. Maclaine interrupts, "The ethnic look surprises us. We notice people from Asia and India, people in turbans, serapes. I do take a spin around when I see that, and I think you do too, don't you, Mary?" And emphasizing his earlier point about dress and weather, he adds: "If we ever walked around our town in September or October like they do here with a jacket and a hat, I think the druggist and the butcher and the baker would ask if we were sick."

A young black couple who are computer programmers in the probation department are my next subjects. Both obviously pay great attention to the way they dress. He's wearing a thick, nubby beige sweater, shirt, skinny wool plaid tie, and slacks. He subscribes to GQ and tells me the East Bay look is one of "earth tones." She adds it's "a more preppied-up look with women in ties, hats, and shawls. This year women are wearing coats."

She's wearing a wool, fringed-bottom skirt and a V-neck jacket with padded shoulders. I notice her purple lipstick and matching nail polish. She tells me she gets her fashion ideas from

TV, from shows like *Dynasty* and *Dallas*. "I like Victoria Principal. I love her style of dress." "Even on the soap operas, they dress real chic," he adds. I ask her about the Italian horn she wears around her neck. "Oh, I thought it was a dog's tooth."

In the corner table, smiling, sipping wine, and kibitzing are a group of middle-aged Italian men. They include a meat salesman, a pawnbroker, an unemployed man, and the owner of Ratto's, Ray Garcia—"the *Padrone*" as his friends call him. They joke about the changes in their hairstyles this year—loss of hair, graying, etc. The *Padrone*, a handsome man with a full head of thick silver hair, takes my questions about fashion seriously. He thinks the East Bay look is "a western look, western boots, shirts, jeans. It's definitely not San Francisco. Even the lawyers here are more casual. See those guys with the *loose* ties. That's casual."

We get into a discussion about the fad of men wearing earrings. The meat salesman asks: "What does it mean? Now, somebody once told me, if you've got one in your right or left ear it means something." His friend, the unemployed man, asks, "Which way is gay and which way is square?" I assure them I know of no meaning, but the meat man grins from above his polka-dot tie, "She knows. She knows." I ask him if he's ever considered just one tasteful, little diamond earring. "I go for a tasteful, little diamond but not in the ear. And not in the nose either. That bothers me. It's flaky. There's no reason for it, and my father would kick me right square in the . . ." He lets his voice trail off, then adds, "I'd do the same for my kids. But look, I sell meat for Del Monte Meats, and I always work with a tie on. It would bother me to have somebody make a professional call without a tie."

I get a contrasting point of view from the work crew who are plastering on the balcony, preparing more dining space at Ratto's. The crew boss tells me, "I'm a country bumpkin type of guy. I have three hundred T-shirts, two pairs of Levi's, five pairs of cowboy boots, and a thousand dollar leather coat when I'm impressing the women." He tells me his name is Tom Garcia. "Put that in your story—it'll give me a feeling of power."

Tom Garcia is wearing a green jumpsuit covered with plaster dust. His hands fly around as he talks, and at one point he accidentally slaps me, leaving a large plaster handprint on the thigh of my black trousers, for which he apologizes. He talks animatedly about the East Bay look. "It's a casual place. You've got everything from people in suits to people like me to down coats. The East Bay is a kind of melting pot of New York, LA, and Chi-*caw*-go," he says, letting me know my accent has not escaped him. "I knew you were from Back East."

He sums up his fashion position: "I go into a lot of nice Italian restaurants here, and you can wear anything you want, and that's what's nice about it because I'll *die* before I put on a tie. It's as simple as that."

I talk to three women who are clerks at "a large Emeryville corporation." They have three different looks, they tell me. "Casual—old clothes," says one; "businesslike—suit, skirt, heels," says another; and "underdressed," says the third, who is wearing a denim jumper. Two wear gold coil earrings that the woman in the jumper sells. They deny that there's an East Bay look, although they admit that if they worked in San Francisco, they'd dress up more. I also talk to two Ivy-League-looking black professional men, an architect and an insurance salesman. Both look handsomely dressed in tweed jackets. They tell me they are Grodin's men. One wears a tie, the other doesn't, but both join the chorus of praise for the optional tie as a pleasant feature of East Bay dress. "It's more laid-back here, less high tension, less competitive," says the architect. "People here are more loose *and* conservative," adds the insurance salesman. "Nobody's worried about how they look because they don't care. You can wear a tie one day and jeans the next." The architect adds, "The East Bay is more racially mixed than San Francisco, especially in the business community. I've heard that Oakland is the number one city as far as integration is concerned. I think it's a friendlier environment than San Francisco, not as status conscious. So you've got more diverse dress."

My last stop at Ratto's was a table of eight men in their thirties who work as computer programmers and engineers at Digital Microsystems. They have a Berkeley look (most are sporting long hair, beards, and functional outdoorsy clothing) because all but one live in Berkeley. Although they probably have a combined IQ of 1,200, they were particularly inarticulate on the subject of clothing. Perhaps they had spent their morning dreaming of accessing a plate of Ratto's tortellini with meat sauce, and I was ruining the mass schlurp-in. One man took pity on my attempt to wring some sartorial satire out of them and offered, "My last shave was August 20, 1968 at the Chicago Democratic Convention. That's when I lost my timezone."

I leave Ratto's and head for my car parked among the sandblasters and dumpsters that are spiffing up the old Victorians and upscaling downtown Oakland. Before I enter the metal shell that will transport me away from all this, I see a crowd huddled together in the doorway of the Baldwin Hotel. As I approach, the group scatters except for the one man who agrees to talk to me and shouts after the others, "Hey, she's cool. She's a writer. A writer."

My informant is a clear spokesman about the meaning of clothes at the Baldwin. "Most people around here dress with clothes that are one style behind. They go to a Goodwill or a Salvation Army to buy their clothes used because most people around here are on fixed income, welfare, or SSI. So it's pretty hard for us to buy new clothes from like Smith's or Capwell's or Liberty House.

"Most people around here, if you look at them, are dressed *warmly*, warmly. They have jackets or overcoats. See, this is the Baldwin. There's no heat in the rooms; there's central heat. The heat's in the hallway, so you have to open your topvent or your door in order to allow heat inside the room. This hat with the visor? That's to keep the moisture—rain—off your head."

He talks about the people who walk by the Baldwin and returns to a fashion issue almost every man I spoke with addressed. "To a lot of people down here, a suit and tie means *authority*, authority. They're from the court building or the police station. They only come down this way between eleven and one on their way to Ratto's or the Gulf Coast Oyster Bar. They just come to eat. After that, after four o'clock, you don't see anybody except the fixed income people."

He tells me he's worked as a janitor, a spray painter, and a cook, but he's been on unemployment now since last summer. I ask him how clothing has affected his job search. "New slacks, a sportscoat, and a sportshirt would help. When you go into an office for an interview, you have to look well. At Goodwill, you can find jeans, but the slacks and suits are too outdated. When I look for a job, I'm going among people who have three-button or four-buttons, and if I walk in wearing a large lapel that's like twenty years old, I stand out. You look odd when you're out of style."

Berkeley Explained

I am walking north on Shattuck Avenue—
Main Street—Berkeley, California. In my
head I hear Elvis, the late King, singing "In the ghet-*toe* . . ." I im-
provise his back-up, the Mighty Clouds of Joy, adding, "the gourmet ghetto . . ."

A young man comes up to me on the corner of Cedar and
Shattuck and asks, "Do you know where I can get any food around
here? I'm new in town." I brace myself against a lamppost because
the question is staggering. Can I answer him in three thousand
words or less? Doesn't he know he's in the heart of what realtors
call "the most dynamic and innovative retail shopping area in the
United States?" Is he unaware that he has entered—da-da da-da
da-da—the Gluttony Zone?

Before I lead him down the gustatory garden path I attempt to
assess his level of knowledge. He arrived in town yesterday from
SUNY Binghamton and has come to do graduate work in micro-
biology. No, he has never heard of the gourmet ghetto. He has
missed the articles about it in *The New York Times*, *Newsweek*, and
The Nation. He doesn't know that the East Coast press loves to do
a dance on how the Berkeley Left has become the food establishment, how "the counterculture has become the counter culture,"
how the radicals now eat radicchio, how the barricades have been
replaced by the wheels of brie. No, he is just a new kid in town
asking what appears to be a perfectly simple question. For him,
and for all the other new recruits, the young men and women who

are even now arriving from the provinces, I'd like to offer this modest guide to Berkeley.

If you dare to wander beyond the campus, beyond the dorms, beyond your "pig runs" and "animal houses" you will find a place that gets curiouser and curiouser. The first rule is that Berkeley, like Tina Turner, never does anything nice and easy. If you keep this in mind you won't be surprised when what would seem to be the simplest of civic acts—from tree trimming to garbage disposal—become issues of heated debate, protest, emotion, and political intrigue.

But let's start with that innocent question: where to get food around here. I answer the young man by pointing out that we have just passed Poulet, the gourmet chicken deli, the Virginia Bakery, Borrelli's, an Italian deli, the Griffon, a new Scandinavian restaurant, and Warszawa, a place that proves that Polish cuisine is more than a Spam upsidedown cake.

Across the intersection is Smokey Joe's Cafe, a monument to the mellow hippie. Next to it, on the site of a former funeral home, there is a complex of shops including Sweet Temptations, a chocolate and yogurt heaven, a Japanese place where you can achieve yakitori, a place that actually serves hamburgers, and one of the innumerable croissant and cappuccino filling stations that have become the McDonalds of Berkeley. (Surely over ten billion served by now.) Never mind that this mortuary mall once inspired angry protests in the community. That and the ability to park nearby are now history.

On the next corner is the Co-op, the Shattuck branch of a chain of cooperative supermarkets. This particular store is one of the largest volume supermarkets in the country. It too has experienced constant political infighting: should it sell the cheapest food, the wholesomest food, or those products untainted by the human or labor rights violations of the companies who make them? Newcomers can join or they can shop here without joining. If the clerk asks for your number you can say "Farmworkers" or "Free Clinic" and nobody will know you're a stranger. You will also want to check out the upstairs bulletin board where you might find a room to rent, a sofa, or your own true love.

My newfound friend and I proceed up Shattuck past the world-famous Chez Panisse and turn the corner to see the natives gather for coffee at a place called Peet's, which sells the sinsemilla of coffee beans as well as a variety of beans ordinaire. I tell him how on mornings here he'll find what my friend Sharon calls the "independently wealthy mothers." These are the ones with working husbands and one perfect babe in an Aprica stroller. We listen as the men nearby bitch about how they're "not gettin' much."

You can even stop in at the Juice Bar for something as mundane as a turkey sandwich, I tell him. Just be sure you have a styrofoam cup in your hands at all times. This is your passport. Anyone caught wandering around the area without a styrofoam cup is immediately suspect. We have little gestapo type officers who may approach you and ask to see "ze cup, pleeze!"

You'll probably want to stop in at Vivoli's for an Italian ice cream. I keep hoping they'll add some truly local flavors like Walnut Square or Nuclear Freèze but so far it's just plain old amaretto and fresh strawberry and stuff like that. Vivoli's represents a success story from one of Berkeley's unique minorities, the lesbian community. Unlike San Francisco, where the gay male community is ghettoized in the Castro district, the lesbian community is mostly mainstreamed into Berkeley life. It is speculated that there is one feminist therapist for every fifty people in Berkeley. A good thing too because you can't live here for very long without needing one of your own.

Nearby is Cocolat (Parlez-vous Berklaise?), recently the scene of a labor strike that forced chocolate decadence lovers to temporarily satisfy themselves with sex. Next door is a pathetic Northern California attempt at a Jewish deli redeemed by its Yiddishkeit live performances including, believe it or not, terrible Jewish comedians. Further up the street is Lenny's, a butcher shop where they'll "sell no swine before its time," and—what else?—another Italian bakery and restaurant. Then there's the Produce Center (always a bridesmaid to the the formidable Monterey Market), where you can get five kinds of berries and four kinds of mushrooms and have a friendly conversation with the only normal person in Berkeley. You'll know her when you see her.

Completing the food mania is a sushi dealer, the Berkeley Fish Market, and Pig By the Tail, or as one neighborhood wag has dubbed it, Pig By the Balls. And last, but not least, we come to the Cheese Board.

Ah, blame it on the Cheese Board, they started it all. And is their face and politics red. This is one of the oldest and most successful food businesses in town. The collective that runs it seems quite uncomfortable with their newfound fame. Not only did they introduce us to the wonders of brie and their mock Boursin and a myriad of goat cheeses, but they perfected that ultimate symbol of the new Berkeley—the baguette. If you play your cards right and have a lot of time to kill, you may be able to score one. In a form of torture, they pollute the neighborhood with the smell of this delicacy baking.

I imagine someday the Cheese Board will organize a mass community therapy-in. The whole of Berkeley will be invited to engage in a huge swashbuckler scene. Some therapist-cum-facilitator will be perched on a lifeguard platform on the grassy road-divider strip and sound the *en garde*. Then we will all pull our baguettes out of their long white sheaths and begin non-violently battering one another. "Have a nice day. Pow! Take that, you knave!"

I have another theory on the Cheese Board and their diabolically delicious baguettes. No, they don't just want to constipate us. I think the plan is to get the whole community hooked and then baguette tease us. First it'll be "Sorry, no baguettes tonight, honey, the collective has a headache." From there it'll progress to "Baguettes for activists only." Before long nobody will get a baguette unless she submits to working for world peace and against nuclear weapons research. They'll franchise out branches to strategic locales: The Cheese Board, Livermore; The Cheese Board, Los Alamos; The Cheese Board, Port Chicago. Believe me, if J. Edgar Hoover were alive today we'd have a five-hundred page report on this small band of ragtag slicers and bakers, and its potential to wreak havoc by baguette denial.

Now that I've told you all about my neighborhood I want you to get out, leave, scram. I saw it first, and it's mine. If you must move beyond Larry Blake's or La Val's, go to somebody else's neighborhood. Wend your way through the maze of traffic diverters to another one of those islands in the Berkeley archipelago. Go to the Elmwood or Westbrae or Shattuck and Woolsey or College and Alcatraz or West Berkeley. There is actually better food to be had in these places than the ghetto. Some neighborhoods you can actually park in.

"But," protests the young man from the provinces, "all I wanted was to buy some bread and milk. That's all. If you really want to explain something, explain why it's so hard to find a place to live around here." (Phew! Couldn't he have asked me something simple like, "How can Reagan be removed from office?")

As I contemplate an explanation of the great Berkeley housing shortage, I hear Gene Pitney singing, "No, it isn't very pretty what a town without pity can do."

I walk him over to Henry Street behind the Safeway store (in North Berkeley, even Safeways have gourmet counters; I hear McDonald's is contemplating the introduction of Quail Mc-Nuggets). I point out a three-story cellblock-like building which extends back a full block to Milvia Street and bears the name Luxor Apts. This, I explain, is a classic Berkeley ticky-tacky circa 1966. Now look at the place next door. Note the porch columns, the stained glass, the elegant entrance. If you really want to know the story of Berkeley, it's told in windows, eaves, and brown shingles. Berkeley is basically a museum of houses, few of them all *that* grand but each magnificent in its details.

The ticky-tackies threatened this character and charm. Speculation in rental housing made tearing down two old elegant houses and putting up a 26-unit Luxor on the same lots a wise investment. Not three blocks from here is a row of ticky-tackies, one of them built on the site of a cottage where Allen Ginsberg reportedly wrote *Howl*. Would the English tear down Shakespeare's house and put up units?

Two forces conspired to stop the ticky-tackification of Berkeley. One was the riots of the Vietnam and People's Park era. Much anger was focused then on the concept that property was more valued than life. People showed their contempt for property by stoning, bombing, and placing graffiti on it. This didn't look so good when the developers brought the investors through for a looksee. The other force was rent control—for years a threat and finally a reality. Some feel rent control was necessary for neighborhood preservation and to maintain low-cost housing. Others feel it represents an unfair limitation on the supply of housing caused by mealy-mouthed no-growthers and argue that it ultimately contributes to gentrification.

"But," the young man inevitably asks, "what about the new building over there with the greenhouse windows, the skylights, and the wood shingles?" Sorry, pal, you can't afford it. Those are for the YUPs, the young urban professionals. They've been lured to Berkeley, in part, by bargains in condos and single-family homes—bargains, that is, relative to Marin, San Francisco, and the Peninsula. BART, a public transportation system convenient to Montgomery Street and few other places, is also a plus. The influx of these commuters has encouraged a new phase of speculation in commercial real estate, as creative capitalists and tax shelter artists sense a rising demand among the disposable income types for sophisticated shops selling unique items.

I give him an example. For days I passed a sign in the window of La Cuisine that proclaimed: "SALE! INGRID PARTY BALLS, $19.95." Curious, I went inside and asked, "What are Ingrid Party Balls?" "I don't know," the clerk answered.

"But you've had them on special all week."

She went and called another clerk. "Are you the one asking about the Ingrid Party Balls?" this one asked.

"Yes."

"I'm sorry," she said, "they're all sold out."

I considered calling up later and saying: this is Ingrid. Any messages?

I ask the young man if he understands now why he can't find a place to live.

"Sort of. But say, do you think there are any vacancies at the Luxor?"

"Don't tell me you want to live there. There are no fireplaces, no built-in redwood buffets, no window seats, no French doors—in short, none of the necessities of life."

"I think I could learn to survive without French doors. You ever try riding your bike from Pinole?"

I am about to suggest Oakland—"just over the rent control border," as they say in the real estate ads—but I can see something else is on his mind. He has one more question: "Do you know where . . . this is kind of hard to ask . . ."

Let's see. He said he was 23. (Was I ovulating in 1960?) "Look, I'm old enough to be your mother, boy. Ask me anything."

"Do you have any ideas on where I could meet girls?"

"Hey! Call us women," I retort—although, as I think about it, "girl" has had a slightly different ring to it since I've turned 35. (What really enrages me is when 23-year-old guys call me "ma'am.")

I try to break it to him gently how hazardous looking for love in Berkeley can be. I suggest he might want to join a men's group just to get the old Yin and Yang into balance before he comes on too strong or too weak to one of these young, assertive, hot-tub-on-the-first-date types. Next I suggest he make the necessary $25 investment in a haircut—one of those no-sideburn, parted-on-the-side specials. The long hair, I tell him, has got to go. I quote my friend Nina, who recently observed, "In the '60s I saw a guy with long hair and thought: brother. Now I see one and I think: mass murderer."

To meet women, he could try the clubs—Ruthie's, the Berkeley Square, Ashkenaz, etc., but I warn him that most of Berkeley closes at 9:00 p.m. Only the nocturnal creatures venture out after that, so he'd better be wary on the streets. Another approach would be to try the bookstores. (You probably think that there are so many bookstores because this is a town of intellectuals, but guess again—Cody's, Moe's, and their ilk have other uses.) I suggest he might be able to impress the right woman with, "Excuse me. Do you know where I can find a copy of Barbara Ehrenreich's book about men and the flight from commitment?" A more aggressive try would be "Have you seen a copy of (*How to Satisfy Your Lover With*) *Extended Sexual Orgasm*? I've already read about ESO myself but I need a copy for a friend." This will surely impress the red stiletto heels type. But what if he wants to meet a "Humboldt honey," an unshaven, Birkenstocked, Botticellian beauty? Here he might try, "I'm looking for a copy of *Death Begins in the Colon*. Do you know the book?"

While this bookish approach may work for recent East Coast arrivals, Californians generally prefer to get physical. A visit to the jogging track at Martin Luther King school may allow for a clever opener, such as "I couldn't help noticing how you never pronate."

Or perhaps on a visit to Strawberry Canyon pool he could manage a quick "You swim laps often?" between strokes. I tell him the odds are even more favorable (one male: twenty females) at an aerobics class. While his head is between his legs, he can look to his right and say, "Good workout, huh?" He could also try hiking in Tilden Park—if he can find it.

Finally, if all else fails, there is Berkeley's favorite sport: hanging out, eating, and waiting for something to happen. So I hand the young man a step-by-step plan: "BERKELEY ON 5,000 CALORIES A DAY."

8:00 a.m.—Cappuccino at Caffe Mediterraneum. Walk up to a What's Left type (you know, Old Left, New Left, What's Left) and ask for an explanation of the mural at Telegraph and Haste. Jog up Dwight to College. Note woman in wheelchair helping blind man cross street.

9:00 a.m.—Vanilla malt at Elmwood Soda Fountain. Discover soda jerk is local sage. Grab a bag of watermelon Jelly Bellies from Sweet Dreams and a cruller from Dream Fluff Donuts. Check out the Ivy Shoppe. (This place, I predict, will be torn down soon, then reconstructed in fifteen years at considerable expense.)

10:00 a.m.—Bear claw and coffee at the Buttercup (the IRS willing). Too bloated to jog or walk. Call Taxi Unlimited and go down to Shattuck. Wander around Hink's—"a great store at home." Look at Berkeley Public Library.

11:00 a.m.—Optional snack at Edy's or Trumpetvine Court.

Noon—Szechwan Hot Sauce Noodles at the Taiwan Restaurant. Revitalized. Run down Hearst Street past Ohlone Park (Who the hell was Ohlone?), noting St. Procopius Church and the Church of the Good Shepherd. Stop at grocery store at 7th and Hearst for homemade tortillas.

1:00 p.m.—Aerobics class at Goldies.

2:00 p.m.—Piece of pie at Bette's Diner. Meet beautiful woman with Mercedes who takes you to see her villa on San Luis Road.

4:00 p.m.—Stagger down to Fatapple's for a blueberry muffin and four cups of coffee with real cream and real sugar.

5:00 p.m.—Pick up ribs at Flint's Bar-B-Q.

6:00 p.m.—Pick up ribs at K C Bar-B-Q.

7:00 p.m.—Irish coffee at Brennan's. Get in argument over best barbecue place in Berkeley.

7:30 p.m.—Phone Herrick and Alta Bates Hospitals. Comparison shop for stomach pumping. Ask when Alta Bates cafeteria is open.

8:00 p.m.—Attend Berkeley City Council meeting. See our two political parties, the BCA and the ABC, in a ten-round exhibition match. (Tuesdays only.)

9:00 p.m.—Stroll Solano Avenue for Mu Shu Pork. Get a marble fudge cone at McCallums.

10:00 p.m.—Tune into KPFA for "Fat Is No Longer A Feminist Issue: A Look At Manorexics."

11:00 p.m.—Fries and Merlot at the Santa Fe Bar and Grill.

Midnight—Rocky Horror Picture Show at the UC Theatre (Saturdays only). See the children of Berkeley disguised as perverts.

As I hand him the list, I add a personal note. I came to Berkeley in the era of Dustin Hoffman's *The Graduate*. We wanted to get out of the rat race, out of the plastic, out of boredom and mediocrity just as Benjamin did. Now the movie is dated. Things have come full circle as a new generation desperately wants a crack at a good job, a home, some status. We, the class of '65, could reject those things when they seemed so readily available.

"*The Graduate* . . ." he ponders. "I saw that on the late show. Isn't that the one where Dustin Hoffman has an affair with an older woman?"

"Yeah."

"Well, do you think maybe I could buy you a drink, ma'am?"

"What? Pollute my body with alcohol and other toxic chemicals? You've got to be kidding, Babycakes. Now beat it. And welcome to Berkeley."

High School
Confidential

O ut beyond the brownshingled houses of Berkeley, past the antique Clare-mont Hotel, the lush forests of Montclair and the rolling hills of East Oakland, there is another world: the world of South County. Every school day from 1966 to 1969 I joined my carpool for the trip South. We were among the many migrant intellectual work-ers, the "wet brains," who leave Berkeley at dawn each morning to teach in those communities that lie geographically and politi-cally to the far right of Oakland.

Today, for the first time in fifteen years, I am making the jour-ney again—not so much as a cultural emissary this time but on a mission of reunion. Today I am going back to my school—let's just call it South County High—to see Jim, my former student. The last time I saw Jim was shortly after June of 1969, when he graduated and I was dismissed from my teaching position. He was a football star then, the school's lone political radical, a dabbler in Eastern philosophy, and a hard-headed experimenter in search of the maximum dose of clearlight acid.

It was with a lysergic glaze in his eyes that he bid me and the world farewell after graduation. Taking only his backpack and his girlfriend, he had his buddy Dan drop them off at the Sierras. I, who hadn't yet heard the word *machismo*, thought he was plain *loco.* His girlfriend, Jeanie, was not only captain of the cheerleaders, she was the daughter of the chief of police. Plus she had three (count 'em—three) big brothers who were also police officers. Jeanie was the darling of this family and the community. I viewed Jim as a dead man. It seemed as though playing football psychedelically had convinced him that he was indeed Superman.

So when I heard, in a letter from Dan, that Jim had not only survived but was back teaching and coaching at South County High, I felt I had to see him. I wanted to learn how he got from there to here and if, after pounding his brain from both within and without, he was still all there.

On the freeway I turn on the oldies station, hoping to hear Janis or The Doors or Led Zeppelin—something to really take me back to those days. "Itchy Coo Park," a song about skipping school to go get high, would be perfect. Instead what I get is Santo and Johnny's "Sleep Walk," and the sound of the Les Paul guitar takes me back to 1959, slowdancing, and my own antebellum school days.

At South County I was the English teacher, the person who made them write essays on "Who Bob Dylan's Sad-Eyed Lady Really Is" or "Why Brutus Betrayed Caesar" or "My Experience with Prejudice." I forced them to consider what exactly Shakespeare meant by "Now is the bawdy hand of time upon the prick of noon." Each day, five classes a day, I would come in, put on a popular record, and make them write in their journals, just for me. I would respond, and in that way have an ongoing private dialogue with each student. Some poured their hearts out. Others wrote endlessly about how stupid it was to write in a journal.

At the time I started teaching at South County, much attention was being focused on the so-called "culturally deprived children" of the urban ghettos. Yet many of the kids at South County had never even been to San Francisco, a forty-minute ride away. They used the word "Jew" as a generic term for thief as in "Gimme back my pencil, you Jew." Once I gave them an assignment to write about their dream job: what they would like to be if they could be anything they wanted, "no obstacles in the way—let your imagination go wild." One girl wrote only two words on the sheet: dental receptionist. I also remember Sherry, a girl without malice or irony, beginning an essay on South County with "This town was built on the slogan 'Leave Oakland to the Niggers.'"

151

Getting off the freeway at South County, I imagine that I am a French cinematographer taking in the classic American panorama. I get out my long-distance lens for one of those shots that shows the phone wires, the traffic signs, and the relentless sadness of franchise America: Finger Lickin' Good, Fix It Urself, 3-Ring Liquors, Pay Less, Save On, etc. Somewhere in the center of the picture is a road sign that reads "No Exit" or "Dead End." And as we drive along past the endless Malls and Towne Centres, my voice-over describes South County as "A blue-collar community built in the 1950s on the site of former lettuce fields. The homes consist of five basic floor plans and the schools are named after early real estate developers. The few old Victorian farm houses still standing serve as funeral homes. It is a hotbed of alcoholism, child abuse, and the American Nazi Party . . . a place where patriotic and racial sentiments have been used to manipulate the populace into voting against their own economic interests . . ." I could go on being condescending and negative. It's easy to dump on South County. But I am here to meet again one of South County's finest, Jim. I will blur my lens a little as I look at him. I wouldn't want him harmed by details in print.

As I am parking in front of the school, I think of an amazing story Jim told me back in 1966. Before Jim was born, his father bought a South County lot and began to build a house on it. He'd come home each night from the foundry where he worked and then go off to work on the dream house. He devoted his weekends to it. As soon as Jim and his brothers could walk they were put to work on the house. After ten years, when it was just about finished, Jim's dad was notified that his house stood in the path of a newly planned freeway. They never moved in. The State of California made him an offer he couldn't refuse.

When I first met Jim he was ripe for the post of teacher's pet. A perfect gentleman at fifteen, he also liked to paint and read Plato. His secure home life and supportive parents were in marked contrast to most of his classmates'. Generally, a student's track reflected his home life. There were five "tracks" at South County: "More Able" was the highest followed by "High" ("Welcome to High English," I would say with a grin), "Medium," "Low" ("Isn't this Stupid English, Teacher?" one girl asked), and "Mentally Retarded." Once I got a call from the mother of a "Low" student that began, "You lousy, commie teacher. What are you doing

152

to Frank? You want him to be a niggerlover?" I soon determined that she was drunk, and objecting to our reading the book *Black Like Me*. (Frank actually resurfaced in my life again, briefly, when he showed up at a VD clinic I was working at in Oakland in 1974. "Can you believe it, Teacher, I got the clap?")

Another time a father kept interrupting my presentation at Parents Night by standing up and shouting "You are teaching blasphemy!" Turns out he was referring to the words "God damn" in the book *The Martian Chronicles*.

The principal, whom we'll call Dr. Muggs, would frequently call me into his office and begin the conversation with "I'm going to have to fire you, Mrs. Kahn." As my heart sank he would continue, "Mrs. Silva called me and said she found a *Berkeley Barb* in Bobby's underwear drawer. He said his English teacher gave it to him. We have no room in this school district for outside agitators." I would explain that I never gave Bobby the paper, that he probably told his parents that to avoid being beaten. That must have sat right with Frederick Muggs, because he always concluded these little sessions with, "Good to get your side of the story."

Lying to avoid beatings was perfectly believable at South County. I remember the time Linda Janes, the girl with the highest IQ in the history of South County, came to my room to ask me to help her get out of PE. Girls were always coming to me asking if I could help them avoid PE during their periods, but Linda had a different reason. She closed the door and pulled the shades in my empty classroom and took off her blouse. She turned around to show me her back, covered with raw sores from the beating she had sustained the night before.

All these images from my days at South County are sharp in my mind as I enter the classroom—more than a little nervous—to see Jim. There he stands: tall, handsome, composed at the front of the room. I take a seat at the back. Third period history is in session. The ninth grade kids look so young! The mood of the class seems closer to nursery school than college. They're at the age when one notices an undeveloped frecklefaced boy seated next to a girl made up like a hooker. They are supposed to be working on their assignment. A pug-nosed girl periodically turns around and forcefully punches the fat little class clown who sits, wise-cracking, behind her. He's obviously in love with her. The class looks more racially mixed that it would have been years ago. (Once I had asked my class to write about their ethnic heritage. A typical response was "Part Irish, part Portuguese, part German, part Cherokee Indian.") The other thing I notice is that these kids actually seem dumber! The kid next to me says to his friend, "What's China? A country?"

Jim doesn't seem upset by the chaos and the ignorance. He goes around to each kid, encouraging everyone, answering their questions patiently and respectfully. I ask the kid next to me what he thinks of Jim as a teacher. "He's different than any teacher I ever had. He really teaches you stuff you can use. He even taught us relaxation. I never had a teacher teach me relaxation before."

At some point the class clown comes up to me and says, "Are you a shrink? Are you one of those people who's here to figure out what's wrong with us?"

Funny he should ask, for that's one of the main reasons I got out of teaching. I *was* a shrink! Like so many English teachers who invite their students to open up their thoughts and feelings, I discovered they actually wanted me to help them with these things. And I tried. I put in overtime. I sat after school for an endless stream of tragic-comic stories. "Mrs. Kahn, my boyfriend touched my breast! Can I get pregnant?" "Mrs. Kahn, I want to leave home and join the army. Should I do it?" "Mrs. Kahn, is it best to be honest or lie in a dishonest world?" As time went by I found myself increasingly forced to abandon literature, abandon grammar, and teach morals, values, behavior. I felt like a shrink, but maybe it was a whole lot more like being Miss Lonelyhearts.

The bell rings to end Jim's class, but a long line of students stays late, to ask one more question, to get one more bit of attention from that rare teacher who really seems to care. When Jim and I finally sit down to talk, we spend a few minutes just looking at each other and savoring the irony of Jim's now being on the other side of the desk. "Well," I begin, "I'm glad you're the teacher and not me."

In 1966, my starting salary was $6,000. South County was at the bottom of the pay scale and the last place I wanted to teach.

Like most of my college classmates, I wanted to teach at a black or integrated school. Interestingly, those schools paid the best. Back then Emeryville was the top-paying East Bay school district, starting at $12,000 a year (twice as much as South County), followed by the Berkeley schools (where everyone wanted to teach) at $10,000. (Today, the Berkeley schools are near the bottom of the pay scale, just above South County.) Jim, after five years at South County, is making $19,000. That includes the $500 extra he makes coaching football (which requires him to work weekends and after school until 7:00 p.m. each night during the season).

"I love it," says Jim. "I mean, it's a job, for one thing, and a lot of my friends don't have jobs. Plus it's a chance to influence some people. If I can get through to just a few of them it's worth it."

"Boy, that takes me back," I laugh. Dr. Muggs was right. I had been an outside agitator at South County. I hadn't wanted the boys to go off and die in the Vietnam war, or the girls to be empty-headed ninnies who supported it. But I had also believed in a lot of things that seem silly or wrong to me now—like the "cultural revolution." It had seemed so simple then: the music and the drugs and the breakdown of the nuclear family were going to be just great. Now, haltingly, I tell Jim that as I had watched him become increasingly strung out, out of touch, I had felt guilty for whatever part my influence might have played. "The power to influence in teaching can come back to haunt you," I say.

"Yes, I know you were worried about me then. You told me that. But really I was OK. A lot of people didn't realize I was really in control then."

"You seemed so wild, so hard to make contact with and talk to. And playing football like that. I really think you had a Superman complex."

"Still do," he acknowledges.

"What happened when you came out of the mountains with Jeanie that summer?"

"The families sat down and it was decided that we should get married. Jeanie voted against it. And I really didn't want to. I mean we were eighteen and just wanted to live together. But we did what they wanted. Then I went to junior college and I started to get really good at football . . . better than I ever thought I could. I was being recruited by Notre Dame and other schools like that. Football was the biggest thing in my life. It taught me strength, it gave me confidence, it paid my college education . . ."

"Fotbal been very, very, gud to me," I interrupt, attempting an impression of Garrett Morris on *Saturday Night Live*. "Actually, I had a hard time with your becoming a jock. As I saw you getting into it, it seemed like your head was getting smaller and smaller while your body got bigger."

"Yeah, I know it's hard to understand, but football really was the main thing that pulled me through. Without it I would have been dead. The thing I really love about the game is how it teaches you that you can't stop, that you have to keep going. Like if you're jogging and you get tired you can stop any time. But in football if you stop or give up you'll get your head smashed."

"Strength is a wonderful quality to have," I agreed. "But I still think it has to be tempered with some sense of limits."

"I learned about limits when football stopped . . . when I graduated it was just all over. I felt like there was nothing left. What was really rough was that football, college, and Jeanie all came to an end at once. Right before graduation I went on a backpacking trip by myself. Somehow Jeanie 'accidentally' left this diary in my backpack. In it she described in detail all her lovers and love affairs including all my best friends on the team. I was in shock. I've only had two or three girlfriends in my life. We got divorced . . . It still hurts to talk about it. So, I came back from that trip to this graduation dinner honoring me, the star of the team. And that's when it hit me that it was over. My dad took it really hard. He lay down on the floor, drunk, at the banquet and started crying: 'It's over. It's all over.'

"Probably the hardest problem I've had to deal with in my life is being an ex-football star. It was so exciting. And then when I stopped there was all this pain—my back, my neck, my arms and my legs. I'd get these horrible headaches. I went to doctors, chiropractors; it's a lot better now."

"Does coaching the team bring back any of the satisfaction?"

"No—it's just for fun. These guys aren't as serious as I was. So it's like my job, it's just guerrilla theater. I do it but I try not to take it too seriously."

I want to know about what South County is like today. Are kids still strung out? What does Jim tell them now?

"Oh, drug use is way down," he replies. "It was just starting when I was in school—the '70s were the real peak years. Now these kids don't use marijuana or LSD so much. Part of it is because many of them try these things when they're younger, ten or twelve, and by fifteen they're tired of them. Another reason is alcohol use is way up. I lost my best quarterback to alcohol. He cracked up his car while he was drunk and he died. I kind of think it might have been better for him to stick to joints."

As Jim talks I remember back to the day Dave Ward fell asleep in my ninth period class. I had decided to play a little joke on him, to "teach him a lesson." When the bell rang I had the other kids stand outside by the windows and watch. When the room was empty, I went up to Dave and shouted "Time for breakfast!" No response. I shook his shoulders. No response. I grabbed him up and started slapping him around his face. It took a full four minutes of slapping to rouse him. When I finally did, he ran out in a panic. No one was laughing. Certainly not me. The next day he told me he had taken six reds (sleeping pills) and some wine before school. He said it was a game he was playing with his friends. "We wanted to see how many reds we could take without dying," he told me.

"You know," says Jim all of a sudden, "you were a great teacher—a terrific teacher." It is good to hear, but frankly it had been easy to be a good teacher at South County.

"One of my major innovations was letting people go to the bathroom when they wanted to," I say laughing.

"Bladder liberation!"

"But really, the other teachers were poor . . . probably burnt out, or too busy raising their families, or moonlighting second jobs, or bowling. Something." The fact was I had no respect for them at all. I still remember vividly the moment in the spring of 1969 when I knew I had to quit. We were having a faculty meeting and Dr. Muggs was describing an "Emergency Plan." The bells would sound and we were to lock our doors and have the students get under their desks. Then we were to stand at the window and watch. "For what?" I called out from my seat at the top of the bleachers in the music room, "I mean, what are you imagining?

Armed troops from Oakland?" At that point, the entire faculty—
all my colleagues—turned around, looked up at me and hissed.
Hissed! Like a bunch of snakes. I must have struck a nerve.

But I didn't quit right away. I had my final review and was
told I would be given tenure. Then one day Muggs called me into
his office. He said there was a budget crisis, so half the English department was being laid off. The coaches (who were already teaching history) would also teach English. "You mean I'm fired? You
can't fire me," I said. "I quit." And, with that, stomped out of
there. My satisfaction was short-lived—that heroic little speech
cost me several thousand dollars in unemployment benefits. But I
was 26 and not one to plan ahead.

Jim asks about the other teachers I used to carpool with. I tell him
about the reunion I had with Carol and Sue last July Fourth in the
mountain town where they live with their families. We all discussed why we left teaching after South County and how we
couldn't imagine teaching now that we were parents. We'd lost our
special sympathy with the students—the kind of sympathy Jim
still has. I ask him if he has trouble with the administration.

"They pretty much let me do my thing," he says. "The '70s
kind of blew them away. They realized they didn't know what to
do with teenagers then. They're happy to have someone who can
reach them. But I worry. It seems like things are really going back-
ward now. They've just announced we have to say the Pledge of
Allegiance again. They want to be sure we're raising loyal, middle-class Americans. Like they just announced the boys can't wear
caps. Well, that cuts the link to their fathers, who are mostly
Teamsters. The fathers go off to work each morning wearing their
caps that say CAT or John Deere or something."

"Reminds me of when they wouldn't let the girls wear pants
because it wasn't ladylike," I say. "If they're not preparing these
kids to be Teamsters, what are they preparing them for? Clearly
not Harvard or Yale. What's going to happen to these blue collar
kids? Their fathers are being laid off. Their rate of unemployment
is five times that of college grads and the college grads aren't doing
so well. What do you say to them?"

"I tell them to scale down their lifestyle. To live simply. I do.
I live in one room. I know I'm a bachelor so it's easy, but I don't

spend a lot of money. I tell them the American Dream was never worth having, that it rested on exploiting most of the people and resources in the world. That maybe it's better to learn to make your own bread than buy a new toaster, that maybe the simple pleasures will be better for them and the rest of the world."

How do you explain teacherly love? It's different than a mother's or a lover's. I feel this for Jim and give him a big hug. Sixth period is starting and it's time to go.

"I still have my journal from sophomore English," Jim calls out.

"I still have the valentine your class made for me," I say, and wave goodbye.

On the way home, the freeway doesn't seem quite so sad. The wasteland may be wasted. Politicians like Jerry Brown and Jimmy Carter, who preached a "small is beautiful, lower your expectations" philosophy, enraged the electorate. But somewhere out there in South County, a few boys and girls are getting some real guidance. ("He really teaches you stuff you can use.")

Jim couldn't tell me what happened to most of his other classmates. He didn't know who died in Vietnam. He didn't know who was sitting alone in her apartment, popping Valiums and drinking coffee. We talked about his friend Dan, another of my favorites, who's now a surveyor with the Forest Service. I told him about Peggy Rogers, who's farming and raising her kids in the country. He told me about Ronny, who's in San Quentin for dealing drugs. I know I'll never forget their faces, their questions, their needs. I'm glad Jim has come back home. Thank God, I didn't let him down.

Amish Chic

When the kid asks, "Mommy, how come Ronald Reagan is president if nobody we know is for him?" you know it's time to show her the real America. Besides, I just had to get out of this beautiful people's republic. Berkeley, where I am a lifer, where I haven't missed a trick (or, for that matter, turned a trick) in almost twenty years . . . Berkeley with its live and let rot, let's-make-the-world-safe-for-dog-caca pretentiousness was stickin' in my craw. It was either a crawectomy or get out of town.

So we came to stand, satchels in hand, me, Paw, and the kids—four for Cleveland. Not that I've heard Cleveland is lovely this time of year, mind you, nor am I partial to people with names like Volvulvovitch or Pryxzynich either. And no, I did not get a deal through Club Med Cleveland. The thing is that my husband has this sister, and she once went to Ohio State to study art—a preposterous idea in itself. There, she met this gentleman sheep farmer and, before you know it, it was good-bye Columbus and hello to a farm ninety miles from Cleveland. Her husband, my brother-in-law, is into genetics. He's bred his flock for multiple births and now shepherds one hundred and fifty baa-baas. My theory on the marriage was that he decided to marry my sister-in-law to introduce a little Jew (or as the country folk say, "je-yew") into his own strain.

The first night on the farm was pure bliss. We were put up in "the wood house," a two-story, barnlike, solid black walnut structure that, like the farm house, dates back to 1830. The music of the crickets, the absence of any other noise, put an end to months of Berkeleynoia. The political factions, the French Hotel, and even my neighbor's Home for Wayward Speed Freaks were all a dream.

In the morning there were oohs and aahs in the farm kitchen as we got out our exotic urban drugs. Filter, cone, and other paraphernalia were exhibited as we prepared our pot of Peet's Guatemalan coffee (don't leave home without it). The brother-in-law downed two cups and had three fields mown and stacked before noon. Reasonably wired myself, I set off on my morning jog down a quiet farm road.

Having just left the brown dying desert of late summer California, the Ohio landscape seemed a verdant jungle of rolling green hills interrupted by stands of oak, maple, or elm, and fields of tall feed-corn. When they talk corn rows here, they don't mean hairdos.

Every bit of land was alive with crops, insects, birds, and wildflowers. And there were these huge blue skies with perfect little cumulus clouds seemingly appliqued on by the Big Fabric Artist in the Sky. It was *Christina's World* as far as the eye could see, open country with only an occasional stark Victorian farmhouse or the clapboard simplicity of the Vermillion Baptist Church, "tower erected 1870." I turned onto the "Johnny Appleseed Trail" (sign courtesy of the Boy Scouts of America) and came upon a granite obelisk surrounded by a cyclone fence. A plaque read: "James Copus and three soldiers killed here by Indians Sept. 15, 1812."

If the trees and the landscape and even the smells were oddly familiar, it's probably because I was born in similar country, although my home was inner-city Chicago. I have noticed how up to age five, a child selects—even in an urban landscape—what is alive. When we took our youngest daughter to San Francisco and asked her later what she thought of North Beach or Chinatown or Montgomery Street, she answered, "I liked all the pigeons." Somewhere in the Ohio countryside I found whatever I needed to remember what it felt like to be a baby on a blanket in a park in Chicago. Once, I had a life before California. Once, I had a home. And as I was running and thinking all sorts of dark, patriotic thoughts like "this is country worth dying for," I heard a young Bob Dylan singing: "My name it is nothing, my age it means less. The country I come from is called the Midwest . . "

161

That night at dinner a charming, folksy 78-year-old man (my brother-in-law's father), a man who traces his ancestry in those Ohio parts to before James Copus and three soldiers were massacred by Indians, a man who is a Stanford class of '28 grad, turns to me over the leg of lamb and asks, rhetorically, "Why don't the coloreds want to work?" He has been railing on about welfare and social security and Roosevelt and the incompetent Geraldine Ferraro and a number of other things that threaten the republic. He has been civil and charming and pulled my chair out for me four times when I stood up and opened doors for me all evening. It's insidious. To be straight, ungifted, and white is really all these people are asking of me.

One night we went to a party given by my sister-in-law's women's club. Twenty-five of the area's finest couples have chipped in to have lobsters flown in from Maine. There was also garden salad and Silver Lady corn, just picked. But this California girl is shocked to discover there is only iced tea to drink (although a few of the men have brought their own beer or scotch, which they do not share). The claim is that wine would have been too expensive, but I suspect a strong temperance strain in the culture was the real reason. Ohio has strict blue laws which forbid liquor sales in unregulated stores and on Sunday. When we did stop at Big Daddy's Kwik Way Drive-Thru Liquor Barn, the only wines available were Cella, Riunite, and Blue Nun. I really hate to be a wine snob, but there wasn't even a lousy carafe of Paul Masson Chablis.

The lobster party was properly upper middle class—no kids except the children of the host family dutifully forced into servitude. My daughters were all too happy to stay on the farm with teenage cousins, sheep, kittens, trout to catch, and a tractor to ride. At the party, the dress was casual, with men attired in L. L. Bean ill-fitting mail-order moccasins and more plaid pants than I have ever seen off the fairway.

The men and women were almost all in their forties, all white, Protestant, married and never divorced, with two to four children. They stood in separate circles chatting outside the barn which was converted into a dining hall, never mixing with the opposite sex at all. My sister-in-law said that a man would not approach a woman who wasn't his wife because that might be viewed as flirting. I thought that flirting was the whole point of such parties! Don't these people realize that there are therapists making bucks off the concept that flirting is necessary for a successful marriage?

Hardly anyone spoke to my husband or me, although they clearly noticed us and stared at us furtively, curiously. It wasn't that they were snobbish or rude, just shy and socially isolated. One woman came up to me and said, "So you're from California? I just got back from Anaheim myself." I introduced myself to a man who is a lawyer in town. He asked me if I was from New York. This, I know, is code for, "I never met a je-yew before."

A woman who is the music specialist in the local schools was shocked when I told her we have no music, art, or PE other than what the classroom teacher provides. "You're kidding. California schools?" she asked. "You've heard of Proposition 13?" I queried. "Oh, the tax savings," she said. "We were all so jealous when we heard you got that." "Well," I informed her, "that would have meant your job."

Later, when we were tearing our lobsters apart like savages, she asked me, "Would you flip if you had to move to Ohio?" "I would find all the Republicans a big change," I answered. "Marge!" she shouted to another woman, "we don't know any Democrats, do we? So you're a Democrat, huh?" "Yes," I told her, "but I've got plenty of neighbors who'd vote for Fidel Castro over Walter Mondale any day."

I'd grown tired of being polite. I'd pretty much given up on trying to discuss the issues. These Republicans seemed so isolated from the problems of urban life that any attempt to talk about it seemed academic. To question Reagan's defense policy or the unfair distribution of wealth was to be a crackpot. But I think that what frightened me most about the uniformity of opinion was the disquieting thought that if they came to my community, they'd probably find a similar rigidity and unquestioning acceptance of the prevailing orthodoxy.

Perhaps the strangest attitudes I caught were the feelings the Ohio people had about the area's only unique minority—the Amish. The Amish are a Mennonite sect who came to the Midwest to escape religious persecution in Europe. Their central belief seems to be that electricity and the internal combustion engine are the work of the devil, and they live a pre-Industrial Revolution lifestyle.

One sees them riding through the town in their horse-and-buggies, dressed in simple homemade clothes in dark colors, long hair tucked in their bonnet. They live apart from American political life, refusing military service, and they are the only group in the country to have won exemption from the social security system. In some ways, particularly their love of hard work, they seem like an exaggeration of their Republican neighbors. One local author described them this way: "They view anyone who doesn't glory in physical labor as mentally ill." My brother-in-law told me about going to the hardware store and meeting an Amish farmer who was gloating about what a good year he'd had. "How much did you make?" my brother-in-law asked. "Twenty-five hundred dollars," the man boasted. The big acreage boys smirked until he added, "but after expenses twenty-three hundred."

My sister-in-law drove us all over Richland County in search of Amish straw hats. We visited the Helping Hands Quilt Shop in Berlin, Ohio, where classic patterned quilts like Ohio Star or Tree of Life or Double Wedding Ring were going for five hundred dollars, and one wondered who got the profit. We also stopped at Sugar Creek, "the Switzerland of Ohio," where they pipe in the Swiss national anthem through speakers on Main Street. It was as authentic as Disneyland.

While riding home, we passed an Amish farm that had a sign: "Maple Syrup for Sale." We stopped and knocked at the door. A woman appeared, and, one by one, her four daughters, ages two through ten, tiptoed out. They had all just unbraided their waist-length hair to shampoo it with rainwater from the cistern. I felt like I'd been riding in a covered wagon for days and had suddenly come upon this vision of warmth and beauty.

She invited us inside. The house was exquisite—polished random plank floors, beautiful old oak furniture, everything so shiny and clean. I thought about the comments I'd heard about the Amish at the lobster party. "The Amish are dirty. They keep a bar of soap for a year."

After selling us some maple syrup, Mrs. Hesselbock chatted with us about her water pump and her windmill, and delighted in showing us her huge New Pioneer wood-burning cookstove with a brick oven and a place to heat water overnight. She directed us to the Weaver farm where we could buy straw hats.

Going up Clear Creek to the Weavers, we passed the one-room parochial school where the Amish teach their own. Mrs. Weaver was as friendly and open as Mrs. Hesselbock. "Have you never been in an Amish home?" she asked with a Pennsylvania Dutch accent. She invited us in and opened the door to the living room, startling her husband, who had fallen asleep on the couch. He was a big jolly man with a long white beard, a kind of Santa Claus in overalls. Yes, he had heard of San Francisco, but he was very curious to learn how we grew our crops if it never rained in summer. We had no crops, we confessed, but discussed the elaborate irrigation system used in California agriculture. Then Mrs. Weaver showed us her beautiful solid oak kitchen sink. "I got it in '49," she said, "as a wedding present." While we spoke, her daughter, who was sweeping the kitchen, gaped unabashedly at my sister-in-law's flaming red blouse.

It was funny how the Amish seemed more familiar than the Republicans. The feeling in the Amish homes was much like that in Northern California country homes I have visited where back-to-the-land hippies are using solar technology and living apart from consumerist society. One almost expected to see E. F. Schumacher's *Small is Beautiful* alongside the only book found in an Amish home, the *Holy Bible*.

In a few days we were off to New York where we hoped to show our children still more things on heaven and earth than are dreamt of in their philosophy. As our taxi pulled up to my pal's Manhattan loft, the four of us donned our Amish straw hats and my husband said, "Let's call this one: 'Hicks Hit Gotham!'"

A Winter's Tale

I guess it's winter coming that makes me miss her again. It was winter when she died. Not a moist, misty California winter but a cold, grey Chicago day. There, in a nursing home in Skokie surrounded by bare trees and brown bricks and railroad tracks, I last saw my mother.

It seemed each time I got in my car for work that winter, I'd hear a hit song on the radio about a horse named Wildfire: "Well, they say she died one winter / When there came an early frost . . ." Doesn't anybody die in summer?

How long is it now? Five years? Six? I honestly can't remember. She died that slow cancer death, that wasting and waiting. But how she shone that winter. A bright star of courage she was for me. And I kept going. I was tough. A couple thousand miles away, I went through denial and anger and depression and all those stages of death and dying. I worked hard at my job, took care of my family, ran thirty miles a week, ate health food, kept going. Some people I knew were preparing for marathons then; I was in training for her death. On one of those sunny November days we get around here, I could forget I had roots and a mother dying back in the old country.

Oh, there was a slam when she died. There was a numbing. And how the snow fell on that long hearse ride to Jewish Waldheim, Pinsker Section, where she joined my father and the other people

166

from Pinsk. We could have been in Russia in that bleak, barren cemetery with the ladies wrapped in furs and the tears that froze.

The hearse driver was an affable fellow. And, indeed, when the conversation between me and my sister fell to dirty jokes and four-letter words, he confirmed that that was fairly typical behavior on the way to the cemetery. A big relief when the funeral service was over . . . a few penis size jokes, a couple of fart jokes, and a few good Polack jokes. Those were for her, the Polack jokes. How she hated the Polacks.

Idell. That was her name. Idell Aronovitch. Although my birth certificate said her maiden name was Aron and she was born in Russia, I know she was born in a *shtetl* near the town of Suwalk, Poland, in Bialystok province.

Her life was hard. Her father was a severe man, an Orthodox Jew, a sheet metal worker. My only picture of her parents shows them both large and frowning, wearing dirty clothes. Idell described the *shtetl*, a typical Jewish village, to me once as a little court of houses. She remembered a fireplace with blue tiles in the center of her cabin. She remembered a constantly boiling pot on the stove that got meat or vegetables when they had them, and that pot was always dinner. She had four brothers and two sisters. One day around 1920 when Idell was four, German soldiers came to the village and abducted the young Jewish men for the army. The Polish authorities encouraged this. They took her oldest brother, Avorum. Soon the family packed and left Suwalk and tried to find him. When it became clear they couldn't, they decided to try for America . . .

> *That blessed land of room enough*
> *Beyond the ocean's bars*
> *Where the air is full of sunlight*
> *And the flag is full of stars.*

How they got to America is a bit of a mystery. She remembered wandering the Polish ports with her family. One terrifying day, she got lost at a fish market in Danzig and thought the Poles were going to have a little pogrom just for her. A few months later she came to America.

Details of the voyage surfaced some years ago when a cousin of mine married an Army intelligence officer—the first military man in the family since Avorum. When they ran a security check on my cousin, they discovered there was no port of entry date for her mother, Ethel Aronovitch, my mother's sister. This helped explain why all my mother's brothers had different surnames—Harry Robbins, Joe Rabinowitz, Eddie Schiff. Of course, she was an illegal alien.

She didn't remember steerage at all, but she did remember Ellis Island. She remembered somebody giving her an orange which she regarded as a rare treasure. And she remembered somebody gave the family some maraschino cherries. Yes, America was looking like the wondrous place where dreams come true. But the man who "gave" them these goodies demanded and got the little money the family had. He was the first bunko artist to prey on the immigrant family.

In the streets of Chicago, she dreaded being teased with taunts of "Greenie! Greenie! Greenie Fazeenie!" The little "greenhorn" did her best to fit in. She studied hard at school, mastered English, and learned to be quite good at the needle, making clothes as fine as any in the stores. She remembered the principal at Kominski School (Chicago was no place to get away from Poles!) lifting her up on his desk so she could display the skirt and sweater she made to the whole faculty. But like her brothers and sisters she quit school in the tenth grade to go to work to help the family.

She sold dresses at Goldblatts, a big retail chain (that recently went bankrupt). While she observed the sabbath and never ate pork, she sure enjoyed sneaking out at night in her chemise dress, her t-strap heels, and her cloche hat to dance the Charleston or the foxtrot. Her one photo from this period shows her with her hair in blonde waves like Jean Harlow, and little semicircles drawn over her eyes where she had plucked her brows.

When I asked her once (after I had spent an agonizing hour in the dentist's chair) why she raised me on Cokes and candies and cookies and cake, she said, "Because I had none of those things." She told me of long hours spent in the charity ward of Cook County Hospital languishing with fevers—rheumatic fever that left her heart damaged, a nervous system disease called St. Vitus' dance, infections that left her partially deaf. No visitors were allowed. She would lie there and dream of the day when she would have a little girl and give her all the wonderful things she could only imagine—dolls, pretty clothes, sweets.

She met my father, Herman Nelson, at the local Yiddish theater. He was part owner and stage manager. He wore silk shirts and pinstriped suits and shook hands with his pinky. He acted as if he had "mob" connections and this impressed Idell. After the plays they would attend banquets with the actors at Joe Stein's Roumanian Steak House or the Cafe Royal. Sometimes they'd go "out steppin'" at the "Negro" nightspots like the Cotton Club or the Club Delisa. She remembered once eating dinner with a man named Mimi Capone. In 1969, my mother sent me an article from a magazine describing how, in fact, the Mafia did use the Yiddish theater circuit to launder money!

Since Herman was also a nice Orthodox boy from Pinsk, there was a wedding. Idell had married up in the world when she moved into the eight-room apartment with Herman, his sickly mother, and his bachelor brothers, Abe, Leo, and Benny. She cooked, cleaned, laundered, and provided emotional support for all of them.

My sister, Myrna, came into the family in happy times, the late 1930's. My father had converted the Yiddish theater into a grand neighborhood movie house. Myrna said that I never really got to appreciate the benefits of our "family position." When I pressed her for a "for instance," all she could come up with was, "We had bubble gum during World War II, and nobody else did."

My mother gained 40 pounds in her pregnancy with Myrna and her curved spine led to further back trouble. She was advised not to get pregnant again. Five years later, she was pregnant with me, and despite a valiant effort in which she gained only twelve pounds, she suffered a slipped disc and severe pain throughout the entire pregnancy. She was told to have back surgery or she would never walk again.

They pulled me from her belly, C-section, during a freezing cold winter's day in the middle of World War II. The radio might have been playing "Till We Meet Again." They whisked my mother off and since she refused surgery, put her in a body cast. Because no one at home could care for me, I was kept in the hospital nursery for a month or two until we were both released. They sent us home with a lot of pain medicine for her, and phenobarbital drops for me to keep me calm so I wouldn't bother her. It was as far from current notions of natural childbirth as you can get.

Also, since my parents were not those kind of modern parents who prepare their children for changes, Myrna (who was five) was told to vacate the crib the night I came home. Needless to say, this little trauma did not sit well with her. In fact, it took us about 31 years to become friends after that transgression.

Idell recovered but never did get much time for me. And what must she have felt towards the little rascal whose conception coincided with all that pain for her? Perhaps that was why I could never draw her away from the cauldrons of gefilte fish and beet borscht that brought forth such joyous belching from Uncle Ben and Uncle Leo.

My earliest memories are of those days after the war. We lived on a boulevard where there were parades almost monthly with the stars and stripes flying. Myrna and the big kids on the block built a clubhouse and started the All American Club. Somebody's grandfather bought them red, white, and blue sweaters and painted the clubhouse similarly. And, since it was a Jewish immigrant neighborhood, those early days were filled with whispers about Hitler and "the camps." Once, while we were walking down the street, my mother saw a woman she knew and burst into tears, hugging and kissing her. Later she said to me, "Did you see the number tattooed on her arm? She was from Suwalk. She never got out."

When she saw old friends and relatives, Idell would speak with them in Yiddish, a language she never taught me. She wanted me to be a modern American young lady (if not a rootless Californian). Each morning I would go out with her to the stores around the corner—the kosher butcher, the fruit stand, the salami factory, a kosher poultry house where you would select a live chicken from dozens clucking in their cages and then an affable Yiddish-speaking man would behead it before your very eyes. We might as well have been in Warsaw. Idell had the best of both worlds then—her old language and culture, her new freedom and spending power.

If some evil soothsayer, some dybbuk, had told us then, in 1948, that within five years all those shops would be gone, that all our friends and relatives would move away, and that we would remain in the community an isolated and depressed nuclear family, we would never have believed it. But that is precisely what happened. The racial Maginot Line which divides the cities of the Midwest and East Coast moved forward, engulfing our block. Poor black families moved in, and in a matter of a few years, every white family except ours moved uptown. City services came to a halt. Garbage and snow were removed last from our part of town. For reasons I never understood, they put a fence around the neighborhood park so you couldn't play there anymore.

That's what happened outside, but what went on inside our house was far worse. I woke up one morning in 1948 to find the mirrors in the house draped. Death had come. My grandmother, my Bubby, was gone. For my mother it would mean one less person to take care of. But for my father, it was the beginning of a long, chaotic crash. He sold his theater because he "didn't want to be around music anymore." He wore black ties for the next ten years. He and his brothers had a series of bitter, brutal fights. Benny and Leo moved uptown. Idell continued to send them pots of beet borscht by taxi from our apartment in the ghetto to their luxury high rises on the lake. Using our address as a front, Benny was elected State Representative from the old neighborhood.

But worse than my father's brooding and mourning was the way he went after my mother . . . cursing her out for the slightest reason, screaming at her on public streets, accusing her of obscene acts I was incapable of imagining at eight or nine. And, finally, he started to hit her.

He'd have maybe one or two drinks. It didn't take much. And then they'd start fighting. He'd always aim at the fat part of her upper arm, where she could take it. After all, without her he'd probably be in an institution and we all knew it.

I remember her black and blue arms stirring the soup. I remember her sitting with those packs of Lucky's and those pots of Hills Brothers coffee, literally crying in her cups. I can hear Nat King Cole singing on the radio: "Pretend you're happy when you're blue / It isn't very hard to do . . ." And, I remember she never fought back, never ran away, just stood there and took it.

I couldn't take it. When he'd go after her, I'd go after him and get him to chase me. I was fast. He'd come roaring down the hall of our apartment after me like an angry bull, and I'd slam the bath-

171

room door in his face and lock it. I'd stay inside there panting until he stopped pounding.

One day after a fight she went into the bathroom and locked the door. She came out, all calm and serene, and went to lie down in my bed. After a while I went to talk to her, but she was asleep. I shook her, but she didn't move. I pulled back her eyelids and couldn't see her eyeballs. I ran to the bathroom and found the empty pill bottle. I was ten years old.

I tried to tell my father, but he just kept saying, "You're crazy, you little bastard." "Look!" I implored. "The pills are gone, and she has no eyeballs!" He just paced around talking to himself.

I got my sister and a doctor. "She's in a coma," the doctor said. What's a coma? A state between life and death, I was told. We fed her coffee and kept her walking all night while she begged to die. She didn't die. She came out of the coma. It wasn't yet winter.

Things continued more or less dismally for another few years; then they got better. We moved to a middle-class neighborhood. My mother got a job she loved, selling lingerie in a shop that catered to prostitutes and transvestites. My father was diagnosed as having uremia, kidney failure. My mother felt better when the doctor said toxins in his blood might have been affecting his behavior. He grew too weak to fight.

I turned twelve and began an adolescent rebellion that was to last twenty years. I focused it on my mother, who had never seemed particularly pleased with me anyway. Besides, if she had been ready to abandon me like that, who needed her?

My sister and I developed regular patterns of disrespect for her. One consisted of making fun of her deafness. We'd yell out words—anything—to get her to respond. Once we yelled out a phrase we learned from the Italian kids. "*Fa'n gullo ate!*" "Yes, coming," she yelled back. This got shortened to "Fon goo!" And, finally, "Fonzo!" That stuck and until she died I called her by that nickname, Fonzo. It was hard to explain to my friends, later, in my twenties, that my mother's nickname came from the Sicilian equivalent of "Up yours."

The rebellion reached a peak one Yom Kippur eve. That night I came home with three of the blondest, blue-eyed Aryan studs I could pick up. We sat down in front of her and played poker into the wee small hours of the morning. It was the only time I ever made her cry and it was quite satisfying.

When I decided to go off to New York, ostensibly to go to college, she and my sister bitterly opposed it. "Don't do this to me," she said. "You're killing me," she said. "Your father is dying." But I had shifted the battleground to within myself. I couldn't save my father. I'd already saved my mother. Maybe if I got as far away as I could for the rest of my life, I could save myself. But I rebelled against that too, and led a life of dissolution that culminated in a severe case of hepatitis and a long hospitalization.

During the two miserable years I spent in New York, my mother called me almost weekly to say my father's death was imminent. Every few months I'd fly home for a final goodbye, but he'd survive. He looked like a snowman then—round, frosty white, and bald. Finally, one November, I flew home for his funeral. I was numb. I went back to New York and read King Lear and poems about winter . . .

> One must have a mind of winter
> To regard the frost and the boughs of the pine trees
> Crusted with snow.
> And have been cold a long time . . .

> Now is the hour of lead
> Remembered if outlived
> As freezing persons recollect the snow—
> First chill, then stupor,
> Then the letting go.

I'd walk around crowded Manhattan in the snow, hearing these poems in my head, feeling like I was encased in ice.

That was the last year of my life I spent in winter. In 1965 I moved to California—the new world where the sun shone with promise. It was my Last Chance state: if life doesn't get better here, I'll give up, I told myself. I remember that first ride into Berkeley on a golden September evening—the clean streets, the pastel stucco and white frame houses, the tan young people in sandals.

Fonzo began to have fun after my father died. She came to see me in Berkeley in the '60s in her white go-go boots. She was hip; no Greenie Fazeenie her. Oh, no. She wanted to see marijuana. She wanted to go on a peace march. "What do you hear about that

Huey Newton?" she'd ask. Or, "How about that Jerry Rubin? A jerk, huh? I like that *A-bie* Hoffman better."

She was trying; but to me, she was an embarrassment. She had always been an embarrassment. Today, when my daughter cringes at me for singing out loud on a Berkeley street—the same street where we've just passed a man who's in contact with Saturn—I try to tell her what it was like to be with my parents. But how can I explain those evenings standing in a swirling wind on the crowded corner of State Street and Lake with my father shouting at my mother, "You fuckin', greenhorn, son-of-a-bitch." Or, sitting in a Chinese restaurant as he told her (in Yiddish) to put the entire teapot in her purse. And she'd do it! Or the times she'd argue with me in the dressing room of Marshall Field & Company to just walk out of the store with the expensive petticoat under my dress. "You're too goddamned honest," she'd say, looking at me with disgust. Embarrassment. I could write the book on embarrassment.

Maybe some of you are those rarest of all creatures, native Californians. And maybe others of you can go home again. Maybe there's a home or a family in South Dakota or Nebraska or Louisiana or New Jersey always waiting, waiting for your return. But for me, the old country is gone, gone as the Poland of my mother is gone. Once, in 1973, I tried to stop in front of my apartment in Chicago to show my husband where I was born. Our car was immediately surrounded by a group of young men carrying baseball bats and wearing leather jackets that said "Vice Lords." I mean, I really can't even get near the house again.

If home is where you come from, then it died that winter my mother died. In the hearse, on the way to the interment, cracking the bawdy jokes, we drove near the old neighborhood. A lot of snow. A lot of brown brick. And a crowd of hostile strangers.

The weird thing about long distance death is that it adds an extra dimension of unreality. She didn't really die. A voice on the phone just said she did. It's the phone's fault. I still can't hear it ring late at night without tensing up and feeling sure someone's died. But who's left?

The interment was brief. What with the snow and the wind chill, five minutes more out there at Jewish Waldheim and we'd all

174

have been ghosts. I got on the plane and a few hours later, I'm walking around Berkeley. No, not just walking—I'm jogging, in my shorts and a tee shirt. Somewhere in the back of my mind I'm trying to trace this path . . . from Poland and Russia to Chicago. Okay, I can follow that. It's just footsteps in the snow. But then to Berkeley? It's a dream! Who am I? What am I doing here?

So acclimatized am I that it only takes a hint of winter to make me think of her. Only these shorter days. Only a little bit of rain.

Yesterday, I was standing in the bank behind a kind of woman one rarely sees in Berkeley. In her sixties, with a bleached yellow chignon, lots of gold jewelry, polished red nails, she belongs to Brooklyn or LA or Miami Beach. She could have been my mother. The back of her neck was in front of my nose. I wanted to reach out and touch it. It's been five years now, but the slightest memory can plummet me to the deepest longing for the physical presence of my mother.

I listen to the young women in Berkeley talk about their mothers. How they raised them wrong, fed them wrong, gave them hang-ups. They are busy rebelling. Mother dumping is the center of their lives, as it was for me for twenty years. Now I feel as if I am across an abyss from them, longing for a mother to dump on, longing to see my mother just one more time.

Maybe this winter will be the end. Maybe this winter, I'll feel "the letting go." Perhaps on some rainy night she'll come to me. She'll be wearing a white, gossamer gown. Her platinum hair will be back in those Harlow waves. A little shower of snowflakes will halolike surround her and she'll lift an icy, sinewy hand to me. Bye-bye, Ma.

Upward Mobility, Heterosexuality, and More Bizarre Trends

Tongue Tied

Ever have someone come up to you at a party and just stick his tongue in your mouth? I'm not talking about a friendly little peck. A friendly little peck is what you were expecting when he approached you. And I'm not talking about some aseptic Hollywood greeting, some dig-my-gold-chain-and-let's-have-lunch-and-discuss-the-project-some-time-Murray kiss. I'm talking about full frontal tonguity! It happened to me.

I had to wonder: am I such a hot little number (actuarial and other evidence to the contrary notwithstanding) that he just couldn't resist? Or does this kind of thing happen all the time to other people? An informal survey taken of the staff of a certain prominent East Bay newspaper indicates that others, too, have been on the receiving end of the casual, unexpected French kiss.

A scientific sampling of this out-of-control group reveals that the incidence of *their* tongue in *your* cheek is on the rise. And—I hope you're sitting down—a certain unnamed male actually confided to me that he has been thus accosted several times. Not, as I know *you* are imagining, by some sex-crazed homosexuals, but by perfectly normal American women.

Just what is the meaning of this? Must we now add to the growing list of previously male diseases such as heart attacks, emphysema from smoking, and workaholism, the rise of oral dominance in women? Before you cry "double standard," let me hasten to say that I am not talking here about sex. The big S involves, to my way of thinking, some kind of flirtation, anticipation, build-up. Certainly it is perfectly reasonable and, perhaps, even a turn-on for women to make the first move. No, what I'm talking about are a whole group of behaviors involving gestures that while in one context may be sexual, in another seem purely aggressive.

Really, is there anything sexual about standing at a party with a fistful of smoked salmon in the middle of a serious discussion about Kirkegaard or Nancy Reagan's gynecologist and finding some casual acquaintance is licking your inlays? To me it is more like the famed anonymous copping of a feel on the subway. Let me explain to those of you who ride BART that BART does not seem to attract the same type of clientele who populate your decaying East Coast mass transit systems. The situation I am referring to is more likely to happen on a packed rush hour train in the bowels of Manhattan. Suddenly you feel an unmistakable grabbing sensation in your most private part. You look up and—nothing. Nobody there but a bunch of stockbrokers bobbing up and down with their noses pressed in the *Wall Street Journal*. Not your central casting dirty old men, but who knows? The beauty of this situation (from the aggressor's point of view) is that you can't fight back. There is no defense against the guerrilla feel-coppers. Just try yelling, "OK, who put his hand on my crotch?" and watch what happens. The brokers drop their *Journals*. People flee your subway car. The pervert is you.

At least with your foreign nationals you have a chance for revenge. There is nothing sneaky, back-handed, or sub rosa about these guys. They will come right up to you on a crowded street, as one did to me recently on University and Shattuck in front of Mc-Donald's, and pinch your most well-padded part. That's right, he sunk his fingers into my tush like tongs grabbing a blintz. In broad daylight, without any previous warning and, believe me, no provocation—he just decided to sink his hand into my Big Mac.

What's a girl to do? You can ignore it and walk around pissed all day. I've done that before. You can, after a certain point, bask in the fact that someone still cares. You can try to "talk it out" with him after making some effort to determine what language he speaks—parla Italiano? Parlez-vous Francais? Eakspay Nglishea? Or you can do what I did, which is go with your instincts and just pinch him right back—an eye for an eye, a tooth for a tooth, a tush for a tush. There is certainly some risk in this approach. Some possibility for misinterpretation of the reciprocity. Some outside chance he will assume he has lucked into a quaint American courtship ritual. Some unseen risk that he will turn bilingual on you and ask, "Shall we get a room?"

However, with the tongue guy I don't think I can return the favor in an even-the-score way. Again, I don't mean to sound sex-negative. I mean, I'm all for it. Some of my best friends do it. I think what actually bothers me most is that the gesture meant *nothing*. Nothing personal. You see, I come from an age, strange as it may sound, when French kissing *meant* something. When you didn't just do it at a party like, "Hi, howaya, here's my tongue, what's your hurry." There seems to be a whole new ball game out there, one in which you're *not* supposed to get excited by tongues, touches, even nudity.

Last year when my wholesome young niece and her college roommate visited from the Midwest, I was trying to think of some California things for them to do. They were planning to go to a New Wave nightclub. I suggested that she might want to go to a hot tub rental place afterward.

"Yeah," she said. "Maybe we could meet some guys at the nightclub and go with them to the hot tub place."

"Deena, I don't think you understand. Generally, you take your clothes off in the hot tub."

"Of course."

"You mean you'd do that with people you just met?"

"No problem."

See, here's my problem: if nice girls are stripping on the first date, what are the sluts doing for action these days?

I know what I'm going to do. Next party I'm invited to, I'm going to get me a black sequined strapless dress. I'll make a dramatic entrance trailing my feather boa over my shoulder behind me. Then I'll walk over to the piano and I'll peel off one of my elbow-length white gloves and toss it carelessly at the crowd. I'll get up on top of the Steinway and nod to the piano player and say, "Hit it, Sam." And then, in a husky but lilting voice, I'll spread the word:

You must remember this
A French kiss is still a French kiss . . .

The Call of the Buck

G ag me with another male empowerment story. How many times must we
read about those same thirty gluttons-for-punishment? (Or is the
sexual battleground actually strewn with more bodies than that?)
Please, stop kissing those poor princes and let them turn back into
frogs. We gals know what's happening at those little bullfrog sessions anyway. The guys are just sitting there in a magic circle,
cross-legged, each grasping his manhood, and chanting: Men on
top. Men on top. Men on top.

Am I wrong? Prove it. Have you got pictures? Why else
would a man I know rush directly out of his "empowerment" session and run to the phone to tell Bernice, his life-long friend:
"Bernice, this is Bernie. Either we make it or that's it." They
didn't make it. That was it. Had he only waited an hour they'd still
be friends, because, like the proverbial German-Chinese dinner, an
hour later you're hungry for more empowerment.

But seriously folks, what I am talking about here is not empowerment, it's endowment—female endowment. I refer not to
the bra cup that runneth over, but to the pockets that seemeth
empty. I want to tell you women out there how to fill those pockets. So why don't all the men who are reading this just—as the
president would say—*bug out*! This is between us gals. (Are we
alone now? Can we dialogue?)

Let's all ask ourselves one little question: what really matters
in life? Love? Security? Health? A perfect body? Yes, these things

are nice, but I'm sure you'll agree they are totally meaningless without something to share it with. That something, friends, is money.

What have women won this past decade but the right not to be called girls, the right not to get seats on buses, and the right not to get married to the person we eat with, sleep with, and worship. But what about the old cash gap—the 59 cents we earn for every dollar he gets. I want to talk about the only really important thing in life: how to get our 41 cents.

In an effort to organize women to seize the 41 cents, I have established the Little Chapel of the Big Pockets. This institution began when I realized that even I was too wimpy to ask the boss for equity. I searched for a Raise Asking Support Group and discovered to my shock that none existed. Thus I turned to this wonderful free enterprise system of ours and began my own small business, the Little Chapel.

Here at the Little Chapel we worship God *and* Mammon. Our slogan: Political Power Comes Out of the Barrel of a Fresh Roll of Fifties. And, if you will follow my four step plan, I, Sister Alicia, high priestess of the four-bit hordes, promise to lead you out of the fiscal wilderness and into the money market accounts. In my program you will learn about IRAs, Keoghs, tax shelters, commodities, options, puts, calls, the Kondratieff Wave, stocks, bondage, and other forms of financial deviance. You will finally learn to make *real* money on the spread. You will go down with the Dow. You will forget the double chin and focus on the triple bottom. And you will learn the difference between the streets and The Street. Not Broadway, suckers, but Wall Street—the bright lights, the pin stripes, the excitement, the roar of the traders, the thrill of the cash.

First, it will be necessary for you to cast a little bread on *my* waters for the privilege of letting me make you rich. I want you to go to the bank right now and remove everything you've got in that puny little account. That's right, every little dime you've worked so hard for, because we're clearing the way for Bigger Things. Then I want you to mail it all to me: Sister Alicia, c/o the Little Chapel of the Big Pockets, 711 Easy Street, Lubbock, Texas. In a few short weeks you will receive through the US mail a copy of my four step plan for gaining control of your life: *Four Steps to Forty One Cents*. I will also include, at absolutely no additional charge, a signed copy of my best-selling book, *Power: How to Get It, How to Keep It, How to Flaunt It*. Briefly, the four step plan consists of:

- Step One: Ask for more.
- Step Two: Ask for more.
- Step Three: Ask for more.
- Step Four: Ask for more.

If the four step plan fails to bring you greater wealth within two weeks, you will immediately be flown to Lubbock, Texas, to our Greenback Spa for economic basket cases. There you will participate in an intensive program designed to overcome guilt about making money, be taught regular exercises towards achieving a personal fiscal fitness plan, and learn to accustom yourself to a steady diet of richness. You will be assigned to one of our specially trained financial therapists who will lower you into a tank filled with crisp one-hundred-dollar bills. There you will sit and caress the money while your therapist guides you toward overcoming your fear of money. You will learn to stroke the bucks and practice the art of transcendental capital accumulation. You will sit in a magic circle with other women, grasping your pocketbooks, and chanting: Buy low, sell high. Buy low, sell high. Buy low, sell high.

Then we will listen to testimonials from previous Chapel members and I will reveal the True Story of Gail. Gail owned the best restaurant in the entire area, just a little counter where Gail would serve me and the same sixty senior citizens every day. Gail would make fabulous foods like pesto chicken salad and eggplant caviar and homemade chili—all fresh, all served like works of art on a platter. And Gail would charge next to nothing for it. Every time I went in I would say, "Gail, when are you going to raise your prices? Two dollars for a meal like this? Do you have any idea what they're charging for two almonds on a lettuce leaf uptown?" And Gail would say, "Yeah, I know, but I guess I just feel guilty having money." "Well, Gail, at least let me write a review of this place. Then thousands of people will rush here with their two dollars and you'll be rich." And Gail said, "But then the old people won't have any place to sit down."

Well, what can you do with someone like Gail? Gail was flown to Lubbock, Texas. Gail was dropped in the tank. Gail was forced to chant: Buy low, sell high. Gail was given a major make-over. And today, friends, Gail is slinging hash at the Santa Fe Bar and Grill. Gail can be seen on nationwide TV in the series *Great Chefs of South-West Berkeley*.

Do you believe that? If you believe, I want you to rush right to your banks and send me your life savings. Then I want you to make ten copies of this article, send it to ten friends, and tell them each to send me their life savings, then add their name to the bottom of the list. Within ten weeks they will receive the life savings of ten other desperate individuals. This plan cannot fail. Act now. Who says women are stupid about money?

G Marks the Spot

If you're the kind of person who hates reading about sex and orgasms, read no further. If you're sick of hearing about the struggle to become orgasmic, to become multiorgasmic ("Once is enough," says my friend Joyce) then you probably won't be interested in the latest scientific breakthrough. It is a breakthrough that came just when we gals almost had it made. Just when we were beginning to inch up from the 59¢ on every dollar *he* made; when the Olympics were recognizing the ability of women runners to go the distance; when we had fifty percent of the men in the Bay Area eating quiche from the palms of our hands, a book appeared that was destined to wipe that smirk off our collective faces.

I am talking, of course, about the volume that put the G spot on the map of America's sexual consciousness. It concerns a discovery that has led millions of women out of the nirvana of whatever-I'm-getting-is-more-than-I-expected into that previously male-dominated hell of performance anxiety. All over town you can hear the anguished cries from the contorted bodies writhing on their Cost Plus Indian bedspreads: Out! Out! Damned spot.

My first encounter with the G spot concept came last April Fool's Day at my daughter's third birthday party. Now you wouldn't think a party for a three-year-old the occasion for a major sexual breakthrough, but so it goes in a town where the children and the grown-ups compete for a life of irresponsible fun. It all began when the dads (who were enticed to stay by a good supply of imported beer) began to use the bathroom. I like to keep some light reading in there, things like the *Smithsonian*, the *Berke-*

ley Monthly, or *Women Against Violence in Pornography and Media Newsletter*—one sitting material.

On this occasion I happened to have left a publication entitled *Sexual Medicine Today* which I hadn't read yet. At some point one of the dads asked me, "What do you know about the G spot?" "I think it's more than a C note, isn't it?" I said nonchalantly, cutting the cake. Somewhere behind a screaming chorus of "I want a flower! I want a flower!" I heard a voice say, "No, it's a place in a woman's vagina which can cause ejaculation during orgasm. I just read that in your bathroom."

Well, I wasn't the only one who heard that little bombshell. One by one, the fathers gulped their beer and raced to the bathroom. The mothers nervously laughed and followed suit. The three-year-olds were left alone to play doctor. Finally, my turn came. There it was on a much-fingered page 14 under the section-head "Developments in Sexual Research: Female Ejaculation Documented." "Although researchers still don't understand the mechanism, they have found that stimulation of the Grafenberg spot—the once-disputed erogenous zone in the vagina which has now been documented in over 400 women—can cause ejaculation."

The article went on to discuss the work, done in the 1950s, by Dr. Ernest Grafenberg, the father of the spot. His findings took a back seat in the 60's to that of Masters and Johnson, who have since dominated the debate as to where, anatomically, orgasm in women originates. Now researchers Whipple and Perry have shown that stimulation of a particular vaginal area (G spot) is associated with orgasm and sometimes the expulsion of a fluid that is almost identical to seminal fluid minus the sperm. Women who had lived in shame and were doing special exercises to control what they thought was urination during orgasm could now go with the flow. However, these exercises to strengthen the vaginal muscles (so-called Kegel exercises named after that arch tormentor Dr. Arnold Kegel) probably contribute to the ability to experience orgasm and ejaculation. Forget your vibrators; there's a new orgasm in town.

I'm not sure what the other parents did when they got home and put their three-year-olds to bed but I for one got out the map and set off in search of Dr. Grafenberg's magic bullet. Fortunately, I realized that I was scheduled for my annual "female" exam in the next week and would have a chance to discuss the whole thing with my favorite professional, my very own gynecologist Dr. Shaun "Dare-to-be-groovy" Westmarin. Why worry about what to do until the G spot comes; why not ask the doctor?

Shaun, as he prefers to be called, had proved himself an invaluable ally three years earlier at my daughter's birth. In fact, I felt dangerously close to that preliberation Schlafly-like stance of being in love with my gynecologist. But what else can you feel towards a highly educated man who is willing to spend his Sunday mornings groveling on the floor of the bathroom in the Alta Bates Alternative Birth Center, pointing a flashlight between my legs and saying casually, "The baby's crowning. Would you like to deliver there on the toilet or go back in the bed?" Hey, no problem, Shaun. My space or yours.

I couldn't bear the thought of delivering a child on April 1 on a toilet. So, I made it back to the bed and during that glorious moment when my daughter came out I heard Shaun, in that same hip monotone, say to my husband, "You want to cut the cord or shall I?" "I'm not that groovy," my husband offered. Then I heard my daughter scream, the crescendo of new life, as Shaun bent forward to separate us and I saw the collar of his shirt where the words "Wilkes-Bashford" stood out to be indelibly associated with this precious moment.

What a man, that Shaun. Can't you understand now how I with my unimpeachable feminist credentials—I who spent a year of my life placing This Offends Women stickers on everything from ads for James Bond movies to nude photos of Gerald Ford—can't you see why I would almost love such a man? So even though he was that most loathesome of all creatures, *a male gynecologist*, I felt perfectly free to open up the innermost questions of my heart or vagina to Shaun.

"What do you know about the G spot?" I asked him as I lay there on the exam table shivering in my paper gown while Shaun sprayed my pap smear. "The What?" he asked (rather uncooly, I thought). "The G spot, Shaun—the place associated with female ejaculation." To my astonishment he looked down at me and said, in that I'm OK, You're Not OK tone, "Alice, isn't this another instance of women trying to be like men?" "Well, I was just wondering what you knew about it. I mean, not that I care that much,"

I said talking faster and faster. "It's just that the fathers at my daughter's birthday party wanted to know. I mean, have you ever found it?" He was silent. "Well, I just wondered if you ever observed it in any of your patients or maybe your wife."

As soon as I said it I realized I'd committed a faux pas. One never invokes the gynecologist's wife. She should remain a shadowy background figure along with Brunhilda—is it?—Grafenberg and Sue Anne—is it?—Kegel and those other sources of inspiration. No, I'd made a mistake invoking the wife. There was nothing left to do but get dressed and pray my pap smear was normal. Hell, even if it's class II, I'm not coming back.

Unfortunately that night was the night we chose to give Chez Panisse one last chance—the cafe, of course. I can't get it together for the months-in-advance reservation the restaurant requires. But I wanted to satisfy myself about the cafe. The G spot could wait; I had food anxiety to deal with. Was there something wrong with me that I didn't like expensive plates of noodles floating in cream or melted cheese in a pocket of bread dough? Or is the famed Chez cafe, as I suspect, the gastronomic equivalent of the Emperor's New Clothes? As the waiter seated us, we soon realized that we were going to be placed among the squeezed-in tables practically in the laps of Mr. and Mrs. Shaun D. Westmarin, MD. Shaun looked up from his meal in horror. He was having the special; I believe it was mesquite grilled Stellars Jay in Raspberry Sauce. I could tell from his look that he'd just been telling his wife about what a hard day he'd had at the office. Probably at the moment we came in he'd been saying, "And then this crazy bitch came in and asked me how to ejaculate."

After that I tried to get the G spot off my mind. Just relax and drop the one-ups-orgasmship bit, I told myself. Then this book appeared entitled *The G Spot and Other Recent Discoveries About Human Sexuality*. The book makes it clear that it wants to validate the experience many women have been having, not create a market for gourmet orgasms. But when you read about the gushers others are having it gives new meaning to that old 50's concept "dry humping." Worse yet, the coauthoress of the book is a woman with the same name as mine!

I want to set the record straight. I am not Alice Kahn Ladas nor was I meant to be. I'm not that groovy. I certainly don't mind being confused with other writers. Norman Mailer, for example; I'd be happy to have people think I wrote any of his books—from a feminist perspective, of course. Or Ishmael Reed—from a woman of no color perspective. Or Alice Walker or Alice Adams; they get great reviews and you can mix me up with them any day. Or confuse me with Alice Waters whose bestselling *Chez Panisse Cookbook* proves the pen is even mightier than the swordfish (she probably thinks the big G stand for garlic). But please don't confuse me with Alice Kahn Ladas the G spot lady. I prefer that you think of me as Alice "Still Searchin'" Kahn.

Dead Beat

Peace, love, good vibes, dope, dayglo, tie-dye, brain damage—all the varieties of hippiedelic experiences were out in force. They came from as far away as Alaska and as nearby as fraternity row to pay homage to the Grateful Dead, a living monument to Flower Power.

I was, until this day, what's known in Dead subculture as a "virgin." This was my first time at a Grateful Dead concert. I came at the behest of someone named SLA, a self-confessed "Alice Kahn/Grateful Dead fan." SLA wrote and offered a ticket in the time-honored tradition of "the first one's free." SLA turned out to be Shelly, a 28-year-old graduate student in demography. We were accompanied by Michael, Shelly's old friend from Washington, D.C. They had been policy analysts in the Carter administration together. Michael was also a colonel in the Air Force. *That* Air Force.

Shelly or SLA or Fay—she had a bunch of names—was an eager guide. ("They call me SLA because it's my initials and because I look like Patty Hearst.") She supplied me with a running montage of data about the concert, the fans, the songs, etc. She had the grad school data collection habit bad. I refused to take notes. Somehow taking notes at a Grateful Dead concert seemed like the ultimate in missing the point.

Shelly's what we used to call a free spirit, a kind of intellectual Holly Golightly. Throughout the day at the Greek Theater, we met her friends, mostly young men, mostly, alas, *platonic*. Tall, in

191

aerobically good shape, with no need for makeup, Shelly is looking for love and studying population demographics. She has not
yet heard for whom the biological clock tolls, but she knows it's
out there.

Approaching the Greek Theater, the tie-dye level was getting
hot enough to burn your retina. Unfortunately, so was the temperature. As I contemplated joining the human barbeque inside,
two young men emerged from the crowd of ticket-seekers and
embraced Shelly with their thin but muscular arms. These, she explained, were not the gay men from her aerobics class for whom
she was looking.

So. Gay people are Deadheads. Government bureaucrats are
Deadheads. Air Force colonels are Deadheads. What next?

When we entered the theater, the woman who inspected our
backpacks also copped a quick frisk of our rearends and stomachs.
A young man ran past us with security guards in hot pursuit. "Go
man, go," shouted the otherwise laid-back crowd and then, when
the guards nabbed the gatecrasher, they cried out, "Let him go.
Don't hurt him. We'll take care of him."

Inside, the theater was a sea of human mellowness. There
were classically attired Deadhead men wearing shorts, no shirt or
a T-shirt from a previous Dead concert, and redneck hats bearing
the ubiquitous skull and roses. Even among the younger ones
there was a certain preponderance of bellies. Beatific men walked
around with spray bottles showering fellow Deadheads as an act of
kindness. Two bearded bellyboys looked at Shelly's white T-shirt
and squirted her breasts, saying, "White. White. Outasite."

We finally located Shelly's other friends, three more men.
They included a young man in felt hat and shades who resembled
the fans at the Hunter S. Thompson so-called "appearance" I once
attended. He, I was impressed to learn, was a visiting professor in
economics from Yale and had been on Shelly's—you should par-
don the expression—orals committee. This learned Deadologist
pointed out a character in the crowd who leads an imitation band
called Jerry's Kids.

I tried to figure out the demographics of the crowd. I would
say they cut a wide swath across the white middle class between
the ages of fifteen and forty. The crowd was disproportionately
male—about 1.7 males to one female. That's about what it takes
for a Berkeley woman anyway.

Shelly's circle of friends later grew to include Paul, a computer nerd (resplendent in tie-dye, one huge beaded earring, and fire engine red toenails), and a recent law graduate who knew Paul from MIT. The budding lawyer—let's call her Sunshine—was described by the others as a true Deadhead. She had lost count of both her Dead concert and acid trip tallies. The latter she swore off twice—once in high school (she started tripping at fifteen) and again after leaving MIT. She was a tall, freckled woman wearing an ankle length lavender Indian cotton skirt and matching tank top, big straw hat, and blue feather earrings.

The assembled audience formed a huge Impressionist painting dominated by flesh tones but dotted with red, purple, marigold, and turquoise. I personally saw no alcohol consumption, nudity, or drug dealing, things I remembered from the free concerts of a decade or so ago. I remembered the great hippie comedy group, the Congress of Wonders, who once did a routine about Jerry Garcia, senior citizen, sitting in the park trying to get a hit off the dope helicopter. Even without helicopters, there was a cloud of smoke above the Greek Theater, and I wouldn't have touched the Kool Aid in that place. Many women were wearing their old hand-crotcheted bras. I decided I should have gone to the attic and pulled out the dress I made from Persian curtains in 1970. There was a lot of skin glistening in the sun, most of it a tanner shade of white. In the overflow crowd of about 10,000 (the Greek seats 8,000), there were perhaps a handful of people of color.

In front of us, an overwhelming array of technical equipment filled the huge stage and rose above it. Unlike Dorothy in the Wizard of Oz, knowing that they do it with machines of this size and complexity makes it even more impressive to me. The machines dwarfed the men who played them, and who had suddenly, unceremoniously appeared. Jerry Garcia was not about to take the mike and say, "You're a beautiful audience. We love you." But surely, no one has ever cut a more striking figure on stage than Jerry Garcia. With shoulder-length, unstyled, rapidly whitening hair and an untrimmed beard, he has become the Doo-dah man incarnate; he has, quite simply, kept on truckin'. He has also eschewed the fitness mania of the past decade as his rollypolly Buddhaness attests. I felt in awe of him, the hippie abominable snowman.

They opened with "Dancin' in the Streets" and almost everyone stood up and began a rhythmic pelvic thrust that was to last four hours as the two guitars, bass, two drums, and keyboard attempted communion with the ten thousand. Shelly would occasionally stop her dancing to recite the lyrics in my ear to be sure I *got* them. "It doesn't matter what you wear / Just as long as you are there." Shelly, gimme a break, I thought. I was trying to act cool at bars that played Martha and the Vandellas when you were in second grade.

I asked Shelly if she thought everyone in the crowd was as smart as her friends. She said she'd decided that the typical Deadhead's IQ was higher than average, although this might not be reflected in the number of years of education.

"A lot of these people live like this all the time," Shelly said, "so it's nice for them to get together with the rest of us." I'd say the crowd included about one to two thousand Northern California plantation owners and support staff types. They'd been caravaning into town all week, following the Dead tour and getting ready for the harvest season. There's enough money involved to have kept this culture alive long after the media declared it dead and while its more urban brethren went straight or burned out.

Certainly that is part of the fascination with Jerry Garcia and Company. Garcia has managed to make the transition from popular artist to cult figure without ever fading away or going to Europe to be rediscovered. He just kept on truckin', mostly with the musicians from the original 1966 Grateful Dead band (Weir, Kreutzmann, and Lesh) and some even from the South Bay jugbands he played in before that. To the dedicated core group of fans, new recruits have been added—young people who remembered the hippies from their childhood but who never got a chance for a whole summer of love. Now, as they face the bleak night of Yuppiedom, they can at least get out the tie-dye and be hippies for a day.

There is another reason the band has survived; as Shelly said: "No one plays the guitar like Jerry Garcia." I always wanted to go to a Dead concert to understand the frequently heard comment that the Dead are never as good on records because "the magic isn't there." The magic presumably lies in "the vibes" between audience and artists. Through the first half, I was still pretty much entranced by the scene although I enjoyed the music enough to eventually stop worrying about where the fire exits were.

The energetic second guitar, Bobby Weir, with his boy-next-door good looks is clearly the love interest. Although he is probably close to Garcia in age he appears about twenty years younger.

At the break or "space" as Shelly told me it's called, I left my guide and headed down to the stage. Space consisted of a drum duet that sounded like it had originated either in outer space or in ancient Egypt. Meanwhile the dancing was getting more, shall we say, avant garde. I noted several outstanding examples of a particularly colorful form of wildlife I had thought extinct—the hippie momma. The mommas were earthy, pre-feminist wild women, into outlandish costume and prone to trance on the dance floor. Perhaps they came out of the woodwork or the Santa Cruz mountains for the show. I stood behind one who wore a handmade purple turn-of-the-century bathing suit complete with purple polkadot pantaloons and matching hair bow. Down near the stage was a Salome who was to complete a four hour dervishlike dance, changing veils with each dance. As I watched she moved through purple and green, saving the white with red hearts for the finale. Another woman, clad in scanty tigerskin, kept her face covered by shaking her blonde tresses over it. As she danced, she ran her hands up and down her torso, frequently holding up her breasts as if they were an offering to the Dead.

The chosen people who knew Somebody were milling about among the speakers. One was a witchy-type woman with actual solid gold claws glued onto her fingernails. Another was a prosperous looking Angeleno showbiz kinda guy with a Jewish *punim* and a nose full of something expensive.

The second set starts and the crowd goes wild for their national anthem, "Why Don't We Do It in the Road?" The hippie momma who has braided her hair with tinsel has reached a 6.5 on the Richter scale and the blond Rastafarian boy next to her has achieved that state where one's eyeballs are buried somewhere high up in one's forehead. The concert is heating up.

Then Garcia slides into one of his sweet, lyrical guitar riffs, and I feel touched. I am remembering the first time I heard music like this and realized it was beautiful. Suddenly, without any warning, I—your objective journalist—am grooving. I am part of that great sea of humanity. We are one. All is possible. I'm in the mandala soup now.

Garcia is a genius. The others are good, even terrific, invoking an American panorama from Santana to Bob Wills to Chuck Berry. But I'm worried about Jerry Garcia. Up close, he really does not look well. It isn't the girth. It's the pallor. Then, that voice comes through the shot nasal passages, singing "Uncle John's Band."

I get it. I understand why all these people want to be part of the mass pelvic rock-in. It's stress reduction in the best sense, a hippie aerobics class. For the professionals, bureaucrats, academics, and kitchen helpers it's a complete escape from the mundane job and its tension-producing responsibilities. For the marijuana growers and dealers and fulltime consumers, it's a validation. For me, it is nostalgia, a reminder of September, 1965, when I moved to San Francisco. It took me about two weeks to figure out I was in the right place at the right time. In his book *The Power Tactics of Jesus Christ*, anthropologist and therapist Jay Haley writes of the late 60's, "The central theme of hippie life was a cult of love which was not confined to male and female relationships but was generalized as an amiability towards everyone."

As I walk away from the concert the image that remains is of the tall, shirtless space cadet with the large leather portfolio. He came up to me and stood about an inch from my nose and asked ingenuously, "Would you like to see some art? Not to buy but just to enjoy." I said "Sure," and he said, totally deadpan, "Most people say 'no' at this point."

Under the Boardwalk

Who can find the slut in the bush? That was the name of the game at the Myth America pageant the year that the usually dull and excruciatingly embarrassing spectacle was given some drama by the publication of dirty pictures of the last year's queen. At stake, of course, was our last shred of national innocence, threatened with extinction on the Jersey shore. Bye-bye, Miss American pie.

Just under the boardwalk in Atlantic City lurked three forces vying for psychological control of the pageant. First, there was Vanessa Williams, last year's defrocked queen and the first black Miss America in history, who swore, "I am not a lesbian and I am not a slut and somehow I am going to make people believe me." Secondly, Bob Guccione, sleazebag extraordinaire, who not only promises *Penthouse* will be publishing a second set of "outrageously shocking" S&M photos of Williams, but who stuns Fred and Ethel Q. Public by announcing that he also possesses dirty pictures of one of this year's contestants. And, finally, there is another force at work here, struggling to defend all that is good and pure and godly in American womanhood and maidenhead, a force we will, for lack of a better name, call Ronald Reagan. So, we waited to see who controlled the pageant and, by extension, the aesthetics of feminine beauty—the lady, the tiger, or the Gipper?

I, like you, did not rush out to buy *Penthouse* just to see the dirty pictures that shocked a nation, although I did try to find one at a magazine rack. Sold out, of course. My curiosity was piqued by a person-in-the-street interview on TV which had a reporter asking people if Williams should have to give up her crown. The typical response was, "I think it's unfair." Then, after being shown the pictures, the response changed to "burn her at the stake." I felt I had to see the photos just to understand what this country is coming to.

After persuading a blushing young man I know to make the drop in a plain brown paper bag, I opened the magazine. I recall being somewhat startled by a close-up of the Labia Sisters, Majora and Minora, as well as one of Ms. Williams on all fours with The Other Woman behind her projecting her tongue towards Ms. Williams's anal opening. This was, of course, particularly shocking because this wasn't just *some* asshole—this was Miss America.

Never missing an opportunity for an intellectual discussion, I used the pictures to stimulate a conversation with some friends on why men like to look at women being sexy together. One friend offered the Doublemint Theory: if one naked lady is exciting, then two naked ladies are still more tit-tit-titillating. Double your pleasure, double your fun. Another theory offered by my friend Dobbie (known professionally as the noted Jungian and Shakespearean scholar, Dr. John Boe) is that men are embarrassed to look at other naked men because that is a potentially homosexual act. According to Dr. Dobbie, looking at two women is safer and free of the latent lust of viewing another man doing it.

My own theory on why men's magazines so often feature lesbian fantasies (or fantasy lesbians) is that we have become so inundated with scenes of nude men and women in movies that it just doesn't seem dirty enough. There's no wildness in it. Sex between men and women has no pictorial shock value. Ordinary intercourse is no longer sexy.

A final theory on the popularity of lesbian themes in male-oriented pornography comes from my old pal, Norm Nudelman. Norm is fond of telling me how much he enjoys a "conversion job." He views a woman's sexual preference for another woman as stimulating, a challenge calling for Norman conquest. In fact, there is more than one man in this town who feels the real proof of his sexual prowess lies in being what Norm might call a "dyke-buster." (Who ya' gonna call?)

Which brings me back (for no apparent reason) to the Miss America Pageant itself. I watched it, as I have watched it every year since my big sister, Myrna, and I first sat at the sixteen inch, black and white, RCA console, munching on Jay's potato chips and saying things like: "Ooooh, she's pretty, Myrn."

"No, I think she's ugly. She'll lose."

"Well, I think she's pretty. Look at those legs."

"But her thighs, Alice, there's fat . . ."

"Ooh, you're right. Yuck."

The show opened with the traditional evening gown competition, where all our national female stereotypes were paraded forth like choices at a bordello. There were East Coast girls who were snotty but dumb, Southern girls who were sweet but dumb, West Coast girls who were tan but dumb, and wholesome Midwest girls with brains like blue skies over Kansas. "Hi, I'm Mary Ann Farrell, a master's candidate in Business 'Ministration at Oral Roberts University . . ." Whoops, did she say *oral*? There goes her shot at the title.

Next came "your host, Gary Collins," a man whose presence only served to remind us of the last time tragedy befell the pageant—the firing of Bert Parks. Parks was a sort of queen-mother to the girls. When Bert sang, "There she goes, Miss America . . ." not only did we get the chills, we got yet another reminder that lack of talent needn't stop anyone in this great land of ours.

Gary Collins introduced past Miss Americas including Suzette Charles, who replaced Vanessa Williams when she was licked. (Charles, who is also, conveniently enough, black, saved the pageant from charges of racism.) Additionally, we met a former Miss California, Debbie Moffet, who literally had her face rearranged by a prominent plastic surgeon to win the crown in 1983. "How was it when you won?" asked Collins. "It was very emotional," said Miss Moffet emotionlessly.

When the ten finalists were announced, you wondered if Guccione, a kind of machismo Liberace, was jumping up and down in his fifteen pounds of gold jewelry, chanting, "Got her! Got her! Got her!" Following messages from our sponsors, a roll-on deodorant whose theme is "never let them see you sweat," and Figurines (that's Fig-*urines*) Diet Bars, we came to the real meat of the pageant—the swimsuit competition.

In a desperate attempt to lend an air of wholesomeness to the pageant and to try to convince us that these gals are more than air-heads, they spliced the question and answer sessions in between the runway walks, the real Olympics of T&A. Have you ever tried walking in high heels, let alone walking in your bathing suit, in front of millions of people, where, one false ripple in a thigh, and there goes your college education? If we could imagine Reagan and Mondale in the middle of a debate, walking down the runway in swimsuits and high heels, then perhaps we would be closer to letting the best man win.

It was in the answers to the questions that I began to respect what Vanessa Williams has done for all of us. "I'm patriotic. I believe in using the talent God has given me for society." "What I really think is important is aggressiveness in men . . ." "I have high moral values. I'm a Christian person." It's enough to make you want to see all these people degraded. The irony of the slut-look in fashion being embraced by these quintessentially *nice* girls (as is the style across the country) cries out for exposure. We want justice, like when conservative state senator Schmitz was exposed as an adulterer and child neglecter or when Anita Bryant's marriage fell apart. Let's give Vanessa Williams some credit: she degraded the pageant as bra-burners never could.

Last, and certainly least, was the alleged talent competition, that painful amateur hour of opera singers, tumblers, ventrilo-quists, flautists, concert pianists, and fantasy torch singers. Enter Margaret Marie O'Brien, Miss Massachusetts, proving not all white girls can sing and dance as she segues from "The Man That Got Away" to "Oh, my man I love him so . . . I'll come back on my knees someday . . ." But, what was this? Miss Texas, Tamara Hext, singing a sweet, little, unambitious version of "I've Got a Crush on You." Please, I thought, give her the crown and get it over with. Meanwhile, all over America, there were men looking into Miss Hext's fetching blue eyes and thinking, "She-yat. I sure hope that Kitchione's got a beaver shot o' they-at."

I'll spare you a critique of the rest of the talent other than to observe that there was more than one "ten" on the embarrassment scale in the group. When it came time for the crown, I noted that Tamara Hext was last runner-up—so much for talent. Finally, when Sharlene Wells, a Mormon from Utah, was named the new winner, I looked back in my notes to see how I rated her. (While bookmakers at the casinos were taking bets on the winner, I'd been rating them for Guccione-proofness.)

Wells, Sharlene:

Talent: Plays harp and sings folk songs. Got to be kidding. Maybe at the Cafe Trieste but not on TV. A case study in smiling when can't sing. All over America people are saying, "Man, that bitch sure can play the harp."

Bathing suit: It took years of self-sacrifice and denial to learn to do this.

Questions: Patriotic drivel. The one contestant you can never imagine posing in the nude.

So, Little Miss Never-Naked took the cake. Score one for the Gipper. Guccione, eat your heart out! Vanessa, write your autobiography in which you tell all: "I am a lesbian and I am a slut and somehow I'm going to make people love me."

Meanwhile, as night falls over Atlantic City, as the beauties without fortune allow their tired smiles to fade, as the moon lies fair above the Atlantic Ocean which "was really something in those days," police search for clues in the murder of Salvatore Testa. Testa, son of alleged Philadelphia crime boss Phil "Chicken Man" Testa, was shot twice in the back of the head at close range with a small caliber weapon. His death was "apparently another execution in a continuing power struggle involving casino-rich Atlantic City," authorities said.

Stress for Success

One reads so much about stress these days it's enough to make you sick. Blame it all on those under-33s, the tail-end of the baby boom generation, the tokhis of the demographic bulge. This is the Me-Me-Me Try Harder generation, the people who are networking, eating to win, going for it like rats in the last marathon before they close down civilization. The result of all this hustling is—Lord have mercy—stress. And stress research.

Take Dr. Hans Selye. As any stress enthusiast can tell you, the good doctor was hard at work looking for physical evidence of stress. He found it. He fished stress out of glands and arteries. He held stress in the palms of his hands. He did this by taking laboratory animals and subjecting them to the equivalent of twenty years on the New York Stock Exchange. Think of the poor mice in little pinstripes enduring all this stress knowing full well they were going to end up in Dr. Selye's cutting room with their shriveled thymuses being held up for inspection. A team of men and women in white coats would then stand around looking at the burned-out mouse, saying things like "Tsk, tsk. Poor Jerry. He never should have put off that trip to Tahiti."

Dr. Selye, as any stresshead can vouch, was no slouch when it came to perceiving the complexity of the situation stressed-out Americans face. He discovered that there is more than one approach to stress management. One man's yoga is another woman's purgatory. Selye believed that the earth's multitudes are divided up into "tortoises" and "hares." The secret to well-being, stressed Selye, consists of deciding which you are and acting appropriately. Take a rabbit and force it to meditate, and you're going to end up with one petrified gland on your hands. Make a turtle earn an MBA, launch him on a fast-track career, and a few years later you'll need jaws-of-life to pry him out of his shell.

But what about those of us who checked "neither"? Sure, the competitive level has been upped by those determined souls born too late for the high salaries and low mortgages of their older siblings. They have increased the pressure to be a rabbit and made a mockery of the mellow turtles. But what of those who fall somewhere in between, those of us who are of the zebra or wild boar persuasion?

Never fear. To help mid-level, societally conscious achievers in evaluating their lifestyles for telltale signs of stress, I have developed a personal stress index (PSI). Based on extensive computer modeling of miserable human beings (MHBs), I have observed ten traits that spell trouble, and ten lifestyle changes that spell relief.

Personal Stress Index

Part A: Circle each statement that applies to you.
1. I never give a sucker an even break.
2. I'm always nice.
3. I go for it.
4. I'm into fads.
5. I rely on artificial chemicals to help me make it through the night.
6. I can't sleep eight hours a night.
7. I have a lover (but I wish I didn't).
8. I exercise every day.
9. I worry about Ronald Reagan.
10. I am lonely.

Part B: Relief.
Unfortunately, relief is not a swallow away. If it were that simple, we'd all be swigging down flagons of relief. No, relief

consists of modifying the afore-circled behaviors. For each stressor identified, apply the appropriate relief described below.

1. *Give a sucker an even break.* It will benefit your Positive Karmic Uptake (PKU).

2. *Don't be very nice.* Very nice people are sickening, and they end up as bag ladies and gentlemen, and you have to survive on discarded Big Macs (which is not a sound nutritional program).

3. *Don't go for it.* Hire some schmuck to go for it, and you take the credit. (This is known as managerial style.)

4. *Avoid fad riots.* Don't take politically correct positions just to be one of the guys.

5. *Avoid artificial chemicals.* Only use caffeine-free coffee, non-alcoholic wine, and no-pain-killer aspirin.

6. *Sleep at least eight hours a day.* The nighttime is the best time for letting the creative genius out of the bag. Consider the following piece of erotica written by a frustrated legal secretary at 3:00 a.m.:

Workers on the dock,
Lemonade in summer,
fresh kiwi—
your penis thinking.

7. *Avoid second-hand stress.* If you have pain-in-the-ass significant others, dump them. You're having enough trouble taking care of numero uno; you don't need dos equis. (But do find someone who is always there for you, especially if you're not all there yourself.)

8. *Don't expect to solve all your problems with exercise.* Exercise is nice but sometimes you will need to use Dangerous and Addicting Drugs (DAD). The DAD approach has its drawbacks, but it is still the most effective stress reduction method known to man. Had Jim Fixx gotten a fix, would he be alive today?

9. *Don't worry about Ronald Reagan.* This is a real waste of your time. Remember, there are three possible scenarios: A) Reagan does decide to start the bombing ("I really mean it this time, guys, no kidding, swear to God") and stress will only be a memory; B) Reagan was reelected, but when the horrible depression comes, it won't be blamed on the liberals; C) Reagan is right, and we all get rich, and we won't care about anything else.

10. *Have a baby.* When all else fails, find yourself a sperm or egg donor and grow your own. It will solve all your problems.

Whatever you do, don't consider suicide when stress reduction isn't enuf. Suicide only opens up another can of worms: is there stress after death?

Pure Gold

Prevailing wisdom, in its infinite smarts, divides all people into two groups: haves and have-nots. Once you get into having, there are many subdivisions but these have always seemed trivial to me when placed alongside not-having. Some years back, when I visited my sister, Myrna, who lives in an upper-middle-class suburb of Chicago, she introduced me to her neighbor, The Artist. The Artist, upon learning that I was from Berkeley, took me aside, blinked her false lashes at me and asked, "Have you got any dope?" Then, to let me know she was a comrade, she whispered in my ear, "We're really very different from Myrna. Our house is the one with the monkey bars in front." Wild and crazy! I'll bet they keep the trash compactor in the living room.

Recently, however, I've been made aware of yet another distinction among the haves. It has to do with putting your money where your morals are, as opposed to just parking it with what we used to call (before we had money management problems) "the rapacious running dogs of imperialism" or "the pig power structure" or Mom and Dad's bank.

It goes by the name of Socially Responsible Investing, this distinction which its followers insist can make a difference in our lives, our future, and, even, our rate of return. It has its prophets as well as its profits. They include E. F. (*Small is Beautiful*) Schumacher and Paul (*The Next Economy*) Hawken. Probably the most well-known entity in this network is the Bay Area-based Working Assets Money Fund which includes on its board of advisors such politically correct heavyweights as food policy maker Frances Moore Lappe and former Berkeley Councilmember Loni Hancock. Working Assets describes itself in *Netbacking* (a publication for socially responsible investors) as "investing in instruments that finance housing, small business, renewable energy, higher education, and family farms," while avoiding "financing enterprises that pollute, build weapons, discriminate against women or minorities, produce nuclear power, treat their employees unfairly, support repressive foreign regimes, or shut down plants in America and shift jobs abroad." Right on, you think, just the place to park the 50 K Aunt Gertie left you from the Lockheed dividends.

But there is a wider network of socially responsible investors—some who even consider themselves more righteous than Working Assets. Sounds vintage Berkeley, doesn't it? To learn more about these people who are bucking the system, I visited Roger Pritchard, who describes himself as "a small business teacher-consultant, a teacher-counselor on socially responsible investing, and a single parent running a cottage industry."

Forgetting that I am in California, I arrive ten minutes early at the Pritchard home and am eventually greeted by my host, who is standing there dripping wet and wearing a towel. While he finishes his morning toilette, I read his literature, which includes the Vermont-based *Good Money*, "the newsletter of social investing and inventing" to which Pritchard is a contributor. I look over his articles on investing in yourself, lending money to friends, and inheriting money. I also note in his biography an impressive education that includes advanced degrees from Oxford (he is British) and Brandeis. The degrees, however, are in those 60's subjects like philosophy and sociology. No Wharton MBA he.

Pritchard's home and office is one of the most beautiful in the flatlands—redwood walls, a large stone fireplace, tasteful wood furniture, and lots of light coming in through the windows. Outside there is a colorful flower garden that Pritchard lovingly tends.

Once dressed, Roger Pritchard sits down and describes his work with a "network of inherited money," his classes teaching people how to start small businesses and invest responsibly, and his philosophy of promoting a regional economy and ecology. "People come to me because they are intimidated by the banks and have lost their skills. People are alienated from their surplus money," he says. "We can't reject the economy, but we can challenge it with alternatives. Social responsibility means acting in accordance with your values—whatever they happen to be. Anybody who is integrated is socially responsible."

I wonder whether this isn't just the Big Chill generation's attempt to buy off guilt for our about-face on the capitalist road issue. I ask Pritchard if he would consider the protagonist of that movie—the guy who made a fortune in Running Dog brand jogging shoes—socially responsible. "Since the business promoted exercise," he says, "and people need exercise, I'd probably consider him socially responsible."

Pritchard then explains the Buddhist concept of "Right Livelihood" that is the basis of his philosophy: "It is doing work you enjoy and learn from. This is the fifth step in the eight-fold path to Enlightenment."

I tell him it all sounds good to me but that I have a little trouble when the distinctions between church and bank statement get blurred. He responds that this root-of-all-evil thinking is my Judeo-Christian hang-up and that the Buddhist path does not preclude good work leading to Enlightenment and, apparently, cash. I ask him if he'd mind telling me how he got the cash for the beautiful house. "I bought it in 1971 for $30,000," he explains. (Right Livelihood is nice, but right place, right time never hurts either.) Then, Pritchard invites me to meet the other SR's at a party at his home.

Needless to say, the idea of attending a party of socially responsible people threw me into quite a tizzy. Add to the usual problems of what to wear and what to bring, the necessity of questioning the social value of all these things, and I begin to understand why I've been so socially sloppy all these years. I decide to wear my hundred percent cotton skirt (Save the Polyester) and then grapple with the big issue that must be faced before any East Bay party: to shave or not to shave. I divide all social occasions into smooth legs, hairy, or stubble OK. A mistake can be unpleasant. There is nothing more embarrassing than showing up at a party where all the other women are looking comfortably Mediterranean and you're standing there with two plucked chickens dangling from your skirt. My razor-sharp female intuition told me this was definitely a stubble OK crowd.

Then: what to bring? He said to bring wine or dessert but *whose*? Without reading a *Mother Jones* investigative story on wineries, you could pick up something that looked safe, say Shady Oak Fume Blanc, only to discover you've bought a Heublein subsidiary. Dessert, was simply out of the question. Sugar, we know, is Very Bad unless you think Cuba, in which case it's good for *them*. And as far as sugarless desserts go—forget it. I baked my last batch of uneaten barf buns years ago. Finally, I found the bottle of homemade wine that my friend Larry Westdal gave me for my birthday. What could be more small and beautiful than a guy who only produces six bottles for his friends? No peasant's grape-torn feet would be on my conscience.

To get into a money kind of mood, the husband and I warmed up with a drink from the Santa Fe Grill's bar. There we could watch the capable and charming bartendress Karen West pour Pinot Noir with one hand and mix a margarita with the other. I didn't see Dianne Feinstein, or even Charlotte Maillard, but I actually counted eight BMWs, six Mercedes, and three Alfas in the parking lot. I was hoping to catch another favorite sight at the Santa Fe: disoriented, hungry punks wandering in from the Berkeley Square Nightclub, acting awkward as hell while being seated, and then leaving after reading the prices on the menu. No such luck.

The socially responsibles were quite a different scene. About forty people were gathered at Pritchard's, munching on corn muffins, yogurt-covered nuts, one fancy chocolate cake, and jug chablis. There were more men than women, and the men were mostly thirtyish and of the new sensitive variety—many potential *Co-Evolution Quarterly* posterboys in the crowd. There were a few women who might be *Mother Earth News* centerfolds—long hair, long dresses, no late 70's sellouts to blow dryers here.

I spoke with John Lind from the Interfaith Committee on Corporate Responsibility. He does research linking human rights abuses with credit risks in third world countries. I also met a man who was a kind of mole working in a traditional irresponsible investment house. Another man introduced himself as a "therapist," although he was actually a psychiatrist. Therapist sounds more

SR. A psychiatrist you expect to pull out a cattle-prod and start zapping you.

I was expecting more of the guilty, inherited money people. Instead, most in attendance seemed to be hardworking people, many looking for investors for their small businesses. Whatever social strata they belonged to, there was, in contrast to the Santa Fe, a notable absence of conspicuous consumption in the crowd.

There was a short presentation by the guests of honor—the Lowrys, from Vermont, who publish *Good Money*, *Netbacking*, and *Catalyst*. They discussed the complexities of determining what was a socially responsible investment. Later in the week, Susan Meeker-Lowry, mother of three, would be speaking at Pritchard's house on "Investing from the Heart." Her husband, Peter Lowry, was seated by her side, making an interesting fashion statement by combining a gold neckchain with hiking boots (plus pants and shirt, of course).

I left the party feeling I had been engulfed in the sweetness and sincerity of a Lutheran singles group; but these people are out to make money, not each other. They seem undeterred by their David and Goliath problem, celebrating the fact that *Good Money* just got its one thousandth subscriber. Even in the Bay Area, there are probably more people ready to come out of the closet than out of traditional investment modalities. The three-piece-suit set is certainly not threatened by this movement, perhaps seeing them as the fringe rather than the cutting edge of a new economy. Yet, I'm sure many new ethical investors will come to the same conclusion as Hazel Henderson (author of *Creating Alternative Futures*) who says, "Conventional economics is a form of brain damage."

Upwardly Mobile

You know me. I'm the jogger. If you live in the Berkeley hills, you have seen me. Almost every day for the past five years I have run by your house. There may be others, but I'm the faithful one—the slightly overweight, slow-moving, young old woman. I am an anthropologist of the streets, studying the flora, the fauna, the earthquake cracks, the bumper stickers. One day while I was heading up, the lady I always see gardening on the corner of Milvia and Hopkins looked up from her camellias and spoke to me: "One thing I'll say for you . . . you're consistent." She confirmed what I'd begun to suspect; I've become a part of your landscape.

When I run up here, I'm not just getting exercise. I'm getting to a place so peaceful that my mind is free to wander except for the interruption of an occasional commentator. Although I don't run in races, some of you have taken it upon yourself to coach me. "Faster!" or "You're going too slow," or "You'll get there some-day," say the old men. The women on my route seem more confident that I'm making progress. "You look great since you started jogging," shouts a woman getting out of her car. "Hi, Skinny," smiles the braided lady who owns the folksy shop near the Solano Tunnel. A real tribute came from the garbage man on Euclid who gave me a clenched fist and called out, "Lookin' good, Baby."

They should be there when I have to pass the teenagers—those brutal critics of the body. The girls look up from their clusters and giggle. I want to grab them by their woven barrettes. I want to pull down their lavender leg warmers and slap them on their tight little Sergio Valentes. In my fantasy I say to them: "Wait until you're 38 and have two kids and are on your third career. Come back and giggle at me then. I'll be 65 and have time to run up to Grizzly Peak every day. What'll you be doing then?" But I don't say it. I just keep moving.

Sometimes the fantasy turns violent. Like the time the chubby 14-year-old boy zapped me in front of Live Oak Park. He looked down at me from his bicycle and said, "Why are you running?" Before I could answer, he finished his sentence, ". . . you fat whore." He rode on toward Walnut Square and it took me until I was in front of the Church of Mary Magdalen to figure out how to respond. First, I grab him down off his bike and push him to the ground. He tries to get up. I give him a right to the jaw. He's down again. I give him another right. Little stars form over his head. I am Popeye and jogging is my spinach.

I never planned to be running out in the streets. I mean, I'm no exhibitionist. I started out jogging at Martin Luther King School track back when King track was nothing but an animal relief station and patch of weeds. I'd occasionally reward myself by driving across town through the UC rush hour traffic to run a mile at the School for the Deaf.

The track there was a lush green field with an unrivaled view of San Francisco. The tree-covered hills rose up sharply behind the eastern side of the field and the pungent growth of eucalyptus functioned like a Benzedrex inhaler. Either the Deaf School track attracted more competitive runners or there's something to my inhaler theory because things always seemed to move faster at that track.

The hills above the track look green and empty, but legend has it that there are many bizarre individuals encamped in the area—part of a growing number of "Reaganvilles" on Berkeley's public lands. Legend or not, once, while trying to go up the impossibly steep trails in those hills, I happened upon an elaborate campsite—sleeping bag, Co-op grocery cart, wood-burning fire. The camper appeared from out of the bush clad in nothing but a lot of hair and a waist belt with samurai sword. I did not pause to interview him.

That was not the only jogging path I've been scared away

212

from. Many world class joggers say that the Strawberry Canyon's upper fire trail is the finest jogging path on earth. Even if the magnificent views of Berkeley, Oakland, and San Francisco aren't enough, the long stretch of flat, soft road is far from any traffic. It was during the drought of '77 that I first came to Strawberry Canyon, and it was there that I learned that I could run long distances and up hills. I was free in the open country, two miles straight up from home. I especially loved being up there all alone. On weekday mornings you might not see another soul. When the rains finally came the road got hopelessly muddy. In dry, hot September other joggers might warn, "There's a rattler ahead." I learned to watch for the branches that moved. Then in 1980, two women were raped on that trail. I could never enjoy it again. There's something about running and looking behind you that just doesn't make it. The fantasy of being alone in the country and feeling strong was shattered.

I try going back to the tracks because I consider it physically risky to run on concrete all the time. King track is now part of a beautiful park—a kind of People's Republic of Berkeley Fitness Center. When I was growing up in slummy Chicago, a pool such as the tree-surrounded jewel at King was something I could only picture in Esther Williams' movies or Florida dreams. Next to the pool is a playground with separate toddler and big kid play areas. I was there one day when some people with clipboards were setting up the equipment. "Who are you?" I asked them. "We're the designers of this playground," he said. He explained that they had degrees in psychology and urban planning (or something like that) and showed me how the equipment was designed to foster various motor skills. This just isn't a swing and sandbox kind of town.

The track itself is now redone in special water-repellent dirt. Dogs are forbidden. Entertainment is provided in the form of Middletown-like parents imploring child soccer players to excel on the well-watered green. At rush hour the track is a kind of adult merry-go-round. To find fifty joggers is not unusual. But it is still a rather low-key crowd. There are groups of women running and discussing relationships, and there are bearded men dreaming of research money. Occasionally one sees a mother jog while pushing her child in an umbrella stroller as if the hook handles were some strange extra-uterine umbilical cord. But mostly the 5:00 p.m. crowd resembles a healthy, bare-your-muscles, singles bar. The last time I ran there I ran very slowly behind a man who said to his friend, "I can always tell a woman's age by the backs of her thighs."

So now I just head for the streets. By the time anyone can count the rings on my thighs, I'm way up the block. In determining my route I sought stretches of flat, shaded streets—a scarcity in the flatlands—except in the shade under the BART tracks, a path that takes you from the creek near Gilman Street to the back door of foundries in El Cerrito. But, alas, this is another also-ran route as again fear won out. On my last run beneath the BART tracks I became aware of a man running behind me. When I'd stop and turn around, he'd stop and duck behind the pillars that hold up the tracks; you know, those places where somebody spray paints "White Fascists Rule." When this guy finally got close to me I began to suspect he wasn't a true jogger. It wasn't just his leather shoes or his polyester pants. It was the pack of Marlboros in his rolled-up shirt cuff above his biceps that gave him away.

And that's how I came to jog in the high rent district. The North Berkeley Hills may be steep but they're nonviolent. According to Berkeley Police Department crime data, the rape and homicide line seems to stop somewhere around Rose and Grove Streets. (Maybe it has something to do with the wait in line at Fatapple's. Maybe they pause for a blueberry muffin and calm down.)

Fear of rape, ultimately, is no laughing matter, so I gave up jogging the isolated paths. The first time I set my sights upward I was jogging on Milvia wondering where I could go to find some shade and avoid stop lights. I was staring up at the Berkeley Hills ridge line and I noticed Indian Rock. I had walked up there many times on those wonderful pedestrian paths that slice through the hills and I realized that even without the paths I could get my feet anywhere my eyes could go.

I went through Solano Tunnel, that monument to post-1906-earthquake development. By extending the Key Route Railway system to the Thousand Oaks area, the tunnel made these hills accessible to those commuters who would take the train to the ferry to San Francisco. Today the tunnel is filled with cars, loud whistlers, horn honkers, and an impressive array of graffiti. The real drawback to running through the tunnel is the carbon monoxide cocktail you inhale. My friend Carol who lives in the Sierras and grows her own vegetables and chickens refused to run through with me. An ear, nose, and throat specialist once told her she had the clearest nasal passages he had ever looked down. When I tried to show her my route, she looked at the tunnel with horror. "I'll spoil my nasal passages!" she insisted.

But for me the tunnel is a transformational experience leading to the stately homes, private rose gardens, and rock parks of a unique community. I run along under the old sycamores and then on toward The Arlington. For some reason most of the people wandering around lost in their cars in the hills are looking for The Arlington. There is something irresistible about a street that takes the article.

At Indian Rock I stop for a drink of water. Why does this water taste particularly good? Is it from some ancient spring? I wonder if it's the same water Indian women used to wash their clothes. I imagine them beating their laundry on the rock now dotted with student climbers. I look out toward the Bay and try to squint out the houses and the bridges so I can see things the Ohlone way. It's an effort. Another presence is here, evidenced by the stopped-up water fountain drain with gum wads floating on the top and the hundreds of broken beer bottles scattered everywhere.

Still, it's a magnificent spot. No wonder John Hudson Thomas, one of Berkeley's premiere architects, put his office right here.

Up the hill I am confronted by one particularly enormous structure that looks like a concrete wedding cake. You can see it if you stand on the corner of Henry and Berryman and look up north. This is the 25-room Spring mansion and its theatrical grandeur would be more at home on Sunset Boulevard. Built by a "concrete baron" who profited from the '20s building boom, it later became an obscure college. The college had to contend with the chagrin of the neighbors who deplore anything public or commercial near their homes. Similar community opposition was raised against a children's dance school and the Shakespeare Festival in nearby John Hinkle Park. Today, I am told, the Spring Mansion is again a private home. All this is on a street that has a sign posted stating: "Private Street. Permission to pass revocable at any

215

time," and signed by the San Luis Court Homes Association. On many occasions, I noticed people walking up this street in their bathrobes. At the risk of getting my permission revoked, I asked a passerby what went on up here . . . a PJ party? A somnambulist's camp? She told me the Homes Association has a private swimming pool and tennis park in the canyon. Strangers are most unwelcome, as she learned when she wandered in walking her dog. She was greeted by shouts of "Who are you? Get out of here! You don't belong here!"

Actually, there isn't that much open space up here until you come to Tilden Park. It's strange to jog along these streets where a Tudor castle is stuffed in next to a craftsman's bungalow. Each house belongs on its own estate with acreage and names like "Paradise Found" and "Windamere Farm." Up here I am frequently delighted at the sight of a City Council member who, like Marie Antoinette playing shepherdess, is pushing the hand-powered mower on the lawn of her mini-hacienda. Gilda, I want to say to her, no wonder you have such a hard time understanding the anti-development feeling in this town. Look at all the parking up here. How would you feel if someone suddenly put up twenty boutiques on your corner? Where do you go for a croissant and capuccino? You drive down to my block, park, and walk to one of the ten new cafes within three blocks of my house!

Although I'm always reading letters in the paper from hills residents denying there's a difference, the hills/flatlands distinction remains a major division in Berkeley. Not only does there seem to be more money, but the lack of foot traffic makes it harder for strangers to case the streets of the hills without being noticed. There are also no shops or developments (with the exception of one block on The Arlington) to attract strangers to the neighborhood. This may be why the crime rate is lower, although the police attribute it mainly to the winding roads that make a quick getaway less feasible. The lack of automobile traffic on most of these streets creates a completely different atmosphere of quiet and serenity. I can run down the middle of the street and hear a car coming blocks away. I can hear the birds chirping. Early one morning I ran into a deer rounding the corner of Southampton and San Luis Road.

The lack of automobile traffic not only make streets quieter, they are, in fact, safer. Of the six traffic fatalities in Berkeley so far this year (and 10 last year), none occurred in the Berkeley hills. While there is an occasional accident—mainly on Spruce Street or Grizzly Peak Boulevard—the threat to life and limb is nothing compared to the accident rate in the Berkeley flatlands, particularly near the busy intersections that cross University Avenue and Ashby Avenue. This year a pedestrian was struck and killed trying to cross Shattuck at Virginia, an intersection still without a light or four-way stop. When it comes to street running, jogging the flatlands may be suicidal.

Who are the people who live up here, I wonder. Are they professors who bought their homes before 1974 when professors could still afford such homes? Are they old Berkeley families? I've seen more than one slim, immaculately dressed, white-haired grand-dame pull the Cadillac out of the driveway. Are the newcomers professional, childless couples? Iranians who got out with the rugs and the cash? Nouveau riche drug dealers or rock stars who shunned Marin? There must be something relentlessly "flatlands" about me, because in seventeen years in Berkeley I have only been in hills houses a few times, and then only at big parties or for Lamaze lessons. I guess that's why I continue to get my voyeuristic kicks jogging up there.

Are hills people different from you or me? I know they're not all rich. I've stopped on my run at an occasional garage sale (the only form of commerce one sees up here), and it's the same old crap as any other garage sale. Once I followed an "Open House" sign to tour a hills home I had seen advertised at well below the usual market price. It was one of many stucco bungalows with beautiful redwood trim and built-ins. There was a creek running out back and I had fantasies of a breakfast nook where you could munch on your bagel and hear little rapids flowing in the rainy season. Instead, I was greeted at the door by an anxious, pasty woman who was quick to tell me they had an estimate of $30,000 to repair the cracked foundation. Her husband, an enormous man, was ensconced in an easy chair watching *Days of Our Lives* on TV. The walls of the room were scarred with floor-to-ceiling cracks and all the curtains were closed. On a little tray table next to the man were a glass of water, eight prescription bottles and a quart of Maalox.

I tend to keep tabs on these houses. I like to see who's getting an addition or whose rhododendron stays in bloom the longest. I know where the party houses are by the cases of empty wine bottles left for recycling. This is my route. Almost nobody else is on my streets except the letter carriers and the construction crews building the additions. I always know when new people move in. It's especially noticeable when the old-timers leave or die and the young people move in. Then the gauze curtains become replaced with Levelor blinds and the earthquake-cracked stairs get replaced. They might repaint the place in grey with light blue window trim or put in a redwood fence with a built-in bench around the front yard.

Once while a family was preparing to move, I noticed a large wooden object leaning against the garbage cans. I vowed long ago that I wouldn't stop running to pick up the nickles and dimes I frequently see glinting in the streets. Don't go down for pennies, as we used to say in high school. However, I confess that I do brake for quarters. And on this occasion I stopped to check out the object in the garbage. The next day it was still there, and the owner was coming out the door. I asked if he was throwing it out. "Sure. You want it?" he answered. I raced home, got the husband and the Chevy, and that's how jogging gave me a solid oak Victorian halltree.

But the real rewards come in the flights of fancy . . . the thoughts of Fred and Ginger waltzing out the French doors of the terra cotta mansion up on Santa Barbara Road. Or my fantasy about the white-haired lady in the wheelchair who's always parked before her picture window. Each day I wave at her. Once her nurse came outside and called to me, "Where've you been?" after I had the flu. So, they do notice me. I imagine the lady communicating to her lawyer: "I'm changing the will. Please see that everything goes to that nice young woman who always waves to me."

Further down Santa Barbara, in a stone retaining wall, is the remains of an inscription: FAIR PAR

What did it say? Fairview Park? Fairy Park? That's it. This is where the Simple Lifers, those zany early hills inhabitants, hung out! This must be where the little Maybeck kids came in their togas to dance and look for ordinary kids who would trade them bologna sandwiches for their seeds and raisins.

I am interrupted from my reverie by a handsome couple jogging by me. "Didn't think anyone runs slower than we do," the man says as he smiles and passes me. Where did they come from? What are they doing here? Are they the forerunners of hoards of flatland escapees who are onto my secret? "Hey you," I shout as their thighs ascend too fast for me to guess their age, "Off of my street!"

Parenting and Kidding

Madonna and Child

Remember when poets used to write things like "Thoughts of a Briton on the Subjugation of Switzerland"? I had one of those inspirational moments recently and I'd like to share with you some Thoughts That Occurred While Watching My 10-Year-Old Daughter Lip-synch the Hit Song "Like a Virgin."

As I watched her eyes roll and her lips pucker up in all the right moves, I considered how she had already mastered the basic courtship gestures of the species. Then I had a vision of what lies ahead for her and I saw this river, this raging torrent, rushing right at her. It was a flash flood of our culture, and in it I saw beer and cars and tampons and Prince and McNuggets and Malibu Barbie and spermicidal jelly and hair dye and *Porky's* and bulimia and Virginia Slims and I don't mind telling you, I was afraid.

What I saw in my daughter's precocious Madonna impersonation was the end of my child. *My* child. She belonged to the world now, soon to be a vessel in that river of no deposit, no return. The best I could hope for was that I'd outfitted her well enough, given her enough of the rudiments of survival, so that when she hits white water she'll make it through. Somehow, I thought I'd have more time, more power, more control, but it becomes apparent, as the hormones that will turn her into a woman begin to flow, that my influence is waning.

It's not as if I ever had this great plan for her, although she was, as we say, planned. It even seems as if birth control was the

223

last time I really had any say in the matter. I remember that during these first months of her life, when she would wake up almost hourly to be nursed, I'd try to go back to sleep reading Dr. Spock on managing the "four-hour intervals between feedings." Four hours! To this day she doesn't go four hours between feedings.

Hurdle No. 2 was trying to get her to sleep. "Just put her down and let her cry," the pediatrician would say. Why don't family albums have photos of these Great Moments in Parenting? What I wouldn't give now for a snapshot of my husband and I as we were then—hovering in a closet with our fingers in our ears watching the timer for the 15 minutes to pass so we could rush to her room and beg her forgiveness.

Toilet training, a subject too gross to discuss with anyone but other veterans of the Potty Wars, was not a major problem for us. I was patient with toilet training because I was in no hurry to terminate my relationship with the individual who often seemed like my only human contact in those early days of motherhood—the diaper man. I remember pacing the floor at 6:00 a.m. with my baby in the last rectangle of clean linen—the other 150 soiled ones lying in state in the so-called "odorized" pick-up hamper—singing my own unique medley of nursery songs: "Oh, Diaper Man, where you gon' run to?" and "God damn, the diaper man" then segue into—big finish—"Someday he'll come along, the diaper man I love."

I had illusions back then of protecting my child from being sacrificed on the altar of the junk culture. She would never eat sugar— just adorable plastic bears full of honey and cups of apple juice instead of cola. The existence of white bread would be utterly unknown to her. She would only watch selected television, nothing but *Sesame Street* and Fred Rogers until she was ready for *Masterpiece Theatre*. And when it came to toys, one thing was clear: A certain molded latex trollop named Barbie would never darken my door.

Even in those early days, before my daughter displayed her gift for jurisprudence by vigorously arguing her case, being a disciplinarian was tough. As a result, I would frequently escape the tension of trying to be a good mother (i.e., one who conforms to the cultural prejudices of her time and place) by getting into the car with a big box of a particularly disgusting candy called Hot Tamales. Then I'd drive around too fast with the oldies station blasting. I'm convinced now that these little bizarre episodes of stress reduction (none dare call it hypocrisy) were what kept me going.

When I began slipping, standards-wise, it was just a matter of not being equal to my child in sheer stamina. Maybe if I had had babies the old-fashioned way—without knowing my career plan from my elbow—I would have had the youthful energy to resist. Instead, one day I just surrendered my child to the sacred triad: hamburger, fries and a Coke.

When "the sibling" was born and I realized I was even less able to cope with two daughters (surprise, surprise), I began to acquiesce to eldest daughter's wishes in a major way. My recollection is it proceeded in this fashion—first junk food, then Barbie, and before too long the kid was rushing home from school to watch *Santa Barbara*.

Surrendering to Barbie (a definite Madonna precursor) was in many ways the beginning of the end. It wasn't just the feminist issue, but ethnic ones as well. Did I want to communicate to my dark-eyed, dark-haired Jewish daughter the message that someday if she bleached her hair, got contacts, had a nose job and stopped complaining she might be lucky enough to land a stud like Ken?

When I bought her her first Barbie, I watched in astonishment as she went off to her room and played for hours. By herself. I remember remarking to a friend at the time, "That little plastic hunk of T&A just bought me the first freedom I've known in four years."

Let me be perfectly clear. I think my daughter is one swell kid. Whether this has anything to do with how I raised her I'm not sure. As she grows more independent, I can see my ability to influence her may be waning just when her need for discipline is greater than ever. She can role-play Madonna all she wants. But let her try to *be* Madonna—a jaded tease—and I'm going to bust her.

She's not going to like it or me. We're going to have to have long screaming fits in which we'll both lose track of what's really important. I'll get so caught up in arguing that she can't wear the black lace see-through dress to school that I'll forget that what I really wanted to say was: Don't go riding in a car with a boy who's had a quart of Wild Turkey for breakfast. She'll get so carried away telling me how ignorant and out-of-it I am that she won't be able to let me comfort her when Ken ditches her.

Why didn't somebody tell me when I had a baby that the real problem was not whether to have an alternative birthing room at the hospital or whether cloth is better than paper diapers, but that someday all that would be left for me to do was discipline? I don't know how other parents feel about it, but for me discipline is bondage.

My child may be living in a material world, she may be a material girl, but isn't she my creation? Perhaps I can put a stop to the impending hormonally induced psychosis. She *is* awfully good at math. Maybe she'll be a nerd. Yes, please Lord, make my baby a nerd.

Forget my official position of throwing her out in the polluted river of reality and seeing if she can swim. Why not just lock her up in her chamber for the next 10 years with her computer terminal and a lot of fancy software? Keep her there until the right boy comes along—the one smart enough to gain access.

Congratulations, handsome prince, you have broken the code. You may have my daughter in marriage. You must understand she knows nothing about triple-pierced ears or Esprit underwear or Calvin's Obsession or snorting anything. She's got no sense of the Rhythm Method. She's not just like a virgin; she's the genuine article.

Lodge Lizards

Sometimes life imitates *Leave It to Beaver* but more often it resembles *Family Feud*. I really don't know how any families are surviving during these times that try adults' and children's souls; but I do think the family that plays together, stays together. So last month we took off for a little family vacation.

It was nice to get out of town for a few days. Ride out on that Highway 101. Get down past Morgan Hill. See where the silicon stops and the vineyards start. See the boutiquing of California agriculture. I, now the old-timer, could say, "Why, I remember when this whole area was fruit orchards." Today the money's in the fruit that gets people high.

In that time-honored division of labor, my husband does the driving and I stare out the window. I look for mementos of El Camino Real, the mission bells and mission markers. I look at the vineyards and the couple in the next car reading *Cabernet Annual*. I watch for the bumper stickers, the best being: Russia Sucks. And I soar with the flocks of birds cruising the green hills of winter. I also try to monitor the fights between the girls. "That's my sticker. Mommy! She's got my Betty Boop." "She's not wearing her seatbelt. OK, if you want to get killed . . ." "You can hold my dinosaur if I can have your calculator."

My husband gets all excited by the oil field near San Ardo. It's been ten years since we drove this far south on 101—since we had children. When we were pregnant (believe me he was in on it) we

227

had big travel plans—Mexico, Eastern Europe, faraway places with strange-sounding names. Now we hardly make it past Oakland. So the development near San Ardo really caught his eye. "Look at all that steam injection. There were a few pumps before, but nothing like this." I stare at hundreds of those big green mechanical birds pecking away at the oil. Just in one spot. Then they're gone. Back to cows and horses.

Where are we going? Are we just a ramblin, ramblin, ramblin kinda family? Hit the road, Jack—the highway is our home? Wish I could say "yes." Wish I could tell you we're just four drifters off to see the world, there's such a lot of world to see. But we're not gypsies; we're bourgeoisies. We've got places to go, things to see, jobs to return to, schools to come back to, bills to pay.

I have, like anybody in her right mind with children, carefully planned this trip. We are going to Cambria. Cambria is as far south on the coast as I think we can get to in one day given the reality of a carsickness-prone kid. It's always a trade-off between the carsickness pills that make her crabby and the ubiquitous prospect of cleaning up vomit. I figure five hours of crabbiness to be the limit of parental nonviolence.

I chose Cambria because I've been to Big Sur and Santa Barbara's too big. Also, my friend, the New York artist with the good taste, stopped there once and told me it was pretty. The guidebooks repeatedly used the term "quaint old village." I read that Juan Cabrillo landed somewhere near there (on a space mission from Queen Isabella). And Cambria is just moments from the fiefdom of William Randolph Hearst, the San Simeon estate that the Hearst family bequeathed to the State of California in 1958. Who could ask for anything more?

I assumed the guilt risk on this trip, having reserved two adjoining rooms at something called the Cambria Pines Lodge (lured by the guidebook phrase "old") and made reservations to tour Hearst Castle. If the vacation was a bust, everyone could blame me. So to soften them up, I made a concession to family life and agreed to stop at a franchise restaurant for lunch—the King City A&W. (It was easier to lift my franchise ban after a stop last Fourth of July at the only "cute, local" joint in Marysville. There, my husband was actually served a Spam sandwich. I wisely avoided culinary risk by ordering a green salad hold the dressing.) After being mollified by the mystical triad—hamburgers, fries, and a coke—the girls cheerfully returned to lockdown and we pushed on toward our destination.

The lodge was a big hit—tiny cabins (built in the 20's), quiet, off the highway. Nearby was the big lodge house, a lovely redwood structure with a garden restaurant complete with a flock of peacocks. They even had a children's menu (!) including fried chicken (the girls hated it anyway, but we only had to throw away $2.95 on it instead of the usual $5.95 or better). They did like the blueberry pancakes at breakfast and I loved the fresh baked scones. There was a nice mix of people at the lodge, even other families. One little girl carried a Cabbage Patch doll with her at all times, and I heard eldest daughter mutter the phrase, "Cabbage Patch bitch."

Best of all, the place included a "health spa" and not just a tepid "hot tub" in a seagull beshatted redwood gazebo. There was a huge indoor heated pool where we swam when it rained, hot tub with jacuzzi, sauna, and several exercise machines. While soaking in the tub we met many locals who come to use the health club— the ambulance driver, a psychologist, a contractor. Is there anything more California than meeting people in a hot tub?

Hearst Castle was a fascinating tour, truly Alta California. Built by Oakland's own Julia Morgan, la Casa Grande (the Big House) sits high on la Cuesta Encantada (the enchanted hill). Sabe usted? That William Randolph Hearst lived como El Rey (like a fucking king!). We were shepherded up the hill in organized busloads. I couldn't believe that the same State of California which can hardly educate its children could operate so efficiently what is described as the second most popular tourist attraction in the United States.

A charming man who resembled an aging Monty Clift led our tour group. Our docent pointed to the palatial table in the medieval dining hall (where a droll Senior Hearst liked to keep bare bottles of Heinz ketchup and French's mustard among the sterling) and said, "Imagine you're sitting here and Cary Grant is on one side and Clark Gable on the other." We returned outside the building, which looks like a mission with the spoils of Europe plastered all over it, and for the second time our leader looked directly at me and said, "You women should be very proud of Julia Morgan who designed all this." Is there something about me that reeks feminist scumbag? (For more on the tour guide see my forthcoming *Sometimes a Great Docent*.)

The other people on the tour were not the gang of Yahoos you might expect. They included a group of German-speaking, stylish young men—probably weirdo cinematographers. There was a big bear of a Russian man who must have felt right at home in a state-owned former private palace tour (although this one was donated, not confiscated). Then there was the woman from New York who looked at the millions in Persian carpeting and asked, "Do you know how they kept the rugs clean?" (22 servants). Nobody seemed to mind my youngest daughter, who got bored and kept proclaiming, "I hate this castle. It's yucky!" But honey, what about this beautiful pool inlaid with real gold mosaic tiles and built at a cost of thirty-three thousand depression dollars? Yuky!

Our bus headed down from la Cuesta Encantada, and we watched for the remains of Mr. Hearst's private zoo—the zebra and buffalo still roaming the hills. What an American sight, the world of William Randolph Hearst—a spoiled brat gone mad. The richest nouveau of them all. Up from Rosebud.

We return to Cambria and look at the shops. It's gone beyond quaint. What it is is cutesy the way any small town with sixty gift shops is cutesy. Every one of them sells two books—*Citizen Hearst* and the autobiography of his beloved Marion Davies. The town's economy survives (as it has since Hearst began La Casa Grande after World War I) on the spoils of the castle.

A few days later, back on 101, heading home we talk things over. It was a good family vacation, particularly because everybody loved the lodge. A sign in the lobby announced that over the next few years each cabin would be torn down and replaced with a luxury chateau (probably with wine cellars). There's really no money in catering to families, is there? Today, the very word "family" seems synonymous with junk as in "family dining at the Sizzler." In the same way "adult" has come to mean dirty as in "adult entertainment." The worlds of the child and the adult seem to be increasingly divergent. They get McDonalds and Smurfs; we get cognac and cocaine. What a thrill when we can find common ground.

230

A special moment in the vacation for me was when I got to watch the sun set at Moonstone Beach. Someone had the kindness to put in a playground right there on the beach. So while my kids were swinging and sliding and running around I could sit in perfect stillness and watch the sun go down. I stared at the illusion of gold steps on the crests of the waves that led to the horizon. Finally, the song that had been in my head all week came out. It was a Les Paul and Mary Ford hit from my childhood. I could hear them singing, seemingly about old California: a world of dark haciendas and sleeping towns. *Vaya con Dios*, my loved ones.

Confessions of a Chaperone

I think I am a typical modern housewife. I have two children. I work at two jobs. I jog four or five miles every day. And I spend my spare time wondering why I never achieve anything and what I can do to gain some self-esteem. Just your normal, post-liberation basket case.

One thing I generally don't do is volunteer. After spending my twenties as a volunteer in various political and community organizations, I made a firm commitment to paid labor in my thirties. Also, since one of my jobs is as a nurse, I usually take an I-gave-at-the-office attitude. So when my oldest daughter asked if I would go with her fourth grade class on an overnight trip to Fort Point (the historic structure at the Golden Gate), I gave her my stock response: no. However, when she made it clear that not going meant turning in my motherhood papers at the door, there was no choice. Low-level guilt I can live with (in fact, for me it is a way of life); but acute, fulminant, you-call-yourself-a-mother attacks are simply unbearable. I was going to Fort Point.

She told me that her teacher said we would be living the spartan life of Civil War era soldiers at the fort, which was built in 1861 (on the site of an 18th Century Spanish fortification). We would have drills, sleep on the hard floor of unheated barracks, and take a two hour watch on the roof in the middle of the night. It was expected that the selfless parent-chaperones—i.e., me—would participate in these activities. I briefly considered copping out on the "but this is pro-military propaganda" line. However, since most of the kids in the class are black, I would glory in the politically correct stance of defending the Union against the Confederacy. Although no battles were ever fought at Fort Point, I could share the fantasy. Look out, Johnny Reb, Longfellow School is on the march. Ten-*tion!*

On the morning of the trip, I sat at my favorite cafe fortifying myself with a cafe latte and reading in the paper how a big storm was expected that night. Fort Point, you recall, is the place with the crashing waves and howling winds that is usually shown with the weather forecast on the days of the worst storms of the year. I went home and put on my two pairs of socks, pants, two sweaters, sweatshirt, and down jacket, and headed to the school to pick up my charges. I lucked out and only had to transport three relatively quiet and completely intimidated (by the impending adventure) girls—my daughter Emma, and her classmates Kimberley and Tasha.

I was priding myself on having resisted the urge to pack a hip flask of whiskey like a real soldier would. But as I drove up Park Presidio, a wave of weakness crashed up against my adult wall of strength. I quickly veered down Geary and stopped at Herman's Delicatessen. Although it was against the rules, I felt a need for some ethno-culinary support before we entered the 19th Century U.S. Army. "How about a quick bagel, girls?" I asked. "What's a bagel?" asked Tasha, who had only arrived from Pine Bluff, Arkansas, a month ago. "Jewish courage," I said.

As we approached the brick fortress which is framed by the magnificent arch that supports the Golden Gate Bridge, movie scenes flashed through my mind—*Vertigo, Dark Passage, Petulia, The Streets of San Francisco*, and many others, all filmed at the solitary beauty of Fort Point. We were assigned to our barracks. Squad Four pulled the one room with replicas of woodplank bunkbeds. I immediately grabbed the one with the authentic straw mattress exhibited on it. Other members of my squad were aghast to see a mother behaving so unself-sacrificingly. One of them, a very big, tall boy named Reggie, began to sulk.

Reggie's sulking continued through the swearing-in, the flag ceremony, and the parade drill in which the children marched under the command of a U.S. Park Service ranger dressed in authen-

233

tic Yankee regalia. All the while, Reggie sat on a bench grieving. I asked the teacher—an energetic, dedicated soul—was Reggie always this broody. Mr. Richardson replied, "He's the one who most needs this. Life hasn't been kind to Reggie. And now he can't enjoy it." Reggie got the straw bed.

The children rotated through four shifts, taking turns at the old cannon (for a mock firing), drill with the flag, kitchen duty for preparing dinner, and the infirmary. Another nurse/mother and I did the infirmary. We taught them bandaging, pulse counting (slipping in a little math), and we plied them with horror stories about 19th Century medicine and epidemics—leeches, open sewage, bite-the-bullet surgery—the works. They seemed to love it.

After a moderately tolerable, but mostly uneaten, dinner of stew and applesauce, the rangers led us on an exciting night walk. Reggie again sulked and refused to come. I think going out at night was weird enough, but into the wooded hillside below the Golden Gate Bridge with waves crashing near us—no way. On the walk, strange girls held onto me for dear life as there were periodic false sightings of snakes and landsharks. We were taken through a tunnel after the ranger checked it for that common urban pest, the ubiquitous wino. It was a beautiful night with little wind and a hillside full of calla lilies glowing in the moonlight.

At bedtime, Reggie would not settle down. We were getting locked into a power struggle. Then he shouted racist epithets at a Japanese boy. That did it. I called him a baby and a bully. He said, "I don't care what you think, Miss Lady." Sleep looked elusive. Then I got inspired. "How about if I get out of bed and tell you a story?" "Snow White!" called the strapping boy. I went over to Reggie's bed. "No, Three Little Pigs," he said. I told him the story with my best streetwise lingo, "I'm gonna huff and puff and blow the sucker down," etc. All the while, I rubbed his back. Miraculously, a little mothering worked, and Reggie was fine the rest of the trip.

We pulled the 2:00 to 4:00 a.m. guard shift. I ran around the barbette tier of the fort, climbing on stone supports that once held guns like the ten-inch Columbians that could fire bowling ball size shells two miles out to enemies that never came. The views of the ocean and the city were breathtaking. Meanwhile, the children marched with rifles, singing the army chants they had learned. I insisted we switch back to old rock and roll songs, and thanks to *Laverne and Shirley*, all my soldiers knew "Going to the Chapel, and we're going to get ma-a-a-rried," which Emma and Kim updated to "And we're going to get di-vor-or-orced." The children also took turns recording their thoughts and feelings in a log book.

That night, as I lay next to my daughter, I realized it was the first time the two of us had spent the night together (away from the rest of the family) since rooming-in at Kaiser Hospital when she was born. I remembered how soft and good she had felt as a baby and how full of hope I was for her. She was still soft and good and full of hope, and I held her hand as we went back to sleep until the 6:00 a.m. tape recording of reveille was sounded. I also thought a lot about big sad Reggie. What his grief was. What his hopes were.

The next morning, the rain finally came just as we were leaving. As the soldiers were being discharged and receiving their commendations, I checked the log book to see what, if anything, Reggie had written. There, on his page, was a near Haiku: At the fort I marched. It was boring.

Responsible for Life

I really don't know all the details of Marvin Gaye's life and career. I wasn't his biggest fan. But I have read everything about him that's been printed since his death. Just when you think you're numb to the news of death, especially celebrity deaths, the headline "Father Kills Son" shocks you with its classically tragic dimensions. I keep hearing Marvin Gaye singing:

Father, father
We don't need to escalate . . .

What was going on between Gaye junior and senior that led to the shooting is something at which we can only guess. The truth lies somewhere along that thin line between love and hate that characterizes all emotionally intense relationships. Certainly the relationship between father and son is one of the most intense.

This tragedy is compounded by several factors. The fact that Marvin Gaye was on the comeback road with a hit record in 1983 rather than at his professional nadir makes it somehow sadder. The fact that the shooting was witnessed by the mother of the victim, the wife of the perpetrator, heightens the tragedy. But I think ultimately what upsets me most in this tragedy is: what is it about being a parent that can drive a person crazy?

I loved Marvin Gaye as a performer. He was beautiful to look at, sang appealing songs, had wonderful rhythm, and adapted his music to the mood of different times. However, it was a strange coincidence that left me feeling a special bond to him. It happened that I was watching a television documentary on the life of Marvin Gaye on the night of August 18, 1974. During the show, I prematurely went into labor with my first child. It was Marvin Gaye's songs and words that were in my mind during the last moments before I underwent what clearly was the most profound change in my life—that of becoming a parent.

In retrospect, it seems to me that all of the other major events in my life—finding a partner, finding work, making friends, trying to feel a part of a community, even surviving the deaths of my parents—none of these things has changed my life as much as parenthood has. It is the one responsibility you can never really walk away from, can't change your mind about, can't get divorced from; there's absolutely no turning back. I suspect that a generation who thinks of parenthood in terms of "should I or shouldn't I have a baby" tends to underestimate the ongoing responsibility.

Not only is parenting unique because of its permanence in a transient world, it is also one of the hardest jobs to do well. Perhaps in a time and place when people felt secure in their values, certain in their outlook, and clear about the future, raising a child was no big deal. I can almost envy people who still live in this time-warp—fundamentalists, people in remote or rural cultures, lifelong ideologues. They must not agonize as I and my friends who are parents do over our children's schooling, sexual orientation, discipline, and sense of values. I often think one of the reasons why so few of us are content to be full-time parents is because work gives us a break from the continual agonizing over whether we are doing the right thing for our children.

Obviously, if your child is not seriously disturbed, is able to get along with others, and is able to learn, you haven't made a complete mess of it. But nobody ever tells you you're doing a great job. There's no merit pay for parents. However, you will certainly hear from the school, from neighbors, from the couple at the next table in the restaurant, if your child is disturbing them. And, of course, you will never get a positive progress report from your child. You'll never hear, "Thanks, Mom, I appreciate how hard you try to make the right decisions that affect my life," or "Dad, I want you to know how much I appreciate your not quit-

ting that job you hate because you need the money to support me."
Instead, what you may get is "Well, everybody else's parents let
them go to *Rocky Horror*. I hate you. I wish I lived with anybody
but you."

At those times when it seems all my efforts are in vain I feel a
sentimental yearning for that carefree time before I had children. I
go back to that night when I was watching TV and listening to
Marvin Gaye talk about his life and how much his parents had
helped him. I remember watching the old tapes of him singing "I
Heard It Through the Grapevine," and "What's Going On," and
"Ain't Nothing Like the Real Thing." And then, in an instant, my
life changed. I felt a sharp jab at the bottom of my eight months
pregnant belly. Suddenly, I was sitting in a puddle of amniotic
fluid. My bag of waters had broken. Life would never be the same.

This past April first was a happy one for me. My youngest, my
Hannah, my little Hanny Bano, turned five that day. I could feel
some pride at having raised two girls through toddlerhood. They
had not succumbed to crib death, croup, or the thousand terrors
that lie out there in a modern city. What's more, I like who they
are, what they look like, what they say. I was feeling the good side
of being a parent, that I must have done something right. Yet on
that same day, Marvin Gaye senior must have felt profoundly different. He took the life he once created.

They said a little thing—an insurance matter—triggered it.
Well, little things mean a lot. Yesterday, in the shoe store, for instance . . . I had taken Hannah and her sister, Emma, for new
shoes. Hannah got the grey sneakers with the pink lightning bolts
and velcro bindings. Emma picked out white Nikes. Then, she
talked me into getting her the fancy dress shoes with the satin
bows. An indulgence, I thought, but why not—she's a good girl.
I was distracted by the tab—one hundred dollars for three pairs of
shoes and four pairs of socks—when the girls asked if I'd take
them out for pizza. I carelessly said yes while I wrote my check.
On the way out I said I was sorry but I was too tired and had spent
too much money already. One girl said, "I hate you. You're the
worst mommy in the world." I said, "I could kill you . . ."

"How sharper than a serpent's tooth is the wrath of an un-
grateful child," says King Lear of his daughters. This wrath can

238

carry me into a rage that borders on madness. The life I labored for and continue to support can so casually insult me. In an angry instant I get a glimpse across the horizon: I see a parent gone insane trying to undo what he had done.

Saint Fred

And so it comes to pass that, at this time of the year, we recount the story of Fred Christ. Who was Fred Christ? you ask. That, of course, was always Fred's problem. He was the kid brother of Jesus Christ. Fred hated being described that way although inevitably he always was. So great was his brother's reputation that poor Fred went through life—not to mention history—unrecognized, unsung, unadored. Talk about your tough acts to follow.

Mary's birthing of Fred was so mundane—in marked contrast to her first delivery—as to go unreported. Oh sure, if you're born in a manger, the son of the Holy Ghost, on the night some super nova appears in the sky, then they flock around, don't they? Then the *National Enquirer* sends half its staff to cover: Miracle Baby Born in Bethlehem; Mother Claims Father is The Father!

Not only was there room at the inn for Fred, but Joseph and Mary were able to book a lovely little bed and breakfast on the outskirts of Nazareth. No wise men attended—only Naomi Schmulovitz, the hot new midwife of Jerusalem. In those days, women gave birth without anesthesia or prepared childbirth classes. So it came to pass that even though her oldest son was staying with his grandparents, during the course of the birthing experience, Mary frequently mentioned him, screaming "Jesus Christ! Jesus Christ!" with all her might.

Even as a young child, Fred remembered basking in his brother's glory. It was always "sweet baby Jesus" this and "sweet baby

Jesus" that. Never a mention of sweet baby Fred. At school, Fred tried hard to apply himself but no matter how hard he worked the brutal comparisons were invariably made.

His mother was totally insensitive to the problem. A workshop on parenting skills was surely in order but Bethlehem was kind of therapy-poor back then. When he was ten, Fred presented his mother with a poem he had written on the meaning of life. "That's nice, Fred honey," she said, "but Jesus was doing stuff like that in pre-school." There was no pleasing that woman. Talk about your Jewish mothers.

As a teenager, Fred was always trying to get the contemplative Jesus to come with him to dances and toga parties, but the older brother was standoffish. When Fred would describe to him the beautiful girls they might meet there, Jesus would refuse and begin to lecture him about "temptations." "Would you come off that holier-than-thou attitude," Fred pleaded, "it's time to have some fun. *Party*. Jesus Christ, you're not getting any younger."

But Jesus had no time for fun and games. He was busy working in one of a chain of self-help carpentry shops that Joseph had established. They were going to call it Christ and Sons but Fred adamantly refused to go into that line of work. So they decided to call it the Savior-Builder Center.

Fred, meanwhile, was getting started in the chariot business and had built a reputation for quality products. His BCW—Bethlehem Chariot Works—was able to outsell the closest competitor, Chariots of Tyre, and the company was grossing in the neighborhood of ten mil. The demographics worked in his favor. What with the anticipated influx of the Teutonic hordes, BCW made a killing on the export market.

Just as business was going great for Fred, the trouble started. Jesus had gotten involved in politics and was causing quite a bit of trouble with the Romans. His brother saw he was getting in deep and because Fred worried about him he tried to warn Jesus to cool it: "You keep this up and they'll nail you to a cross."

Around this time, Fred met a lovely woman, Ethel of Galilee, and they got married. They begot Ralph, Anita, Neal, Joanne, and Little Ricky. Fred was named vice-president in charge of product development and finally Chief Executive Officer at BCW. His mother, however, remained unimpressed. Fred's worst fears for his brother had come to pass but even after his death Jesus' reputation grew. In the eyes of Mary, product development just couldn't hold a candle to dying for the sins of others.

Fred, however, continued to prosper and provide for his family despite the notoriety of his brother. Indeed, Jesus' reputation was proving to be something of a political hot potato for Fred and so he decided to change his name to something less Jewish sounding, Fred Cowan.

The name change, while a practical move at the time, sealed the fate of Fred Christ. Had he maintained his family name he would surely have made it to history not to mention the San Francisco *Chronicle* (Ear Muff Found; Believed to Have Belonged to Fred Christ—Part One in a Series on the Ear Muff of Turin). Fred, of course, would have loved to tell it like it was back then but nobody cared to hear the gospel according to Fred.

So it has fallen to me to tell the not-so-greatest story ever told. How, you ask, did it come to pass?

It happened last Christmas. Having partaken of the ritual drinking of the eggnog I sat (slumped really) down on the couch and began to feel a warm radiance pass through me. I was staring at the fireplace where the stockings were hung from the menorah with care and trying to imagine Santa Claus arriving. No matter how old I am or what my religious beliefs, I have always been fascinated with the idea of the man in red, the sleigh full of gifts, the all night flight to every good little boy and girl in the world. I want to believe in that. And as I was imagining him up there, suddenly a figure emerged from my fireplace. He was wearing a beige toga and knee-high leather cross-strap sandals.

"Where did you get that fine footwear?" I asked him. "Sandals Unlimited went out of business a year ago."

"You can still pick up a pair in the West Village. But that's not why I am here. My name is Fred Cowan nee Christ. I am here to tell you my story. I ask only that you get the quotes right."

We talked through the night. Fred insisted on boring me with little details like how he was better than Jesus at basketball and stuff like that. Finally, I said to him, "Fred, it's been close to 2000 years now and still you bear a grudge. Isn't it time to let go of your anger?"

"That's why I want you to tell my story, the story of an ordinary man who happened to be the brother—make that half-brother—of the alleged son of God." As an example of his obscurity, Fred reminded me, "When's the last time you heard about a kid running home from Hebrew School because he was pursued by a gang of strapping gentiles shouting: 'Cowan-killer! Cowan-killer!' All I've ever wanted was a little attention. Get me that and I'll rest in peace."

With that he vanished, faded into the soot and dust of my uncleaned fireplace. And the rest is, by now, legend. Fred Christ—working stiff, family man, sibling rival. Come on, folks, let's give him a break. Oh, come let us adore him.

Panic in Wheedle Park

Raising kids in Berkeley—or "parenting" as it's fashionable to say—can seem like an exercise in frustration. Take last Sunday morning, for example. A beautiful day. The kind of day, I foolishly thought, a family *should* take a walk.

OK, I admit it, I had a bee in my bonnet. I wielded a heavy hand. I committed an unconscionable act against the very nature of New Age let-the-kid-do-its-thing (even play-with-its-thing) Parenting. I coerced them. First, I forced them to get dressed. Two innocent girls, ages 3 and 8—before 10:00 a.m. on a Sunday morning, yet. Brutal, you say? You can't imagine what happened next.

I made them walk. That's right, I forced them to lift their lovely little china-flats up and down on the pavement. The eight-year-old was pretty easy. After all these years, I have, of course, broken her spirit. The three-year-old, however, remains a complete rebel to the iron will of her mother. She will not be moved. Asserting her human rights she employs her favorite tactic, the sit-down strike. On every block. She usually waits until some UC student, newly liberated from her own brutal parents, comes along to glance sympathetically at the poor child who is being made to walk.

When the sit-down strike fails, my little Rosa Luxembourg moves on to her next favorite and frequently most successful tactic: the full decibel assault. With a range and a power that challenges Beverly Sills she blasts forth her lament. But thank God it's

10:30 a.m. Sunday morning in Berkeley. The lotus eaters are still asleep. Not even the tormented screams of a forced-to-walk child can penetrate these bungalows long used to barking dogs, screeching motorcycles, and amplified guitars.

My husband is perhaps the innocent victim here. Dragged into my program, he becomes my unwitting partner in child coercion. His mistake: not having a plan for Sunday morning.

After a few blocks of sit-downs and scream-outs, even the little one is in line. She tries a few feeble bargaining positions. "Can I get some gum?" "No." "I'm hungry!" "We're not going to a store." "I'm thirsty. I need some ice cream." "Sorry."

Now that we're out and moving, albeit like leaden prisoners on a chain gang, I decide to pull out the carrot—the good news—the raison d'être for the walk. In the corner of my eye, I recalled seeing, several days earlier, new play equipment at the neighborhood park, "Live Oak." "We're going to Live Oak," I announce buoyantly. "*They've* put up some wonderful new climbing structures!"

Later, in retrospect, I realized how I was essentially undone by that vague pronoun reference; but nobody else asked who *they* were. All my poor, beaten girls could ask in their piteous little voices was, "How much further to Live Oak?"

Finally, we made it. The long, tortuous, six block journey was behind us. The life-threatening race across the Shattuck Freeway was history. There through the autumn elms of Berryman Street stood Live Oak Park. Like a mirage gleaming in the sun, the new, two-sided slide beckoned.

My husband and I, weak from the false victory of making the girls walk, began to search for a bench. It was then that the braided lady in overalls approached us. Wielding a hack saw and a shovel, she crossed the sandbox towards us.

Some little physiological warning light went off as she approached. Some slight tensing around my sixth cervical spine told me this Sunday morning Sybil bore me no happy news. I guess I always knew I shouldn't have gone off in Berkeley in search of "family" recreation. Better to force the kids to sit still in the Cafe Med while I down my coffee or let them loose on Art Goldberg and the other hangers-out.

Last week I tried the Tilden merry-go-round. Not bad if you don't mind Castro Street and are in the mood to explain to your kids about Gay People. Then there's the potential embarrassment of the three-year-old approaching the lovers, gawking at them, and shouting "Mommy, why is he kissing him?" I know the world is full of opportunities for learning. I'm just looking for some time off.

The week before I tried the Berkeley Flea Market. I guess it's escapist of me but I didn't want to have to explain to the kids why I thought the man at the booth started beating the woman who stole his records. Who is Carole Terwilliger Meyers and what fun things is she doing with her kids in the Bay Area today?

Sure, I was looking for something easy when I came to the park. Something along the let-the-kids-play-while-the-grown-ups-talk motif. But the braided lady came up to me, stared into my eyes, and said, "Are you here to help us put up the play equipment?"

"No," I answered honestly, but naively.

"Don't you want your children to be able to use the playground?" she fired back.

Whoa, wait a minute. I didn't realize that I had stumbled into a from-each-according-to-his-ability-to-each-according-to-his-swingset situation. Somewhere in my head I heard a young Dan Siegal shouting, "Let's take the Park." But Dan, now that I'm old and feeble and exhausted from six blocks of disciplinary duty, I don't want a Peoples Park. I want a Department of Parks and Recreation to make my park for me. I thought of falling down on my knees before the braided lady: Please, please give us a day off. This is parent abuse. We worked all week. Yesterday we did the shopping and the laundry. Please, lady, don't make me build a park today.

I thought about her. What a saint. She probably had four kids at home throwing oatmeal at her. She probably works all day at a word processor but still finds time for face painting at night. I'll bet she never *made* her kids walk.

But instead I got mad at her. "OK, kids, we're leaving," and I grab the poor, bewildered girls (who were displeased by the "unfinished" playground anyway). She can't guilt trip me, this madonna of the motorskills development. Oh no, I've been steeled on the politics of guilt. I've run the gauntlet of Free Clinic boxes and grey whale savers down by the Co-op. I've learned to throw out personal letters from Ed Asner and Gloria Steinem and Paul Newman as if they were so much garbage. (The Republicans don't give you the politics of guilt. They don't start with the assumption that people are nice. They know us to be the self-serving scumbags we are.)

The braided lady eventually gives up on me. She sees a new couple with baby in stroller arriving. They too leave the park. I find them at the French Hotel drinking cafe lattes while the kid who could've used the new play equipment sits strapped in his stroller at the Cafe. They tell me the braided lady followed them for a block before she gave up.

So much for a family outing in Berkeley. We come home. My husband is free to do the crossword. I start reading *Edie,* the biography of a great American speedfreak. The kids are planted in front of the tube watching the Shirley Temple reruns. Someday, when no one is looking, we'll sneak over to Live Oak Park and cop a slide. Like we used to say: It's a free country.

The Kids Are Alright

Once, Howdy, you were my whole existence. You pulled my strings, Doody-boy. When I heard, "Hey, kids, what time is it?" it wasn't four-thirty at all. No, it was Doody-time—time to escape from all those people who didn't love me, who told me to be quiet, stop shouting, stop running, stop acting "like a wild Indian." In Doodyville, I was wanted. I knew I had found my people in you, Howdy, in Buffalo Bob, and in Clarabell the Clown whose seltzer bottle I dreamed of squirting at my enemies in some pre-terrorist fantasy. There was also mean old Mr. Bluster (who looked like my mean old Uncle Charlie) to hate. And, there was the Flubadub to laugh at, and—especially for me—there was Princess Summerfallwinterspring. If I was a wild Indian like all the grown-ups said, then at least I was like her.

It was all because of you, Howdy Doody, that I was not alone. I did whatever you asked me to, cowboy. I held my nose and drank my Ovaltine; I gobbled down bowls of Rice Krispies, listening for the snap, crackle, and pop; I made Mommy put Bosco in my milk. The fact that your name also represented a certain bodily substance that we were forbidden to talk about—why, that only increased your mythical powers in the Peanut Gallery community.

Friends at home, perhaps you too remember some, ahem, *role model*, some television character that you wanted to be like. Maybe it was Captain Video or Captain Satellite or Captain Kangaroo. Maybe you remember Smiling Ed and Sabu the Elephant Boy and Froggy the Gremlin, or Kukla, Fran, and Ollie, or Shari Lewis and Lambchop, or Mary Hartline, or Bozo (no, not the President, the clown, silly). Or, maybe you remember Miss Nancy from *Romper Room*. Oh no! Did I say *remember*? Friends at home: Miss Nancy is alive and well and taping in Oakland!

I hadn't quite appreciated the fact that Miss Nancy incarnate was just moments from my door until last spring when Hannah, recently turned five, asked, "Mommy, can I be on *Romper Room*?" Later, halfway into the application process, after we have sent in the photo, after we have composed the essay on why Hannah would make a good Romper Stomper, I begin to wonder: what will the neighbors think? You see, I know that someday when Hannah is on that therapist's couch listing all the things her parents did wrong, right there next to "let me eat junk food" and "used sarcasm as a discipline method" will be: "let me watch TV." Even as I write this, I can see the brows going up all over town: so, now we know about Alice Kahn—the one who lets her children watch (tsk, tsk) television. Worse yet is the fact that even though Romper Room has won endorsements from groups across the country, your average hepcat Berklander views the program as "sickeningly sweet." If you're going to sacrifice your child's brain before the tube, it had better be one of those hip, Sesame Street-wise, inner-city-type shows.

Nevertheless, here we are, driving down Martin Luther King, Jr. Way to the KTVU studios at Jack London Square, and the tension is mounting. It has been mounting all morning as Hannah put on the white lace dress with the pink sash that she picked out for the show. She has never worn a dress like this before in her life. We bought it off the $2.99 rack at a schlock house in New York, fighting our way among Puerto Rican mothers and Chassidic Jewish fathers for the bargain. Hannah obviously feels like a queen in this dress, but we are not bowing fast enough. She's getting edgy.

I have packed the bag with a change of clothes and a non-candy snack as Miss Nancy's letter instructed. On this Saturday, we will tape the Monday and Tuesday morning shows and return the following Saturday to do Wednesday through Friday. (You try explaining this manipulation of reality to a child who just wants to know, "But when will I *be* on television?")

As we pass Children's Hospital (and I give my usual silent prayer of thanks that we're not going there), Hannah announces,

"I'm not going to do the shows." "You have to," says her sister, Emma. "No, I don't." Then the screaming begins. Then the shoving. Then the hitting. "You girls stop it," my husband and I are screaming. Drop me at the corner, I think. I want to run away from it all. Why are we doing this? Whatever made me imagine that we could succeed as a family? It's a trap, a cyclone, and I'm stuck in the center. Let me out of here.

By the time we arrive at the security gate of "There's Only One 2," we are calm and serene, a model family ready to move into a model home in Mr. Rogers' neighborhood. We enter the lobby where the other Romper Stompers are sitting with their families. The performance anxiety is so thick you can cut it with a knife. Compared to the tension level in there, our family seems as relaxed as street corner winos. Only an occasional "Be still, Becky" interrupts the silence.

The children gathered around the monitor in the KTVU lobby—watching Steve McQueen in *The Blob*, no less—are a capsule of current-day kidobilia. There's a Cabbage Patch dress, rainbow Velcros, a Smurf backpack, and a Snow White dress (a reminder that even from the grave Uncle Walt is still calling the shots). I wonder how the first Romper Stompers looked as they sat around the studio in Baltimore in 1954 waiting for the first broadcast. Was there a little boy in a coonskin cap next to a kid with mouse ears or a girl in a gray felt skirt with pink poodle dogs? Were they clutching a hula-hoop or a bubblegum-colored Spaulding rubber ball, or a Tiny Tears doll? Were their parents asking repeatedly, "Do you want to go to the bathroom?"

A perky young woman wearing a headset comes into the lobby. She is Jamie Hutchison, stage manager for *Romper Room and Friends*. "OK, Do Bees, ready to go?" We follow her through the maze of corridors in the airy attractive building that looks out onto the Oakland estuary. We pass the news room which I am tempted to rush into just for a peek, but, imagining the headline: "Mother Runs Amok in Studio," I proceed with the others into the Green Room. There, we leave our stuff and the parents ask five or six more times, "Are you sure you don't have to go?" A few mothers park their daughters in front of the enormous bulb-studded make-up mirror for a last minute hairdo check.

We now follow Hutchison past the *Dialing for Dollars* set (the only non-news or non-public affairs program that originates at the local station besides *Romper Room*). We pass the huge lighting board with hundreds of wires going off in a million directions, and enter the chilly studio. There, standing in between the grassy outdoor set and the schoolroom indoor set is Miss Nancy herself—not larger than life, exactly, but surprisingly tall nonetheless. She immediately takes control of the situation, going up to each child and shaking hands and calling them by name. "Hi, Aaron, do you know who I am? I'm not Dennis Richmond, am I?"

One by one, she takes Becky, Nicole, Edgar, and Rashaun on the set. Then she says, "Oh, you must be Hannah. And this is your sister, Emma." Hannah's eyes light up like a sunrise as she says, "Hi, Miss Nancy" and she takes her hand. I can practically see her stepping into that little box—a fantasy I'm sure every child has had—and entering the make-believe world of televisionland. She's in the looking glass now.

With no further ado, the *Romper Room* theme song plays. Let the games begin. They are actually taping! No rehearsals, no nothing. What you get is what you see. While the friends at home are hearing:
Bing Bang Bing Bong
Hey nonny new
Rompity Stompity
Romper Room . . .
Miss Nancy continues her introductory patter. "How many of you are in kindergarten? First grade? Married?" Then the show begins. I'm amazed. There's just Jamie Hutchison and two camera men and all the fancy computerized equipment you can imagine—boards that control the klieg lights, dangling microphones, powerful cameras that can catch the most elusive of spirits.

The parents and siblings are sitting in a corner in two rows of chairs, craning our necks to see beyond the cameras, watching on the monitors what we cannot see right in front of us. When we do get a close-up of our special sweetie-pie darling, we light up with pride. Our mouths freeze in smiles that seem ready to crack into a flood of tears. I see Hannah's face fill up the TV screen and I am just overcome. She is so beautiful. Surely, I have done something right in my life to deserve such a child.

Miss Nancy is talking without any cue cards. "Today, friends

251

at home, we're going to talk about eco-*nom*-ics. Hmm-mmm."
Soon she is asking Hannah to go get the flag for the pledge of allegiance. Oh, no, I worry. Hannah is a Berkeley kid. She won't know the pledge. Everyone will be shocked. They'll have to stop the tape. But Hannah says the pledge right along with the others. (Later, she explains, she learned it from television. That, of course, is the risk of the medium. You never know what they'll pick up.)

They go to a cartoon segment featuring a character named Granny Cat. The cartoon, like the basic format of the show, comes from Baltimore, home of Romper Room Enterprises, a family business that was started by Bert Claster, husband of Miss Nancy Claster (the first Miss Nancy) and father of Miss Sally (who succeeded her mother and is now vice-president of the company). The show is the longest running preschool program on television. Romper Room Enterprises sends out format scripts and cartoons to its various affiliates (or "markets," as they say in the biz), including Miss Nancy in the Bay Area, Miss Soko in Los Angeles, Miss Peggy in Moline, Miss Martie in Witchita, Miss Diane in Lincoln, and Miss Molly in New York. The six Misses reach 1.4 million children in 35 US cities, Canada, New Zealand, Japan, Borneo, Australia, Thailand, and Saudi Arabia. This is the Jackson's Victory Tour of children's entertainment. Miss Nancy, of course, adds her own personal and local touches. I think of the Berkeley McDonald's with its ferns and natural wood trim and old-fashioned pictures.

Miss Nancy is asking the friends at home what they know about gasoline. "We put it in any vehicle that has an *internal combustion engine*—oh boy." She brings out the familiar Do Bee symbol, a maniacally smiling insect, a blatant example of speciesism if ever there was one. "Do Bee careful with money," Miss Nancy is saying, "it's as precious as gasoline." At this point the parents in the corner of the studio gasp. A man has entered holding a chimpanzee in leopardskin diapers. (I wonder if they show the punk chimp in Borneo or if this is for Oakland's eyes only.)

The first show is over and we are told to go to the Green Room for the kids to change clothes so that on the set it will look like another day. In the dressing room, it is strictly the mothers' trip. One mom unceremoniously yanks out her daughter's barrettes. "You're going to have a side ponytail and that's that." Another mother scolds, "When Miss Nancy talks to you, you answer. You understand? I don't want you to be wandering around looking all over the place. You hear me?"

The dads look disgusted but seem powerless to stop it. They mostly sit around eating the raisins and nuts that were brought for the children's snack. One dad has a portable battery-operated TV set and is watching a boxing match. There is a television in the Green Room but it will only show Channel Two. I wonder if the dads are unhappy about the number the moms are doing on the little girls. I suspect that they feel they have no right to intervene since the women do most of the child-raising. (Interestingly, the two little boys on the show have no dads with them.)

Hannah comes running off the set saying, "I love it." She quickly changes clothes, combs her hair, and is ready to go back for more. She pauses in the girls' dressing room to watch a mother spray her daughter's hair. She has never seen anything like it.

I worry that Emma, my oldest daughter, will feel left out of all this attention. Most of the parents are communicating a "get out of the way" attitude to the non-performing siblings. Miss Nancy has let them know that they will be introduced on the air in the second show. Miss Nancy takes care of everybody.

I try to chat with some of the parents, but they are too tense to talk. I go up to the brother of one of the little stars and ask, "Were you ever on television?" He looks at his shoes and his dad immediately shouts, "You look at the lady when she speaks to you." I feel guilty for causing him the trouble.

What is this experience for the parents—a quiz? Is it the final exam in Preschool Child-Rearing 101? Why have we decided to subject our children to the microscope of the camera? I thought it was for fun (for them), but maybe it's really to see what we have done, what we have created. And, to the extent that the mothers have poured their heart, soul, time, and dreams into these children, they expect a return on their investment. They expect the children to perform, to show that in five short years they have mastered the social code. I realize that I have my expectations too. While I had decided that Hannah's natural beauty needed little enhancement from elaborate hairstyles or that her personality and intelligence required no coaching from me, certainly a part of me was praying, "Please, don't let my child pick her nose or masturbate on television."

By the second show, I am in awe of Miss Nancy. She is a bundle of energy, poise, and good humor. The fact that *Romper Room* goes on the air without rehearsal, lacks the big production budgets of shows like *Sesame Street*, and manages to tape five shows in one afternoon, with two groups of kids, is a testimony to her skills as performer and producer. She is a benevolent dominatrix, an attractive woman with a jaw so strong she avoids profile shots. Her toughness is tempered by enormous, expressive eyes and dimples you can sink a fist in. She is one of the few women I have ever been able to get my husband to confess he finds attractive.

The Tuesday show begins and we get more singing ("Just me and my body / having some fun . . ."), magic mirror, safety chief, more talk about eco-nom-ics, and more cartoons. While the commercials and cartoons are running, Miss Nancy readies the kids and the set for the next segment. Meanwhile, the floor crew kibitzes about such diverse topics as legalized gambling ("I tell you we're going to get dog racing") and their careers ("Can you put *Romper Room* on your resume?"). At one point Jamie Hutchison quips, "If we could record headset conversations we could blackmail everybody in the building."

Emma gets introduced on this show and, as her face fills up the screen, I think it isn't because I'm her mother—anyone can see she is just gorgeous. And then the chimpanzee in diapers is brought on to plug Marine World. He grabs at Miss Nancy's eyes and plays with her face as she continues talking, without blinking, about treating animals well.

We come back the following Saturday to finish taping the shows that will begin on Monday. Some of the family tension has diminished. The girl who had to have the side ponytail now has her hair set in a perfect symmetrical roll of curls. I am able to talk to two of the mothers. Both run family day-care centers out of their homes, one in Pleasanton, the other in Redwood City. One mother comments, "The kids will never get this much attention again."

Most of the fathers have begged off this time. My husband comes, but he and Emma get bored and snoop around the prop area where the remains of *Creature Features* are being laid to rest. I later find them in the Green Room munching on the snack we brought for Hannah. That preschool atmosphere is contagious is evidenced by my husband's regressive tone when he says, "Guess who we just saw? Elaine Coral, the newscaster, came right in here and combed her hair and *you* missed it. And we saw the sportscaster Mark Ibanez's Cadillac in his reserved parking space—the biggest Cadillac on earth. You missed *that* too." He is sitting there smirking and eating pretzels, and then he starts singing, "Rompity, stompity Romper Room . . ." What next? A request to sit on Miss Nancy's lap?

While Thursday morning's show is being taped, a father walks into the studio. His wife looks up at him and glares, "*Your* daughter was asking for you," she says. I see him shrink down into himself like Jack being stuffed back into the box.

One boy, Edgar, merely changes his shirt for the next show. His mother is upset because she brought along a pair of pants that are too big, and she forgot his belt. Not wanting to risk his pants falling down on the air, she decides against a complete outfit change. Back on the set, when Miss Nancy holds up a piece of rope and asks, "What do we use this for?" Edgar shouts out, "A belt!"

The children are singing a counting song and counting parts of their body. Hannah is standing next to Miss Nancy:

Count on your fingers
Count on your toes
That's how the counting goes.
Count on yourself,
Count on your friends . . .

Someone whispers, "She touched Miss Nancy's butt!" Miss Nancy, however, is not fazed by it. Miss Nancy could mug and ad lib her way through anything. "Boys and girls, do you know how many states there are? Do you know what state we live in? No, not confusion . . ."

She shows a cartoon about greed and then asks Hannah, "Do you know who's greedy?" I feel my knuckles popping up. I feel my spinal muscles contracting. I know she's going to say, "My mom." But no, she names the appropriate character in the cartoon. Phew.

By the time we get through with the fifth show we are relieved. I am amazed that the six five-year-olds made it through without going bananas. Afterwards, we celebrate with dinner at Jack London Square. Probably all the other families are celebrating too. We will all remember this special event as a happy occasion, a story for family legend. Like other family occasions—graduation, a piano recital, even childbirth itself—the pain will be forgotten.

A few days after the shows have been aired, after my child has been immortalized in a video cassette (maybe by the time she's fifty we'll own a VCR and can play it), I go back to KTVU to interview Miss Nancy. I don't even know what to call her. All I know is she works hard for her money.

Entering her office is kind of a shock. It is a tiny subspace in a maze of little spaces divided by four-foot-high padded walls. Miss Nancy, adored by thousands, in that tiny little cubby—for shame, KTVU. It's like finding the Tooth Fairy in a fleabag hotel.

From this office, Miss Nancy plans her broadcasts, selects from the hundreds of applicants the little Romper Stompers who will make the show, and personally answers all her mail with an autographed photo or a Do Bee postcard. At one point I ask her if she gets a clothing allowance. She does not, she says; it's a sore point since the IRS just audited her and refused her wardrobe deduction. She opens the little closet in the cubby, which is stuffed with dresses and shoes, and says, "This is Miss Nancy, her clothes, her shoes, her make-up. Anybody could jump in this closet and be Miss Nancy."

Actually, it's hard to imagine anybody being a better Miss Nancy than Miss Nancy. She started out her life as Ruby Rose Visek of Milwaukee, Wisconsin, an only child whose mother worked ("so I watched a lot of television"). After studying radio and television at Madison, she got a credential to teach, and worked in the public schools in Connecticut with disabled kids and as a speech pathologist. But her resume also includes such non-standard work experience as: "tapdancing box of 'Old Golds', Gay Freedom Day Parade" and "Game Show Contestant: $18,000 winner *Name That Tune*; $300 winner *$20,000 Pyramid*." The latter had her playing opposite a young man named David Letterman.

Her work experience also includes doing stand-up comedy at the Holy City Zoo and the Boarding House. This explains the witty patter and the mugging—but "Miss Nancy, doing sex and coke jokes?" "Well," she says, "I didn't do *that*."

In person, without the TV make-up, she is even more vivacious and attractive. She is wearing a bright pink knit dress that is cut down low in back. I'm trying to figure out where Ruby Rose stops and Miss Nancy begins. I suspect that she occasionally has the same problem.

"I think it's finally happened. I have finally become Miss Nancy. I'm proud of that. I think Miss Nancy is a *great person*," she laughs. "She's warm and loving and she enjoys what she does. I have to be her because I might meet a kid somewhere. Like when I was in Marshall's in Newark buying my *Romper Room* clothes, I met a little girl. I go there once a year and fill up a shopping cart. My clothes have to be colorful and lightweight and slimming and movable, so it's a big deal. Anyway, I'd been there three hours and I suddenly realized I didn't have enough to pay for all this stuff. Then this little girl comes up to me and says, 'You *are* Miss Nancy. *I* knew it.' Her mother looked embarrassed. They'd obviously been arguing about who I was. So I smiled and said, 'Yes I am.' What I wanted to say was, 'Do you have any money? I need help!' "

Off camera, Miss Nancy uses the name Ruby Petersen (her ex-husband's name). She found her job through a want-ad in the *Chronicle* advertising for a teacher. When she was one of the ten finalists out of 180 applicants, she was asked by Miss Sally (vice-president of Romper Room Enterprises) if she would consider changing her name. Miss Ruby presumably sounded too racy— "The teacher with the heart of gold?" quips Ruby Petersen. She says that even the dress she's wearing wouldn't be appropriate. "Why?" I ask. "It's short. It's knit. It's cut low in back. Too va-va-*voom*," she says.

Although she wanted to be a performer, Petersen views her work on *Romper Room* as mainly teaching. "Television is a dirty, nasty, disgusting business. I wouldn't be in it if it weren't for the kids. I've seen over a thousand children on the air and I get 50 to 100 letters a week from kids at home who think of me as their teacher. Maybe they have an older sister or brother who goes off to school. Just look at the pictures, Alice."

She's careful to use my name often, to personalize our conversation, to make me feel special as she does with the children. I had also noticed how hard she tried to balance the children on the show, racially and sexually, and how hard she worked to give them all equal attention. She opens a drawer stuffed with letters, kid art, and photos for Miss Nancy. She holds up the snapshots like a proud parent. "When I perform, I don't think of a huge audience. I think of this three-year-old in front of the TV with her blanket." She passes me the photo. "Oh, here's me." The last is a child standing next to a TV set that has Miss Nancy performing on it.

"When I saw Rita Moreno in 1970 on the *Electric Company*, dressed as a tomato, I thought, that's it for me. That's my ambition. I have my life's work cut out. I do make more than a teacher—not that much more, but I love my job. I know how hard it is for teachers now, especially in California. You're almost embarrassed to say you're a teacher because people feel sorry for you. They know you're working for a low salary, and a lot of people think working with children is the worst thing you can do.

"When I started in this job I had people tell me they thought it was the most repulsive thing. There must be something wrong with me that I could stand working with kids, or I must be a complete phoney. To me, it's like being in a religion, like being a nun. People say, you want to live that way, *cloistered*, surrounded by children. There are a lot of people who just don't value being with kids. But I prefer children to adults. They're short and I'm tall." She laughs. "But really, it's all honesty and wonderment with children. You have a chance to explore everything anew. Children don't disappoint you. With adults, it's not always that way."

On the wall of Ruby Petersen's cubby, along with all the letters and drawings and photos from children, is a large picture of KGO reporter Bob MacKenzie. (MacKenzie recently left KTVU news.) "He's my boyfriend," Petersen explains. "Sometimes we'll be out together, and adults will come up to us and say, 'Oh, Bob, you're so wonderful,' and he'll say, 'This is Miss Nancy from *Romper Room*.' They'll go, 'That's nice. We love you, Bob.' Then a kid will come up and say, 'My God, you're Miss Nancy!' and I'll say, 'This is Bob MacKenzie from Channel 7,' and they'll say, 'Very nice. Oh, Miss Nancy, we love *Romper Room*.'

"I remember the first time I got recognized. I was at Fairyland

and this three-year-old looked at me and stopped in her tracks. My heart melted. I gave her a Do Bee sticker and my picture. I think I was more excited than she was. Sometimes when I send out pictures I think, these are going to be on refrigerators all around the world. Once, some friends of mine in Greece had my photo on their wall. A family from California was visiting them and the little girl saw it and she said, 'You *know* Miss Nancy?' They, of course, knew me as Ruby from Connecticut."

I ask Ruby Petersen and, later, stage manager Jamie Hutchison about the potential for mishap on a show that is done virtually live (they do almost no editing.) Petersen explains that she listens selectively and edits, on the air, the off-mike comments of the kids. "For instance, once I asked the kids the color of the blue box I was holding. A little girl raised her hand and said, 'My grandmother died.' She was not on mike, so I just said, 'That's right, blue,' and kept going. She was a little confused but happy that she got a positive response. Later, I expressed my sympathy.

"One time, we did stop the tape. A little girl looked at me and said, 'Me go pee-pee.' Odd language, I thought, and then she just blasted off her pants with this huge torrent. It was a bigger puddle than the llama made the week before."

"Every so often we have a stage mother like Momma Rose in *Gypsy*," says Jamie Hutchison. "We had a girl on who only wanted certain toys and she'd start crying if she didn't get them. Her mother screamed from the sidelines, 'You get up and play. Do you hear me?' Finally, the mother walked on the set and started spanking her.

"Ruby is very good at sending subtle signals on the air," Hutchison says. Once, when Jack Parmeter was on the floor crew, Ruby was doing jack-in-the-box, but the kids were watching the monitor so what you heard on the air was, *Jack-in-the-box, Jack-in-the-box, Jack turn the monitor, Jack-in-the-box.*"

On the set, Hutchison never says, "Ruby." She explains: "Miss Nancy is someone they never thought they'd see and talk to. It's important for kids to have the illusion of a person to look up to. I want to leave that illusion. I love to watch their faces when they see her and meet her. They're shocked. It's really *her*. I suppose they thought she was just this little thing in the tube. Others are scared to death. They scream and run. Some are overwhelmed by the studio and the cameras. It does look medical. I thought when I was little the equipment and the wires looked like something in the doctor's office."

Hutchison grew up in Hayward, Calif., the daughter of a KGO-TV engineer and "a mom who wanted to be sure our biggest problem was what to do after school." She watched *Romper Room* as a child and believes it's been democratized since her Do Bee days twenty years ago. "I remember when I was little, they used to pray. They don't do that anymore. And they used to have expensive toys with the *Romper Room* label—now it's just stuff any kind can find around the house. Also, they used to have Do Bee and Don't Bee. Now we only have Do Bee. It's all positive."

Ruby Petersen also insists the show has changed with the times. She visibly starches up when I ask her if she doesn't think the show is just a bit too . . . well, *square*. "No, I don't, I truly don't think it's square. Now, sometimes I'll look at myself riding around in the safety chief hat and think, is this any way to make a living? But it is fun. The music is different now, much more hip. You think it's the same, Alice but it's not. Do Bee is about it. We have all new puppet characters, and they speak to subjects like moving away. I always refer to the grown-up at home, not mommy and daddy. I don't say, 'In your backyard,' but, 'in the hallway of your building or wherever you live.' I say 'friends at home,' because we stress getting the child involved. We reflect our environment—the market we're in."

I ask Ruby Petersen, who is almost 39, if she has children. "I'm sorry that I don't have kids now, but it was never right. Perhaps that's why I can do this. People who live in a strictly adult world don't understand why I love my work. They're just so maxed-out being warm or patient or giving to their boss or whoever that they cannot imagine giving any more. But they don't know what they'd get back working with kids.

"Sometimes, I'll be driving up to Tahoe and I'll pass the names of towns that I've gotten mail from and I'll think, 'There's a Do Bee there. They'd die if they knew I was in town. Maybe I should call them.' It's fun to think that there are people who are going to remember you or have this postcard from you for thirty years. It's a kick."

I Remember Silky

Tolstoy said it: "Happy families are all alike." Well, my family was different. And strangest of all was my father, a man who introduced himself as "the Silk Shirt Kid" until his dying day. They were all weird— Silky (as we called him), my mother (aka "Fonzo"), and my sister, Myrna Lou. In this family, I was the sane one. I think that's why I've always liked living in Berkeley. It's the only place, outside of my family, where I've felt like the sane one.

He died half my life ago, Silky. I can certainly recall the bitter feelings I had towards him, the anger at the way his madness dictated our lives. But, more often, in dreams, in reflections, or in crystal clear memories inspired by an old song or a smell or, perhaps, a movie image, I remember warmth, loving feelings, and the benefits of his uniqueness. It's fortunate, I think, that our relationships with people who are important to us don't stop with their death. There really is all of time to work things out.

Father's Day inevitably brings forth the question: who was that man I called my daddy? When I look at the Hallmark cards with pictures of duck hunters, or men in V-neck sweaters, or pipes laid casually on leatherbound books, they seem no more appropriate to evoke his memory than they seemed proper greetings when he was alive. I can still hear the rabbi who spoke at his funeral saying, "He was a quiet violin playing in the background of life." This man did not know my father. My father was a bassoon blasting from front row center.

261

Let me tell you what it was like going out with him in the old Chicago neighborhood. He'd take me on long walks from the time I was four or five years old. We'd start out by going to the shoeshine parlor. There, Silky would get his big felt hat blocked and his shoes shined while a man named Jesse, who worked there and was a ventriloquist, would throw his voice so that my shoes appeared to be talking to me. It was at the shine parlor that I noticed one of my father's bizarre traits. He would imitate the ethnic style of whatever person he happened to be speaking with. I think other men of his generation did things like that, but with my father it was a matter of degree. He'd tell the black men at the shine parlor about how he saw Mamie Smith and Bessie Smith and the Beef Trust Sisters at the Cotton Club and Club Delisa, all the while speaking in a black dialect with them. It came close to Lenny Bruce's classic routine, "How to Entertain Your Negro Friends at Parties," but I don't think it was condescending. The really weird thing was he'd continue to speak that way until he encountered the next ethnic type.

He was, in fact, an incredible interviewer—totally uninhibited, gregarious, charming. He would just walk up to a stranger and ask, "What are you?" If the answer was "Irish," he would say, "I was raised with the Irish," and start speaking with a brogue. If they said "Polish," he would start speaking Polish! He seemed to know enough of each language he encountered to have brief conversations which I couldn't understand but that brought him closer to the strangers we met.

At night, we'd go downtown, the Silk and me. We had our route that included the Greyhound Bus Terminal and the Illinois-Central Train Station. On muggy summer evenings, we'd get a vanilla malt from the fountain at the train station. Or, on one of those snowy winter nights, we'd get a hot chocolate and enjoy the coziness of the restaurant off the bus station waiting room. Then, he'd start speaking to the people who were heading for Des Moines or Green Bay or Terre Haute or points further east or west, asking them where they were going, what they were, and did they have a job, kids, a mate. Nobody ever refused or seemed offended. I suppose it helped that he had a child with him, but even big cities were like small towns then. People were friendlier in 1950.

Later, he'd stop at a bar—always a bar—and he'd tell me to wait outside while he used the bathroom. He'd be gone a long time, and you didn't see many little girls standing outside of bars on State Street late at night. Once, a man asked me what I was doing there and after I explained, he took me up to my father, who was having a drink and charming a group of men and women. It didn't seem like anything so awful to me, but my father nearly killed the man for bringing me inside.

There was a funny undertone of violence about him, although he never struck me. There was some history with the Mafia, but exactly what that was about I could never clear up with him or my mother before she died. Ostensibly, he made his money as a theater owner. He ran what had been a live Yiddish theater in the 30's, and then a movie theater from the 40's on. He thought of himself as a showman. He told me later, when I was a teenager, that he used to leave me in my crib in the balcony of the theater with an usher named Big Ben. Big Ben was an enormous man, tender as he was big. My father liked to take him out to eat and gather crowds around the table while he accepted bets on how much Big Ben would consume. I once personally observed the man eating six bananas with the peels! But, for some reason, whenever my father introduced Big Ben to people he would say, "this is my bodyguard." He also frequently alluded to a man by the name of Legs who, he said, was "my chauffeur." Now, what kind of man has a bodyguard and a chauffeur? What kind of man has associates named Big Ben and Legs? These questions never even occurred to me until years after his death.

He spoke of the moment when he decided to "go legit" like it was the major event of his life, somewhere between a graduation and an epiphany. Exactly what "going legit" consisted of, I could never quite understand. He said, "I did it because I had a little mother who I loved," and I subsequently understood it to mean some point at which he severed all ties with mobsters.

I know a bitter fight took place between Silky and his brother, Charley, when I was about eight. They had sold the theaters they owned and went partners on a hotel, the Alexander. Uncle Charley sold half of his partnership to a man named Fred Evans. Evans had two bodyguards. When the Silk objected to the sale, he and Charley had a brutal, physical fight. I know it was particularly frightening to me because, even though I was in the room, I still can't remember which one of them pulled out the gun.

Charley was, at that time, head of the billposters' union. My Uncle Ben was a judge. And my Uncle Leo was a state liquor commissioner, although he also owned a nightclub called the Planet Mars. The brothers were well-connected, which among the immigrant communities usually meant the Mafia. No shots were ever fired between my father and his brother. The Silk bought him out, we became poor trying to pay back all the "legit" loans he took, and two years later, Fred Evans, the unwelcome partner, was found on a Chicago street, gunned down—as they say in the media—gangland style.

Silk never talked to Charley again. He remained legit and bitter to the end. But when he went out to restaurants, especially fancy ones, he would affect a mobster style. Although the silk shirts had long since gone, he wore the striped suit and wide-brimmed hat of the Mafioso. To call him Runyonesque would be putting it too cutely. He'd walk up to the maitre d' at the restaurant, hold out his pinkie and say, "Little finger only." Then he'd shake fingers with the befuddled, officious man in the tuxedo. Next, he'd say, "I'm a friend of the Fischetti Boys . . ." If this didn't get an immediate rise out of the headwaiter, he would drop other names like Gimpy Schneider or Three-Fingers Murphy. He might explain, "I was with James J. McGrat, the boss of Madison Street, before he bought the Columbia Burlesque Wheel and went bust. You got a table for me and my little family?"

Soon, we would be ushered into a private dining room. Two waiters and three busboys would stand around granting our every wish. The owner would bring my mother one perfect rose and tell my father what beautiful daughters he had. At the end of the meal, my father would request and receive a bowl of cream and a fresh napkin. He'd then proceed to wash his hands with these things. The waiters and busboys would look on as if it were a perfectly normal occurrence.

As he left, he would say, "If one of the Capones comes in, tell 'em the Silk Shirt Kid says, 'Hello.'" Then he'd smile, tip his hat, and be gone.